Cases in Early Childhood Education

Stories of Programs and Practices

Amy Driscoll

Portland State University

Allyn and Bacon
Boston • London • Toronto • Sydney • Tokyo • Singapore

Editor-in-Chief, Education: Nancy Forsyth
Editorial Assistant: Christine Nelson
Marketing Manager: Ellen Mann
Editorial-Production Administrator: Eleanor Sabini
Editorial-Production Service: TKM Productions
Cover Administrator: Suzanne Harbison
Composition Buyer: Linda Cox
Manufacturing Buyer: Megan Cochran

Copyright © 1995 by Allyn & Bacon
A Simon & Schuster Company
Needham Heights, Massachusetts 02194

Library of Congress Cataloging-in-Publication Data

Driscoll, Amy.
    Cases in early childhood education : stories of programs and
practices / Amy Driscoll.
        p.   cm.
    Includes bibliographical references.
    ISBN 0-205-15021-7
    1. Early childhood education—Case studies. 2. Classroom
management—Case studies.   I. Title.
LB1139.23.D75   1994
372.21—dc20   94-17402
                                                    CIP

Printed in the United States of America

10 9 8 7 6 5 4 3 2 1   99 98 97 96 95 94

Photo Credits: Frank B. May and Amy Driscoll

These cases of "out of the ordinary" programs and practices are dedicated to two "out of the ordinary" individuals:

To my soulmate, Brad Eliot, for his support through this year of travel and story telling, for his spectacular photos, and for being my constant and valued source of affection and inspiration.

To my colleague and friend, Bob Dematteis, whose personal and professional life story will always be a lesson for hundreds of early childhood educators who learned from and loved him.

Contents

Preface

For the past 16 years, much of my professional life has been directed toward the preparation of teachers. Although sometimes worn by the demands of this work, I have found continual satisfaction and inspiration from watching individuals flourish as teachers. However, one source of significant discontent and concern has persisted: the discrepancies between what my teacher education students are taught and what they observe in practice. These discrepancies have been well documented in the research literature, and their effects are discouraging. Furthermore, such discrepancies bring anguish to the struggles of beginning teachers as they attempt to teach in ways that are not supported by some school cultures. As many as 60 percent of those neophytes abandon practices in which they believe. Discrepancies even extend to the professional lives of *experienced* teachers as they yearn for a peer community of support for their experimentation and change.

My concerns about discrepancies prompted me to develop cases about situations that are not traditional for a "case approach" to teacher education. Let me first describe my intent with respect to the content of this book. Until now, most cases used in the teaching profession have focused on problems that teachers are confronted with or are unable to respond to effectively. The justification provided is that these problems portray the "real world" of teaching. In all my years of working with preservice teachers, however, I have never heard one of them express a wish to see more examples of classroom problems. As Kathy Carter (1993) aptly expressed it, "Images of teacher deficiencies are plentiful." What I have heard instead, from numbers of preservice and beginning teachers is, "I wish I could see some of these good ideas in an actual classroom." This book of cases responds to that wish.

One of the reviewers of *Cases in Early Childhood Education,* an early childhood teacher educator, may have spoken for many of us when she said, "My students don't see anything like these cases described. I wish they *would!*" The educators in this book teach in truly child-centered classrooms and make decisions that are based on children's needs. In addition, they have all gone beyond providing quality programs and have taken the risks involved in being *different*. Each of the cases in this book describes programs and practices that go beyond quality for children—they are "out of the ordinary."

Yet, the educators are not perfect, and the programs do portray problems! Most importantly, the case descriptions provide ample stimuli for discussion, problem solving, decision making, and, above all, reflection. They are a "positive source of insight" (Mitchell, 1981), however, rather than a crisis-focused way of learning. The detailed stories in this book describe the "real world" of teaching just as much as the crisis-centered mini-stories.

This book demonstrates innovative programs and above-average teaching, but a careful look below the surface will reveal to readers the real-world problems and issues that are part of teaching. Such depth of analysis is exactly what novices, and even the very experienced among us, need in order to examine their own practices. In the past decade, we teacher educators have stressed decision making and reflective practice as the most significant teacher behaviors. Responding only to crises and problems, though, seems to promote a reactive stance to teaching rather than a reflective one. *Cases in Early Childhood Education* provides a look at quality programs, committed individuals, and appropriate practices in the context of educating real children and serving real families in real communities.

Some teacher educators have suggested that teachers use cases as "proxies" for practicum experiences. The cases in this book take the reader to 10 distinct classrooms and communities. They are an alternative to visiting and observing the actual site, and in doing so, they provide a common experience for a group of students or teachers.

The cases in this book are also unique in terms of format. Because they are intended to take you, the reader, into the minds and classrooms of teachers, they cannot be brief, nor can they be narrow. A legal case or a case in the field of medicine demands a description of the overall picture so that professionals can make decisions, negotiate, recommend, and plan. In similar fashion, the cases in this book portray the broad scope of a day from beginning to end. They take you into the community, acquaint you with the major individuals, and allow you to see the minute-by-minute happenings in the classrooms.

These case descriptions are not aimed at "right answers." Instead, they are intended to help preservice and beginning teachers develop a repertoire of approaches and responses. More importantly, they demonstrate that classroom problems are subtle, multifaceted, ongoing, and sometimes insolvable. For experienced teachers, this text provides comraderie in risk taking, support for new practices and change, and inspiration for teaching according to one's beliefs about children.

Suggestions for using these cases appear in Appendix B at the back of this book. These suggestions provide alternative approaches for teaching with cases or for using cases for in-service and professional development programs. They are framed for varying levels of experience and expertise. Also, each chapter concludes with discussion questions and issues.

In closing, I wish to express appreciation to those who helped make this book possible. I am grateful to the many individuals at the 10 sites I visited. They were patient with me and very giving of their classrooms, their time, and their explanations, thus making it possible for me to take you into their minds and classrooms. Their stories are truly gifts to us all.

For the painstaking research that helped me find these innovative cases, I thank Kelly Driscoll and Amy O'Neill, who spent many hours in the library searching the literature. For ongoing dialogue about the concept of case descriptions and the potential for their use, I am grateful to my editor at Allyn and Bacon, Nancy Forsyth, who studied and learned about cases as intensely as I did during the past two years. For careful reading of these cases, I gratefully acknowledge Kerry Driscoll and all my reviewers: Ione M. Garcia, Illinois State University; Joan Isenberg, George Mason University; Vicki LaBosky, Mills College; Ann Marie Leonard, James Madison University; and Doris White, Virginia Commonwealth University.

And finally, for his wise critique and loving support, I am grateful to my husband, Brad. He waited patiently while I traveled and he shared my enthusiasm for each case description when I returned. His own writing served as an inspirational model for my own.

References

Carter, K. (1993). The place of story in the study of teaching and teacher education. *Educational Researcher, 22* (1), 5–12.
Mitchell, W. (1981). *On narrative.* Chicago: University of Chicago Press.

1

A Conversation About This Book

You and I will be traveling thousands of miles together in the pages of this book. Since we'll also spend many hours together observing in classrooms, I'd like to get acquainted before we leave on our journey. Perhaps a conversation about these cases and the experiences ahead of us will get us started.

First, I must tell you that these cases are not the traditional, intense, problem-solving type. They are accounts of my visits to 10 programs in the United States and Canada, each with a description of the community and people, and a narrative of a full day of observation. Consequently, these case descriptions are longer than traditional case reports and have the potential for broader and more varied interpretations. Later in this chapter I will describe some of those possibilities for you.

I want to assure you that these cases are authentic. Sometimes there is a tendency to suspect that a classroom story isn't real if the teacher isn't struggling with one difficult problem after another, or if she or he is actually modeling appropriate practices. The teachers, parents, and administrators I describe in these cases enthusiastically consented to have their names and their conversations used in the case descriptions. The children's names were changed to assure confidentiality, but the classroom situations in which they appear were not changed or adapted in any way. What is especially authentic about these cases is that the problems and issues presented are just as subtle as they usually are in "real" classrooms.

You will probably have questions about these cases, especially about how I found the schools and programs or how I decided on particular sites. I'd like to satisfy those curiosities in this first conversation. I would also like to admit that I have some expectations of *you* as well, and I'll talk about those before we begin our travels. I truly hope we won't be strangers when we move on to Chapter 2.

1

Why I Wrote This Book of Cases

When I tell you about why I decided to write this book, you will get to know something about my background and my professional life. It may not be very different from yours. Ever since I began teaching (first grade in Hamburg, New York), I treasured visits to other teachers' classrooms. I can still remember how significant those visits were to me as a neophyte in the profession. Later, as a new preschool teacher, I signed up for program tours when I began attending the annual conferences of the National Association for the Education of Young Children. Those visits were powerful learning experiences for me. It's one thing to read about an exciting program, but it's quite another to see a program in action. Dorothy Watson (1989) described it well when she talked about teachers' understanding of the whole-language philosophy: "A single visit in a whole-language classroom is worth more than a hundred definitions, for it is in the classroom that the definitions, the theory, and the stated practices come alive" (p. 134).

My visits to classrooms have continued over the years, and today, as I prepare teachers, those visits provide rich examples and explanations for my students. No matter how vividly I describe teaching approaches, my students always lament, "If only I could see it working in a classroom" or "I want to see a teacher who does it." As for my own teaching, even after more than 30 years of watching teachers and children, observations of new programs and practices continue to challenge my beliefs and cause me to reflect.

Decisions I Made in Writing These Cases

Acknowledging the importance of classroom visits to my own professional development led to my first decision in writing this book—to take you, the reader on a visit to an actual classroom for at least a day or more. The "case approach" to instruction usually involves brief narratives that focus on actual problems, situations, or issues. What I have done is to blend case methodology with narratives, or stories, of classroom visits. When one watches teachers and children all day, there is no need to compose classroom problems or issues; they are woven into the very fabric of the daily dynamics. They occur naturally as teachers and children interact in diverse settings. This means, of course, that the problems and issues vary depending on who is reading the narrative; the cases become somewhat individualized by the reader. In short, each of you can bring a different philosophy and set of experiences to your reading of these narratives.

As I made decisions about the development of this book, I was reminded that one way adults learn is through their own and other people's stories. Jerome Bruner (1990) even encouraged people to make better use of stories to understand cultures and to build relationships. My hope is that you and I will create a kind of community as we interact through the stories in this book. Teachers and other professionals

often wish for peers who are willing to experiment or change their approaches, or who model appropriate practices for young children. This collection of narratives responds to that need for community among teachers, and extends to an even wider community that includes students of education, parents, policymakers, administrators, and the general public.

Kathy Carter has argued convincingly that "the analysis of story is of central importance to the field of education" (1993, p.11) if educators are going to face issues and make changes. The sharing of case descriptions in this book also responds to that argument.

As I began to write the first few cases, I was reminded of another characteristic of stories (Bruner, 1990), and that is the influence of the narrator. As my own thoughts, interpretations, and responses kept seeping into what I wrote, I made decisions about my role as the author of this text.

My Role: Anthropological Implications

As an anthropologist writing about programs and practices, I wrote from participant observations, acknowledged my biases, and actively sought an understanding of the culture of each group I visited. My role in writing these cases emerged when I recognized my interpretations and let them flow into the narratives. As I traveled and visited schools and programs, I envisioned you, the reader, at my side. While observing teachers and children, I asked myself, What would the reader like to hear or to see? I knew from my own experience that you needed to hear actual conversations, to watch specific learning activities, and to step into real classroom environments. But I also wanted you to experience the energy I absorbed from these encounters, to be refreshed by the enthusiasm of the teachers I observed, and to have the opportunity to reflect on the conversations and interactions I witnessed.

Whenever I experience a professionally stimulating situation—an excellent speaker or an especially dynamic conference—I come away with a mental and emotional restlessness. That kind of restlessness prompts most people to reflect, to question, to discuss, and, sometimes, to change. My observations of the various programs and classrooms caused me to feel that restlessness, and I wanted you to experience it with me. However, as I wrote the first few cases, the traditional "scientific" reporting format fell short of providing you with the same kind of experience I had during my visits. Experience means "living through or partaking in a common meaning" (Van Manen, 1977), and it wasn't until I decided to use my own voice that I felt you and I could achieve that common meaning. I had been holding back my delight, my questioning, and my discomfort, thus denying you the richness of the experience.

This change in my participation affects you. I will be asking you to participate in the cases differently from what you may have intended when you opened this book. David Burger (1992) aptly called this kind of participation "living in the case." Let me describe what that phrase means and what it holds for you as the reader and fellow traveler.

Your Role: Anthropological Implications

By now, you probably have some idea of what I expect of you. You see, once I allowed my voice and emotions to enter the case descriptions, I couldn't ignore the implications for you as the reader. "Living in the case" demands an equally intense commitment from the reader as well as from the writer. What does that commitment mean? For one thing, it means imagining yourself as a participant observer. For another, it means that you need to be free of distractions, both internally and externally. Leave your setting and put yourself next to me as I approach the Denver Indian Preschool with its unique curriculum woven with legends and tradition. Be ready to engage in lively conversation with an energetic teacher team in Victoria, British Columbia, as they plan and assess the development of their kindergarten and first-grade children.

Viewing different cultures as an anthropologist requires significant time for observations. Therefore, I encourage you to read these cases at a leisurely pace— most importantly, read only one case at a time. Ideally, you wouldn't visit different programs or classrooms several days in a row. Take the time to "live in the case" and reflect on your visit before making a transition to the next one. I've spared you the details and hassles of travel, but I urge you to visualize yourself actually leaving your surroundings behind. Join me in the visits without your day-to-day concerns. If you do, I think you will be surprised at how much you will learn—how much you will construct your own knowledge.

Potential for Cases: What Can They Mean?

If you are currently a teacher or preparing to be one, your tendency may be to look at the cases as models. Quite honestly, I never intended these visits to yield models. Models are structures that are meant to be transferred intact to people and places. This won't work with the cases in this text. For instance, it could be inappropriate to try to replicate the integrated bilingual day-care center of downtown Montreal in my hometown or yours.

I anticipate that another initial response to these cases will be to look for specific knowledge or techniques. Walter Doyle (1986) confirmed that teachers often seek "how to's" when they visit other classrooms. That's a noble purpose, and I do think that many of the cases will accomplish that for you, but I hope you won't stop there.

Doyle (1986) suggested that you can go beyond that first response to one of problem solving and decision making. To do so may require you to analyze the classroom situations with me. You may find yourself questioning how *you* would handle a particular situation, even when it looks like the teacher responded appropriately. I also hope that you will disagree with some of my responses. And at the end of each chapter, I pose some questions and issues to encourage your involvement at this level. You may find that you will need to reread an individual case in order to increase your awareness.

You can stop after Doyle's problem-solving and decision-making stage, or you can proceed to a more complex response. The third response to a case calls for reflection—using your own understandings and applying them to the context being described. That means you will momentarily have to put aside your own classroom situation or your current experiences, and attend to the complexity of the particular classroom setting and school community in each of the cases. John Dewey (1933) called this "reflective action," and it requires a sophisticated integration of theory and practice on your part.

This book provides opportunities to reflect on the practices of others through the lens of your own values and philosophy. Again, you will need time for this. You may want to reflect in a journal or you may want to make this a collaborative reflection with colleagues. I have found that powerful discussions occur when professionals share their individual responses to a case. At the end of the book, Appendix B gives suggestions for using these cases for classes in higher education,

in-service programs, or individual professional development. Because problems and issues are often subtle in classrooms, some strategies for "looking below the surface" are presented. Selma Wasserman (1993) suggested that we, as educators, develop the capacity for such vision as we consistently "make meaning" of what we see or hear in classrooms.

Selecting the Cases

The most common question asked by almost everyone who has heard about my travels has been, How did you select the programs or classrooms for your book? I think that it is important to share my rationale for selecting the cases as part of this initial conversation.

I began my search with professional periodicals and published reports describing schools and programs. The literature on individual early childhood education programs provided a beginning and from there, I relied on my "people-to-people" connections—colleagues throughout the United States and Canada. After that, I'll admit that much of my work was intuitive. As I contacted directors, principals, and teachers, I listened to both the substance and spirit of their statements. When I heard descriptions that were threaded with strong philosophical commitments and with children at the heart of the work, I made my plane reservations.

I was intentionally looking for programs that were "out of the ordinary." Most of these programs wouldn't be found in your neighborhood or school district. Some would say that such programs aren't "realistic" or relevant for observations, especially for beginning early childhood educators. I disagree. Because these programs are *not* ordinary, they can expand one's perceptions of what is possible in early childhood education. I feel strongly that such a broad vision is needed to respond adequately to the diverse needs of today's children and families.

In addition to finding unusual or "out of the ordinary" approaches, I looked for a full range of practices in both the program focus and related issues. I wanted private and public programs, a range of ages and grade levels, and a representation of diverse program types. Appendix A contains a matrix that lists the name of each program, its location, its focus, the age/grade level of the children, and relevant issues.

One other requirement for selecting programs or schools was that of a fairly long history or a "track record." I wanted to write about programs with a certainty that they would be around when this book was published.

By now you have some understanding of why we are heading to Honolulu or to Houston. I've shared my vision of the potential for these cases and you've heard my expectations. Remember to leave your day-to-day cares in the closet as you proceed to Chapter 2. Our first destination is New York City and a private school that nourishes creativity. Get ready to be part of Angela Pino's class and join me as we "live in the case."

References

Bruner, J. (1990). *Acts of meaning*. Cambridge, MA: Harvard University Press.

Burger, D. L. (1992). *The importance of living in the case*. Paper presented at the annual conference of the American Association of Colleges of Teacher Education, San Antonio, TX.

Carter, K. (1993). The place of story in the study of teaching and teacher education. *Educational Researcher, 22* (1), 5–12.

Dewey, J. (1933). *How we think*. Chicago: Regnery.

Doyle, W. (1986). *The world is everything that is the case: Developing case methods for teacher education*. Paper presented at the annual meeting of the American Educational Research Association, San Francisco.

Van Manen, M. (1977). Linking ways of knowing with ways of being practical. *Curriculum Inquiry, 6*, 205–228.

Wasserman, S. (1993). *Getting down to cases: Learning to teach with case studies*. New York: Teachers College Press.

Watson, D. (1989). Defining and describing whole language. *The Elementary School Journal, 90*, 129–141.

2

City & Country School

Encouraging Children's Natural Curiosity and Creativity

Caroline Pratt began her educational experiment in 1914 with a group of young children and a room full of blocks in a friend's apartment in Greenwich Village. She was inspired by the *play* of children, and from her observations, she developed a belief in their ability to create and test knowledge about their world through play, especially play with blocks. Pratt's simple beginnings have slowly expanded to the respected City & Country School that receives visitors from all over the world. The school serves approximately 130 children, ages 2 through 13, and is located in three old brownstone buildings in the same New York neighborhood where Pratt's dream was initiated. The first school provided experiences in the country and combined them with in-school experiences that reflected the city life of the children. The name, City & Country, was intended to communicate those program components.

The school has seen "good times" in the early days of progressive education, with support from John Dewey and Lucy Sprague Mitchell, and later in the 1960s with a revival of progressive ideals. It has also seen "hard times" in the depression and post-Sputnik years, with financial difficulties and pressure from the "back to basics" movement. However, the school not only kept its doors open during difficult times but it also maintained a commitment to "learn from children" (Holz, 1993). The staff at City & Country maintained an openness to children's ideas, direction,

9

and abilities—the same philosophy advocated today by teachers in the name of "developmentally appropriate practice."

Today, City & Country School has a healthy enrollment, and 95 percent of the children live within a five-block radius. Thus, it has remained as it began, a neighborhood school. Tuition costs are average for a New York private school, but the school has an aggressive recruitment policy and 31 percent of the students are on scholarships.

With only a brief history, I am determined to learn more about this school that has maintained progressive education for almost 80 years. Before heading to New York City, I decide to read more about Caroline Pratt's beliefs to begin to understand what I will see at City & Country School.

A Preview of the Program

I am aware that many programs profess to "learn from children" and do actualize the philosophy, but there's a clear reference to more than philosophical commitment in the material describing City & Country School. Frequent reference is made to materials and environments that seem out of the ordinary. The ideas of Caroline Pratt help me understand this uniqueness.

I learn that when Pratt began the school specifically for young children, she crafted wooden blocks for her program. The wooden unit blocks she designed have become a basic material in early childhood education programs all over the world. Today, those blocks are the mainspring of curriculum in the Lower School, the program for children ages 2 through 8.

My preview takes me browsing through photos of the City & Country classrooms. I see extensive and intricate block play but note that blocks are not accompanied by an abundance of materials found in other programs for young children. I don't see the usual shelves full of materials; in fact, the classrooms look somewhat bare. I try to visualize children in them and it's a struggle, so I decide it's time to leave the photos and see the real thing.

The Surrounding Community and the Community Within

A major thoroughfare, Avenue of the Americas, is my first glimpse of the neighborhood surrounding the school. As I walk down the street, I am surrounded by the sights and scents of various ethnic foods, exotic clothing, and sometimes bizarre art objects. The sidewalks are full of people, young and old: babies in strollers, young children holding the hands of adults, 10-year-olds walking in pairs, teenagers in small groups, and adults of all ages drinking from "carryout" cups of coffee, rushing with briefcases or briskly walking dogs. Along the sidewalk's edge are temporary vendors, selling paperback books, old clothing, handmade jewelry, and household bric-a-brac. The sidewalks are full and the movement is energetic. Unfortunately, there's no time or space for stopping to enjoy the sights and sounds this morning at 8:30 A.M.

When I reach West 13th Street and walk the few blocks to the school, the scene is transformed immediately. It feels like a neighborhood: trees border the street, apartments and condominiums are clustered in brick buildings, several charming cafés reach out to the sidewalk, and children and adults are coming from every direction. Taxis pull up in front of City & Country School, depositing children of all ages, some accompanied by adults and some on their own.

It's a noisy, festive setting as children and adults greet friends, gather belongings, and head for the school entrance. The sign announcing the school hangs to the left of the door, and its colorful, whimsical lettering and graphics reflect the feeling of this arrival scene at City & Country.

The front door is locked and I must ring the bell to be admitted. Once inside, I find myself surrounded by a variety of activities in the spacious but crowded hall. Parents are leaving messages with the office staff who are available through a large window that opens into the hallway. Others are dropping off household items and toys for the annual Spring Fair to be held later this week. Some of the older children depart for their rooms while younger ones remain with parents in the entry hall.

Teacher Insights

I have decided to observe 3-year-olds during my visit to City & Country School. Their teacher, Angela Pino, is assisted by Aki and Nanci. In preparation for my observation, I interviewed Angela beforehand. I realized almost immediately that she teaches at City & Country because it's a "fit" with the way she wants to work with children. Angela described her teaching role as one of "facilitating children's talk and decisions" and "taking their cues." The kind of climate she wants in her classroom is one where children have the feeling of "I can do"—not "maybe I can" or "I wonder if I can." Angela stated, "We try to bring out in them what they know or want to communicate, and sometimes what they don't know they know. Often, we're simply providing the language for them to express what they know."

Angela's ideas about her role and the classroom climate are consistent with the school's intent to "encourage children's natural curiosity and motivation to learn." I'm anxious to see her facilitation in action and how she responds to children's activities, ordinary routines, and problems that arise. What does that encouragement look like in practice?

With these and other questions emerging, I look forward to observing Angela and to seeing children interacting in their school environment. When I arrive, I'm told that the 3-year-olds are in the upper play yard. I also learn that the play yard is on the roof of the building! So I follow children and parents up four flights of stairs to the roof.

An Outdoor Environment

As I step out on the green carpet, I am immediately intrigued by two scenes. The first is a wall of cityscape, a panorama surrounding the area. It's an unfamiliar backdrop for a playground. Rooftops, skyscrapers, and smokestacks blend with the sounds of traffic and human activity below and envelope this colorful oasis for children.

The second scene is a conglomeration of equipment not typically found outdoors. Around two sides of the yard I see six large (4′ × 4′ ft. and 3′ × 3′) wooden crates, each with one open side; about 20 long boards (6′); and an abundance of square (15″ in. × 15″) and rectangular (15″ × 30″) hollow blocks. On another side is a shelving unit with buckets arranged in a row on one shelf, paintbrushes on another shelf, and plastic bowls on another—but no paint! On the last side are handcarts for moving the large blocks, and ladders with hooked ends and rubber tips to hold them in place.

Several children are already "on the roof" (to use the local expression) and the three teachers—Angela, Aki, and Nanci—greet them and their parents. I watch 3-year-old Devon and his father as they experiment with a rubber dome that is supposed to "pop" when it is flattened on a smooth surface. Devon pushes his straight blond hair out of his eyes and begins to demonstrate for his friends. When he's not successful, his dad tries to explain why it isn't working on the wooden crates. "This surface isn't quite smooth enough to work. Feel this surface. Probably too rough. It's not like the surface we used at home."

I get the impression that he's deliberately using the word *surface* over and over. I continue to watch, noticing that he doesn't seem to be in a hurry to leave. Devon asks his dad to get out his homework to give to his teacher. His dad explains to Angela, "This is Devon's homework. Devon dictated a song that he's been wanting to teach the class. He insists that you don't know it, so we wrote it down to bring."

Devon shows the song to Angela, who looks at the words and agrees that they don't know his song about mosquitos. She adds that they will be happy to learn it.

At this point, Devon notices me and asks his dad what I'm doing. After I briefly explain my work, Devon's dad asks him if he'd like to tell me anything about his school. Devon begins without hesitation: "All these kids do different jobs. They build different things with the blocks. Kids do different work in the school."

His father tells Devon that if I write those words in my book, it will be Devon's quote. Devon asks, "What is a quote?"

"It's when someone writes down what you say. That's a quote. She may say, 'This is a quote from Devon.'"

This explanation seems to satisfy Devon and he moves away to join an interesting building project taking shape in the corner of the roof. His dad bids him good-bye with, "Have a great day! Those sneakers are good for jumping."

Emmet and Jason go past me with a handcart. There are two square blocks on it and Jason is sitting on them.

"Bronx Zoo. This is where I get off," announces Jason.

Jason jumps off the cart and Emmet gets on. "I want to go to 13th and 7th and 4th Avenues," says Emmet.

They travel to the other side of the roof, playing out familiar scenes from their city life.

Children continue to arrive with adults. Some adults hurry off and others linger. At 9:20 A.M., three adults are still chatting with Angela and Aki or involved in children's play. I learn that Kristin's mom is going to spend the morning with the class. She, like all other parents of the children at City & Country, is encouraged to observe her child regularly. Kristin is hesitant to leave her mother, and clings while watching her friends. Her mother suggests that they pretend that it's a regular day. They kiss good-bye and her mom says, "Have a nice day." Then Kristin goes off to play with three girls who have built a "house," and her mother stays to observe the activity.

Three-Year-Olds Learning about Their World and Themselves

At this time, Vanessa arrives with a doll, and Kristin's mom asks her the doll's name. Vanessa replies, "I can't remember her name."

Kristin's mom asks, "What could we call her until you remember her name?"

Vanessa pauses for a few seconds and responds, "Baby Renata."

After a few minutes of playing with Baby Renata, I see Vanessa take her doll and place it in a very large red canvas bag on a shelf near the entrance. I had previously seen Devon put his dome in the same bag. Vanessa then moves to watch Kristin and three other girls who are adding blocks to their "house." Vanessa watches for a while and then turns over a large crate for herself. I remain to watch the other four girls in play: Elizabeth, Nina, Alicia, and Kristin. Elizabeth is considerably smaller than the others, and she is obviously portraying the "baby." She has crawled into a lower section of the "house" and is curled up "sleeping."

One of the girls asks, "Baby, want to go out for breakfast?"

Elizabeth crawls out and sits on the nearby handcart. She is pushed by Kristin around the edge of the play area and then returned to the "house." Elizabeth does not talk or walk during the next 30 minutes of play. She makes numerous baby sounds and crawls, tapping her peers when she wants something or "crying" for attention. Later, the girls put Elizabeth on the handcart again, saying, "Baby needs a checkup," and head to the doctor's office.

An Opportunity to Observe Angela's Facilitation

Two boys, Eliot and Justin, are inside a crate near the "house" activity. They occasionally watch the girls' drama and then slip down in their own crate to whisper. Eliot gets out of the crate and gets two ladders. He carefully sets them on their sides on opposite sides of the crate, then slips back into the crate. The crate is now a baby crib inhabited by two "babies" who "waaa" and rub their eyes. This is a brief activity—one that ends with Justin suggesting, "Let's play Peter and the Wolf." He adds, "I'll be the wolf," and jumps out of the crate. He begins to skip around the play area. Eliot joins him and they run around. Eventually, they begin to chase Devon. They catch him and begin to take him back to their crate. He protests loudly, and Eliot and Justin interpret his protest as a dramatic involvement in their play. Their drama intensifies and they become more fierce in their wolves' roles. Angela Pino observes apprehensively, waits and watches the trio, then moves in with a question to Devon:

"Are you pretending to object or are you really upset?"

Devon tells her that he doesn't want to be captured and is upset. Angela encourages him to tell Justin and Eliot and then moves out of the area. She stops to listen to Devon tell the others, "I don't want you to take me away because I'm not playing with you." At the same time she's listening, Angela also observes Vanessa, who has been building a "house" of her own now for about 30 minutes.

I, too, watch Vanessa's activity. She notices me and explains, "I'm building a house. I've never built a house before. I'm building a window. And there's a bunk bed and a ladder," she adds, pointing to different areas of her construction. I continue to watch and she continues to build for 10 more minutes. Then she gets a bucket of water and a paintbrush, and paints her house for 10 more minutes. While I watch Vanessa and glance at other activities out of the corner of my eye, I can't help but notice that Angela and her assistants frequently pick up some of the materials that children appear to have finished using. I hear them "talking their actions" aloud to the children, such as, "I'm just going to put this ladder over here, so if you need it later, you'll know where it is," or "I'm going to stack these three boards here so that you'll be able to use them to build when you want to."

Angela explains, "We feel that teaching children this age to clean up after themselves *during* play interferes with spontaneous play and creative activity. Afterwards, we all stop to pick up and ready the area for tomorrow. Then we're fostering the idea of group responsibility."

Sarah arrives at this moment, and her mom quickly explains that they just returned from a trip. Sarah is immediately surrounded by Kristin, Alicia, and Nina, with "baby" Elizabeth crawling after them. The girls clamor, "Sarah, will you work with me?"

Angela intervenes, sensing Sarah's hesitancy, "I think that Sarah needs a little time before she makes that decision."

The girls continue noisily, and Angela says quite firmly, "Give her a little space." She looks at Sarah, then continues, "Sarah's not going to decide right now." I've been watching Sarah's face and she now looks relieved to be rescued by Angela. I reflect on whether I would have intervened, but I quickly realize that I don't know Sarah the way Angela does.

The girls leave and return to their "house." Demetri has been standing nearby and watching the scene. As soon as it is quiet, he says confidently, "She's going to work with me first because I'm going to marry her." Demetri was right about Sarah's decision, and she goes off with him to his "bat cave." They crawl in the cave of crates and boards. After a minute, I hear Demetri ask, "Do you want to be a lion boy or a lion man or a tiger boy or a tiger man? Which animal do you want to be?"

Sarah doesn't answer. She gets a bucket of water and a paintbrush, saying, "We have to paint this 'cause bad guys put dirt on it and glue." Demetri gets a bucket and brush and joins her.

Management Routines at City & Country

At 10:00 A.M., Angela begins singing, "Who is ready? Who is ready? For the pick up meeting? For the pick up meeting?"

Her song becomes, "Justin is ready. Nina is ready. For the pick up meeting. For the pick up meeting."

Soon everyone but Devon is sitting on the carpeted floor of the rooftop. He's sitting on top of a crate, and when Angela asks him to come sit on the floor with the group, he responds, "No." Angela gets up nonchalantly and lifts Devon to the floor without a comment. She proceeds to the routine for a pick up meeting as if the incident never occurred. The children hear her give the pick up assignments:

"Emmet—boards."

"Justin and Vanessa—squaries (their word for the square blocks)."

"Nina and Elizabeth—handcarts and ladders."

"Demetri—buckets,"

Angela continues until all the children have their assignments.

Cleanup is amazingly smooth, and during this procedure, I notice little adult intervention. I watch Demetri searching for buckets and Justin sorting through piles of blocks for "squaries." When children finish, they are urged to "check one more time for squaries or boards," or whatever they were assigned. They are also urged to take "pebbles out of hands and pockets so we can go inside." Soon, the yard is back in order, but a number of children are complaining about their hands being hurt. Angela gathers them on the carpet again, and when she has their attention, begins, "Lots of people have been complaining about people squeezing other people's hands. That's something you know a lot about. Who can say anything about squeezing people's hands? What do you know about squeezing people's hands? Why don't we like it?"

Devon responds without hesitation, "Number one, because it hurts them, and number two, because it's a rule in this school."

Angela agrees and asks, "What can you do instead of squeezing people's hands?"

Devon again jumps in with, "You can just play."

Angela accepts his idea then continues with, "Your friends don't know what you want when you squeeze their hands. It doesn't tell them anything. When you use your voice, you get to tell them exactly what you want."

After this exchange, the children begin to walk down the flights of stairs to their classroom. On the stairs, I note several levels of handrails, one low enough that the 3-year-olds can reach easily and hold while walking. I hear, "Take me out to the ball game . . ." sung on the way down. By the time we reach the third floor, there is emphatic volume to, "And it's one, two, three strikes, you're out, at the old ball game."

When the children reach their classroom, they are reminded that they have "rhythms" today. As they take off their shoes, I hear another old familiar song, "Do You Know the Muffin Man?" but I hear phrases that aren't so familiar:

"Do you know the hot dog boy?"
"Do you know the pizza girl?"
"Do you know the old cowboy?"

Nurturing Creativity as Children Learn about Themselves

The singing continues as the children walk to a small gymnasium where piano music is heard. Joan Morgan greets them at the door and encourages them to come in and move the way the music makes them feel. The music is supplied by a pianist playing a grand piano. When the music stops and Joan has the children's attention, she begins a discussion about frogs, crocodiles, and snakes. The children know a lot about frogs and snakes but little about crocodiles. The only information about crocodiles comes from Emmet, who says that they make a ticking sound. This causes Joan and most of the children to pause, until Nina says, "He's talking about the crocodile in *Peter Pan*." A brief discussion occurs about whether ticking is a real crocodile sound. It's obvious that there is confusion among the children. Joan suggests to the children that they might go to the library and find out more about crocodiles.

For the next few minutes, Joan encourages the children to move with some "frog jumps," "crocodile crawls," and "snake slithers." The pianist varies the music for each creature, and the 3-year-olds vary their movements.

In a few minutes, the children are sitting on the floor again and Joan tells them, "The next music is about things that fly in the sky." She asks for suggestions and gets many:

"Airplanes."

"Helicopters."

"Blimps"

"Balloons."

"Kites."

"Sea gulls."

"Flags."

"Fairies."

The last idea is rejected by Nina, who comments, "Fairies are not real." A lively discussion begins, and Justin, who originally suggested fairies, insists that they are real. He places his hands on his back and says, "They have wings back here." His friend Emmet adds that fairies are real and then he begins to describe ferryboats. When the discussion wanes, the music begins again and the children fly around the gym. I hear Jason say, "Let's get to the airport and get the engines going. We need some directions."

For a few minutes I observe birds, airplanes, helicopters, and some less identifiable flying objects. Then Joan challenges the group with, "Now listen to the music and see if you can guess what's next."

The pianist plays the melody for "Humpty Dumpty" and the children hurry over to the edge of the wall, sing the rhyme with the piano, and fall at the appropriate time. They ask to "do it again" and their request is honored. After the second time, Joan suggests that they need music for the line that begins "All the king's horses." She asks, "What kind of music would it be?"

Devon begins to make the sound of galloping, and Joan responds, "Yes, galloping music." Soon, children are galloping around the room.

When the rhythms time is over, Joan says to Demetri, "Demetri, you asked about balls but we don't have time today. I'm going to write 'balls' in my book so that I remember to have balls next time we're together."

When I comment to Joan about her enthusiasm for the "rhythms class," she informs me that she leads these classes for all the children in the school. She adds, "I did rhythms here when I was a child." Again, I get the clear impression that Joan Morgan is at City & Country because she wants to be there—very much for the reasons that Angela chooses to be there.

Back in the classroom, a simple snack of saltine crackers and juice is on two of the tables—a long rectangular table and a circular one. Children pour their own juice and pass the baskets of crackers. As they enjoy their snack, I look around the room and see an environment similar to what I had previously visualized from the photos. The walls are bare except for a string of children's paintings around the room. There are collections of paintings for each child, hung one upon another and clipped together. I investigate and find that each collection represents about two months' worth of paintings—like a hanging portfolio. When I express curiosity, Angela explains, "We don't send paintings home with the children every day. First, we don't want to communicate to children that you paint in order to have a painting to take home. You paint because you *want* to paint, and there's value in that. We save the paintings for parent conference time—to review with parents, to look at changes, to study the expression."

I also notice multiple shelves of blocks, probably more blocks than I'm used to seeing in most early childhood education settings. In addition, there are several shelves of accessories: one with wooden people figures, one with wooden trains, and one with colorful squares of fabric. When I see Angela removing the fabric squares from the shelf, I ask her why. She explains, "When there are accessories, especially these, their building activity stops early. Their structures aren't very elaborate, not nearly as tall, and I don't hear much planning. I'll put the fabric out later when their building is advanced. I have experimented and tried it both ways. You wouldn't believe the difference in their structures."

I consider Angela's explanation and make a mental note to watch this phenomenon closely when the block building begins. In the meantime, Nina has finished her snack and is standing in the center of the room, chanting, "Who would like to work with me?" She repeats it twice, but gets no response. She tries again, singing, "Celia, would you like to work with me?" Celia nods her head "yes" and joins Nina. Angela bends down and gets face to face with Nina and says, "Did you notice that when you use someone's name, then you get a friend to work?" Nina nods her head, and goes off to the block shelves with Celia following her.

As the other children finish their snacks and leave the tables, I notice that Aki, one of the assistant teachers, also leaves the table and goes to an area that has a water table and two paint easels. Several children go straight to the easels and begin painting. I wonder why they're not wearing the usual paint smocks or aprons, but I'll wait to ask later. Nanci, the other assistant, is on the opposite side of the room with a woodworking bench. Emmet gets a saw and asks to cut some wood. Together, they put a long piece of wood in a vise, and Nanci guides the beginning saw strokes.

During this play period, I note that Angela does a lot of observing and note-taking. There are various forms around the room: a checklist with motor tasks such as skipping, jumping, galloping, and the like; a list of children's names with descriptive comments and recorded dialogue; and so on. I also see Angela intercept children who appear to be wandering: "What are you ready for?"

"Are you ready for clay, or paint, or . . ."

"Sit on the windowsill and think about it until you're ready for work."

Angela makes note of Devon's wandering, and comments to me, "When children wander, it may mean that the environment and materials aren't doing what they are intended for. Of course, there's also real variation in the children. Devon needed and still needs time to observe and comment on everyone else's work. But we do feel that children should look busy at City & Country, or we need to check on what we're doing."

Again, I reflect on the decision to intervene and the importance of knowing each individual child. I am also struck by the frequent use of the word *work,* both by children and by the teachers. I remembered reading Pratt's passionate expression about children's work:

> *Children have their own meaning for the word play. To them it does not, as it does to adults, carry the ideas of idleness, purposelessness, relaxation from work. When we began our school we had named it a "play school," as a telegraphic way of saying that in our way of teaching, the children learned by playing. It was the children who made us, early in the school's history, delete the word from the school's name. To them it was not a "play school" but a school, and they were working hard at their schooling.*
>
> *How hard they work, only we who have watched them really know. They do not waste one precious moment. They are going about their jobs all the time. No father in his office or mother in her home [remember—this was written in 1948] works at such a pace. For a long time I was principally afraid that they would exhaust themselves in this strenuous new kind of school. (1948, p. 9)*

As I watch the block building, I see the intensity Pratt was describing. Angela moves about the area engaging children in conversation about their block structures. After about 30 minutes, she returns the fabric squares to their shelf. Soon, children are using them with their block building, and I hear Justin telling Angela, "We made a movie theater . . . and then there's different shows . . . and people came to the show before the movie was started . . . and then the show was starting" and he points to a fabric square hanging from a block. He pauses with uncertainty. Angela asks, "Is that a curtain?" He nods with noticeable relief and says, "Yes, a curtain."

Celia and Nina, who were later joined by Alicia, have built an elaborate structure with many levels that extend over about nine feet of floor space. The girls have been thrilled to be together, giggling and talking loudly, and are now talking about going to Nina's house after school. Angela reminds them, "Sometimes when you plan things with other kids and the moms or dads aren't around, the plans don't work out." They listen and look serious, but then go back to their planning. Angela adds, "It's still fun to plan and think about it."

As Angela moves about the room observing, I use the opportunity to ask about the lack of paint aprons. She explains, "We don't want to communicate that getting paint on your clothes is like getting dirty. We also want to preserve the spontaneity of the child's work process. Parents are well informed and know that children wear only "school" clothes here—that is, clothes that children can get dirty or paint spills on, or whatever."

She and I notice that Sarah got bumped with a block. Sarah glances our way, looking a little sad, then heads for the mini-refrigerator near the sink in the corner of the room. I watch her open the tiny freezer door and take out an object to put on her head. My curiosity takes me to her side to get a better look. Now I can see that she has an empty film capsule filled with ice. Sarah looks quite satisfied and moves on. I check the freezer and see five more capsules there, waiting for the usual bumps that a 3-year-old encounters.

A quick survey of the entire room shows me that Vanessa is painting her fourth picture, and there is a child painting on each of the sides of the easels. A fifth child, Jason, also wanted to paint, so paper is taped to a nearby table and paints are provided so that he doesn't have to wait. I also notice that Devon and Eliot are at a small table working with clay. They are sitting right on the table and are very involved with manipulating the grey substance. Several children seem to be missing, and when I ask about them, I learn that they have gone to the library with Aki to find some information about crocodiles.

My survey of the room also shows me that Emmet has been sawing his board the entire time. I hear him say, "I'm getting tired. Maybe I should finish tomorrow." Nanci shows him how little wood is left where he's cutting, and he decides to finish. As he gets closer, he gets quite animated and checks his own progress often. After 25 minutes, he saws through his board and has a small chunk of wood of which he seems quite proud. Nanci encourages him to sand the rough edges, and lets him know that he can paint it the next day if he wishes.

Once again, I remember that I want to check the block building now that Angela has added the fabric squares. I can see six elaborate block constructions. I am somewhat amazed that the children have not had any problems bumping into each other's work or wanting the same special block. The amount and variety of blocks probably keep the need for sharing at a minimum, so the activity remains fairly peaceful. But I wondered about the potential for knocking structures over, especially with all the movement of children in the area where the constructions stand. When I commented on this, Angela described their work with children during the first few months of the year. She explained, "We began with a rule—you have to be able to walk between shelves and constructions, and between constructions themselves. Frankly, it wasn't for management and discipline reasons as much as for communicating how important the building is. We're trying to teach respect for children's own work and for other's work. At the beginning of school, when buildings fell, we helped to rebuild them immediately to communicate how important their work is."

I look again at the construction spread over the floor and the spacing is obvious. The routine is well established. I survey the variety of work. In addition to the movie theater, there are twin towers built side by side; a large pyramid structure with tiny colored blocks on the top arranged carefully in a pattern; a room with two beds made from blocks with dolls on each bed; another room with tables built from blocks with dishes on each table; and finally, a very extensive "castle" with "bedrooms, and dining room, and kitchen, and den." I look for the source of the dolls and the dishes, and see that they are from the water play area.

I move to observe the water play activity and notice that next to the water table is a shelf of dolls, metal dishes, and egg beaters. Interestingly, in the water table are

six large bowls full of water. At this time, Vanessa and Kristin are each bathing a doll in their bowls. I wonder about using the bowls and can't help but think that this strategy makes emptying the water a lot easier than emptying the entire water table. I check with Angela once again who explains, "The bowls are to ensure that each child has his own space and that things don't float to someone else's space. For threes [3-year-olds], it's more appropriate than sharing the large water table space. The space between the bowls is community space and there's usually plenty of water there before long. The children really do well with the individual bowls."

Angela is now moving about the room, telling individuals and small groups of children, "Five more minutes until pick up meeting." After the five minutes pass, she announces that it is time for a pick up meeting. As children assemble, she sings, "Nina's here with pink tights, pink tights, pink tights," and on to "Emmet's here with a polar bear shirt, a polar bear shirt, a polar bear shirt." Before the pick up assignments are given, children describe their block structures:

"I made a castle, and then I made a library, and then I made a kitchen."

Justin talks about his movie theater again.

Nina calls her tower-like structures "volcanoes" and adds, "Volcanoes are very hot."

Sarah contributes, "Vanessa pushed on my leg and I didn't want her to."

Angela nods and adds, "Did you hear that, Vanessa?" Sarah didn't want you to push on her leg."

Sarah repeats her complaint, and Vanessa responds, "It's because you were talking to me."

Angela prompts, "Can you tell Sarah why you don't want her to talk?"
Vanessa answers, "Because I was working."
The situation appears settled, and Angela moves to announcing pick up assignments:

"Justin—trains and people."
"Nina—cylinders."
"Alicia—butteries" (their word for blocks shaped like buttresses).
"Emmet—squaries."
"Devon and Kristin—scraping clay."

Again, the cleaning process goes smoothly. I notice that Elizabeth doesn't participate. She curls up on the floor, continues her role of "baby" with gestures and sounds, and watches others. Angela notices and goes to Elizabeth, talks with her quietly (I can't hear), and soon Elizabeth is gathering dishes for the shelf by the water table.

Nanci sits in the middle of the block construction area during the pick up and orchestrates with, "Here's some squaries, here's some butteries," and so on. She reminds Nina, "That's building, Nina; that's not picking up."

I watch as Eliot diligently folds the fabric pieces neatly in squares. I also notice that the table scrapers, Devon and Kristin, are working intensely to remove every bit of clay from the table. They are using putty knives, and when they finish the scraping, they wipe the table with small sponges. All around me is pick up activity, and when it's completed, I realize that the total cleaning procedure took only 12 minutes.

The children are again gathered around Angela for singing and a story. Angela has Devon's song sheet in her hand and she tells the children that they will learn his song about mosquitos. She asks Devon to lead the song and tells him she will join him in the singing. He does so, and after the first time, other children join in. At one point, when Angela is trying to figure out the rhythm of one line, Devon asks for the paper and proceeds to sing the words as if he is reading them.

Next, Angela shows the children a book, *Fix-it,* by David McPhail (Hutchinson, 1984). It is obvious that the children have heard it before because they predict what will happen page by page. At the end of the book, Angela asks, "Is Emma a girl or a boy?" Most of the children cannot decide. For those who do voice an opinion, Angela asks, "How can you tell?" Children suggest that the toys and clothes are clues, but there continues to be no agreement. Angela asks, "Did you notice that I said *she* and *her?*" Children chime in, "Emma's a girl."

During the entire song and story time, Aki and Nanci have been placing children's lunch boxes on the tables, opening the boxes and varied containers within them, and placing the lunches on small paper plates. There are a lot of thermoses and plastic containers with airtight lids. I wonder why children don't open their own containers or arrange their own lunches. I have learned by this time that there is a reason for this procedure, and Angela explains, "Children stay here for lunch for social reasons. With 'threes,' it could take the whole lunch period for them to get everything opened or arranged. Our goal during this period is not independence or fine motor skills. It's social development. The other aspect is that it's done for management reasons. It frees up the teachers to stay sitting at the tables to interact socially with the children."

"We're ready to go to the tables," Angela tells the children. "I'll say a word that rhymes with your name, and when you hear it, go to your place." She repeats these directions, and adds, "If you have trouble listening, close your eyes and listen carefully." Emmet says, "When I rub my head, it helps me think." Angela agrees, and says she's ready to call out the rhyming words. Before she can begin, Devon says, "Bevon Crutman" (his name is Devon Strutman). Angela responds with delight, "That's a hard one—good for you." No one else makes an attempt, so she begins to make up rhyming names and the children move easily to the tables for lunch.

Angela's description of lunch time, and the social reasons for children staying, is played out before me as I observe a calm, conversational meal. Nanci has a plate of pineapple, and asks, "Do you know what this is?" when children ask about her lunch. The guesses include cauliflower, cheese, grapefruit, and pineapple."

I hear other conversations:

"Melissa's mom called to say that Melissa is sick. What do you think could be wrong with her?" Answers ranged from "a stomachache," to "a cough," to "an ear infection," to "a hurt eye."

"What kind of sandwich do you have today, Vanessa?"

"Jelly."

"Jelly! That's half of what Nina has today. She has peanut butter and jelly."

As children are close to finishing both food and conversation, Angela moves from child to child, holding a sketch of the two tables used for eating. She asks each child to tell her where he or she would like to sit for snack and lunch, beginning the following week. As children indicate their preferences, she labels the spot with the child's name. I hear, "I want to sit in the place where Elizabeth is sitting" or "I want to sit where Eliot is sitting" Angela, noting my interest, describes this routine: "In the beginning, I sat children next to individuals that I wanted them to get to know. The last time we changed places, I let them choose their friends and arrange themselves. This time, it was interesting and unexpected. They seemed focused on who was sitting in the *place* they wanted. They didn't even attend to being next to anyone in particular."

As the children leave the table after lunch, I hear, "I'm going to sit where you were sitting." I ask myself what this behavior tells me about 3-year-olds, but no answer comes readily to mind. Angela seems just as puzzled as I am.

Most children get assistance from Nanci or Aki as they gather leftover food and containers and place them in lunch boxes. Angela, in the meantime, has placed six sheets of manila paper in the water table with six small wooden boxes of large crayon pieces. On a small table nearby, she places wooden puzzles, all fairly complicated and difficult. She then places on the floor two large tubs of colored plastic buttons and beads with thick strings. I also see Angela place small pieces of tape on the edge of a shelf near the water table.

The next 25 minutes is a busy time as children do their afternoon work: coloring, assembling puzzles, stringing beads, and continuing the make-believe I witnessed all morning. There's a pleasant hum of activity in the classroom. Puzzle pieces become animals and make sounds during the assembly process. Kristin and Alicia sing "Old MacDonald." From the bead/button stringing activity, I hear, "I'm sewing a necklace for you" and "I'm sewing a shirt for you." Buttons become "cookies for the Cookie Monster" and puzzle pieces become "radar guns." As the activity slows down, I notice that some of the children roll up their drawings, get their own piece of tape to keep the tube rolled, and place their roll next to their lunch boxes. They appear to be taking their drawings home and I wonder why.

As I watch, I also reflect. "It is May, and routines are obviously well established. No one has been reminding the children of what to do. I also reflect on the transitions of the morning, and the word *smooth* is the best descriptor. There are two explanations for the smoothness: routines that are appropriate for large group transitions, and wherever possible, transitions are mostly individuals moving from one activity to another.

Soon, the room is full of adults. I notice diverse roles among the people picking up these 3-year-old children: parents, grandparents, babysitters, and nannies. It's a different group of adults from those who brought these children to school earlier today.

It is also time for me to leave, but before I go, I decide that I need to observe what classrooms are like for children after they leave the "threes" room. I sense that City & Country is a place where it is important to see the "big picture" as a way of better understanding what I have observed in this one classroom. I'm curious again. What do 5- and 6-year-old children do with the blocks, and how does the curriculum address math and literacy content? Are there more accessories?

Looking Beyond the "Threes" at City & Country

When I visit the class of 5-year-olds, I am immediately aware of the central role of block building. I learn that 5-year-olds are the first class to sustain their work and leave their block structures up from Monday through Friday. I see a weekly chart of "Ideas and Builders" and note a focus on "real-world" structures. In addition to building community structures, these children are able to paint streets, paths, water, and parks right on the floor of their classroom with real water-based paint. Signs on the structures tell me that these are primarily collaborative building projects, with the participation of two to five children. This age group goes on many field trips, primarily to visit buildings in the community. They are sometimes impromptu trips, involving a small group of children for whom a need arises, such as an interest in seeing a particular building. Sometimes, the trips involve the entire class.

During group time, the 5-year-olds discuss construction problems. In the rug area, where these meetings are probably held, I see a "meeting map" displaying everyone's place to sit for the meeting. I also see many signs, in children's handwriting, labeling most items in the classroom, as well as many structures in the community of blocks. I learn that there is a weekly routine that involves the children visiting each other's buildings. The visits and the tours that result are done through the same wooden people that I saw in the "threes" room. The 5-year-olds, however, make paper fronts for the people, adding to their realistic quality. These characters then "talk" for the visitors and for those giving the building tours.

The remainder of the 5-year-olds' day is scheduled with mathematics, reading and language arts, art, science, and other curriculum content, generally in an integrated approach.

The "sixes" are off on a trip, so I proceed to a class of 7-year-olds. I notice immediately that there are no blocks, but I learn that blocks were used until Spring break, then put away. Earlier, using the blocks, the "sevens" worked out details of constructing a city. I see a large floor plan, notes from city meetings, and lists of city work.

At this time of year, the city is well underway, with most buildings constructed. It is May and the buildings are made from wood that has been cut, nailed, sanded, and painted by these children. A group of children represent the electric company and they are running wires through all the structures and connecting them to a central structure. The "water company" group is doing the same thing with tiny pipes. These groups have assembled research journals with the information they need to run their companies. Again, there are many signs, messages, detailed paper fronts on buildings, and paper clothes on people and animals.

When the children reach the age of 8, their studies are extended from their own city to other cities, their country, and the world. They have spent up to six years building a solid understanding of their own community and developing research skills to learn about other places and people. At this time, the 8-year-olds are spending a week in the country as part of their study of the Oregon Trail and the explorations of Lewis and Clark. While away from the city, these children are cooking their own food in ways similar to the pioneers' cooking, sewing clothes for themselves, building simple equipment that they read about in stories of the Oregon Trail, and keeping journals about their lives as pioneers.

After leaving the other classrooms at City & Country, my reflections take me back to the 3-year-olds and their classroom activities. I visualize the energy, the imagination, the curiosity, the interest, the initiative, and the exploration of those children. Those qualities are sometimes discouraged or stifled when children leave early childhood education settings to make way for "work" and "real learning." City & Country School provides a program that promotes those qualities in classrooms for the youngest to the oldest children. The noise and activity levels throughout the school tell me that the involvement stays just as intense as children get older. The school is indeed continuing the tradition intended by Caroline Pratt to "make the years of learning, the school years, meaningful."

Questions and Issues

1. Reflect on Angela's rationales for routines and decisions in the classroom. Do you agree or disagree? Can you think of other "out of the ordinary" routine or unusual decisions that demand well-developed rationales? Discuss these.
2. If you were in the position to replicate the City & Country curriculum with blocks as the mainspring, what obstacles would you face?
3. In the 3-year-olds' classroom, you observed a number of adult interventions. Identify these situations and respond to them.
4. You also observed a number of examples of adults respecting children's needs and ideas. Identify these situations and analyze the communication messages.
5. The pick up meeting appeared to be more successful for cleaning a large amount of materials than strategies observed in other programs. What contributed to its success?

References

Cartwright, S. (1990). Learning with large blocks. *Young Children, 45* (3), 38–41.

Gehlbach, R. D. (1991). Play, Piaget, and creativity: The promise of design. *Journal of Creative Behavior, 25* (2), 137–144.

Gelfer, J. I., & Perkins, P. G. (1988). Using blocks to build art concepts: A new look at an old friend. *Early Child Development and Care, 30,* 59–69.

Green, V. P., & Schaefer, L. (1984). Preschool teachers play materials preferences. *Early Child Development and Care, 14* (1–2), 85–92.

Hirsch, E. (1974). *The block book.* Washington, DC: National Association for the Education of Young Children.

Holz, K. (1993). *City & Country School: A model for progressive educational philosophy in practice.* Paper presented at the annual meeting of the American Educational Research Association, Atlanta, GA.

Karges-Bone, L. (1991). Blocks are not (circle all): Messy, expensive, difficult. *Dimensions, 20,* (1), 5–8.

Nourot, P. M., & Van Hoorn, J. L. (1991). Symbolic play in preschool and primary settings. *Young Children, 46* (6), 40–48.

Pratt, C. (1948). *I learn from children.* New York: Harper and Row.

Tegano, D. W., Moran, J. D., & Sawyers, J. K. (1991). *Creativity in early childhood classrooms.* Washington, DC: National Education Association.

Wassermann, S. (1992). Serious play in the classroom. *Childhood Education, 68* (3), 133–138.

3

The Child Development Project: Longwood and Ruus Elementary Schools

"Caring Communities" Where Children Develop Cooperation and Responsibility

Picture an elementary school in a neighborhood where the mobility rate can be so high that the "front door of the school feels like a turnstile" (Davini, 1992). Visualize a neighborhood of homes in disrepair, imagine the abandoned cars sitting in front yards, and envision the dangers that accompany the prevalent drug traffic. Picture some of the children coming from extreme poverty or from homes in which adults "rule" with hard discipline. Look into some of the classrooms: The climate may be tense, learning may be minimal, and rewards and punishments may be the only way to maintain order. Consider the feelings of some of the parents who know little about this place called school and whose involvement, at best, is limited to an occasional back-to-school night.

Those scenes are now "history" in some of the neighborhoods of Hayward, California. Two of the schools in those neighborhoods are Longwood and Ruus Elementary Schools, and many of the children (about 70 percent) who attend those schools have lives with multiple risks and severe stresses.

Today, one can drive through the neighborhoods surrounding Longwood and Ruus and see homes restored with fresh paint and colorful blooming yards. Today, two or three families get together and buy those homes so that their children will have a good place to live. The "drug corridor" is gone, and the neighbors keep a vigilant watch over their community. The schools are characterized by children helping each other, by caring relationships within classrooms and between class-rooms, and by management and discipline systems in which children have "a voice." Parents are involved in family homework and cooperative projects, and at home, many parents now involve their children in family decisions and responsibilities.

Principals, teachers, children, and parents at Longwood and Ruus Schools talk with both pride and passion about the changes in their lives. The changes came about as they participated in the the Child Development Project, or the CDP. The project was not intended as a panacea for the problems in the Hayward neighbor-hoods and schools. However, the changes instituted as part of the CDP had a "ripple effect." That is, they became an impetus for changes outside the classrooms and outside the schools.

What Is the Child Development Project?

Before traveling to the Hayward schools of Longwood and Ruus, you deserve an answer to your question, What is the Child Development Project? A description of the project will give you a preview of what is ahead in our visit. More importantly, the major components of the project will provide a framework for watching the interactions in those schools. To describe the project in answer to your question then, we need to look briefly at the beginnings of the CDP.

The Child Development Project was initiated in the San Ramon Valley Unified School District with generous funding from the Hewlett Foundation in 1982. Simply stated, the CDP was a program for promoting "prosocial" values and behavior in the schools. Another way of describing the project has come from Alfie Kohn (1990), who observed in the San Ramon schools. He described a "kind of immersion for the students, saturating all aspects of their school experience and some of their time at home as well" (p. 172). In 1988, the program was introduced at two elementary schools in nearby Hayward. Longwood and Ruus offered a contrast to the white, affluent suburbs of San Ramon. How would the Child Development Project affect the Hayward children's attitudes, behavior, and achievement? When I listened to teachers, administrators, children, and parents in the Hayward community, I was convinced that the effects would be as positive and encouraging as the data from studies of the San Ramon schools.

According to the Hayward stories I heard from teachers and parents, children were definitely developing a prosocial orientation. Simply stated, they were becom-ing caring individuals. Parents were becoming involved in children's schoolwork, especially in projects that promoted families learning together. Teachers were experimenting with a number of cooperative approaches to learning and classroom management. And the schools genuinely felt like caring communities—"places where children feel valued, connected, and responsible to others" (Schaps & Solomon, 1990).

This background information still does not answer the question of what the Child Development Project really is. Another way of responding to your question is by describing the major components of the CDP. The first component is the curriculum, or content. The content of CDP is sometimes a package of specially designed lessons or activities. But more often, texts, reading materials, stories, and other educational materials are used to communicate perspective taking or to model prosocial behavior. The most prevalent example is the literature used for literacy and social studies. The selections are rich with models of friendship, altruism, feelings, cooperation, empathy, helping others, and being responsible. These selections also describe situations of discrimination, bias, irresponsibility, selfishness, and competition, and are used to promote discussion of values and behaviors.

The second component, the method of teaching, is based on the belief that children should teach children. Teachers arrange and facilitate learning groups and learning pairs; children learn from their peers and from older students. Tutoring is common.

In terms of classroom management, the CDP approaches are described as "developmental discipline." Children make active and important decisions about how their classrooms are organized, and take much of the responsibility for maintenance of routines and problem solving. This role for children is directly related to the third component, the context of the learning experiences at Ruus and Longwood.

The context, or climate, is characterized by frequent, spontaneous, caring behaviors and minimal behavior problems. Teachers and children form warm relationships. The goal of CDP is to create an environment in which children will want to learn and help each other.

The final component is the caring adult to guide and to facilitate prosocial behaviors in children. CDP teachers enforce principles of fairness and model the values that they teach. Parents get involved in assignments, projects, and schoolwide activities that provide opportunities for them to be models too.

A Framework for Our Visit to Hayward

Rather than spend an entire day in one classroom selected from the many classrooms for young children in the two Hayward schools, we will visit as many as we can in one day. You will have a series of vignettes—short visits—to some of the kindergarten, first-grade, and second-grade classrooms at Longwood and Ruus Schools. This will allow you to see the "big picture" of the Child Development Project and the varied approaches of CDP rather than how one teacher implements the program.

I approach the entrance to Longwood School by crossing a large expanse of pavement on which there are faded paintings of world and U.S. maps and a diagram of the solar system. In the window just ahead is a colorful poster representing the countries of origin of the students and families of Longwood. Approximately 73 percent of the children at this school are minorities, and 81 percent of the children at Ruus are minorities. I later learn that the average number of languages spoken in the classrooms of this school is seven.

Vignette #1: High-Flying Buddies

As I enter a kindergarten classroom, the children are sitting in a circle at the front of the room. I hear the children singing "Good Morning to You," then "Buenos Dias to You" to each other. Then Roberto stands up next to the teacher, Linda, and the children sing, "Here is Roberto, our child of the day." Their song goes on to say that they like Roberto and that he is a good friend. After this, the children sing the days of the week in English and Spanish, count in both languages, and likewise describe the day's weather. When SuSu begins to bother the children next to her, Linda requests, "Please help, either by counting or by not disturbing others."

As Linda and the children finish their morning routines, the children's older "buddies" arrive. I watch as the third-grade children seek out the kindergarten children with whom they are paired. The third-graders are from a bilingual class, and I notice that many of them are non-English speaking. Nevertheless, they approach their younger buddies with confidence. Caring is communicated through smiles, hugs, hand holding, and warm conversation.

The buddies go to an outside courtyard where Linda's parents have set up a display of kites. Mr. and Mrs. Rogers are retired and they travel all over the country. In their travels they collect and fly kites, so they have an extensive and impressive collection. The children are also impressed and there are lots of "ohs" and "ahs" over the vivid colors, the sizes, and the intricate designs. Most of the kindergarten children are sitting in the laps of or encircled by the arms of their third-grade buddies. Just then, a blond, blue-eyed child arrives and is told to find her buddy. She hesitates and looks at the group. She immediately sees her dark-skinned buddy waving and smiling to her, and hurries over to join her.

Mr. and Mrs. Rogers show the kites one at a time, telling interesting details about the names of kites and where they came from. All of the children appear keenly interested. Occasionally, there's a question: Why does it have such a long tail? Where do you hold the string? Soon, Mr. and Mrs. Rogers inform the children that they can take the kites to the nearby playground and fly them. I am impressed by the trust and the ease with which they part with their precious collection. Linda suggests to the children that kite flying might not go as well as they would like due to the lack of wind. There is genuine disappointment in her voice. The children, however, take off with the kind of enthusiasm that will not be daunted.

There are not quite enough kites for every pair of buddies to have one, so two pairs of buddies share kites and do so easily. I watch and listen as children struggle to get the kites flying without much help from the wind:

"All you have to do is run with the kite and it'll go up," an African American, stocky, third-grade boy says to his freckled kindergarten buddy.

"Touch the string—help me hold it," a petite Asian kindergarten student says to her Hispanic third-grade buddy.

"Wow, it's going fast, right?" asks a shiny black-haired Japanese 5-year-old.

"Let Pierre do it," reminds Tai to the other set of buddies sharing the kite.

These pairs of buddies are used to such communication; they get together several times a week for a variety of activities. Once a week they have lunch with each other, and once a week they participate together in a recycle unit. They also have "reading pals" one day a week. There are also both social and academic activities scattered throughout the month—parties for special occasions, field trips, publishing celebrations, art projects such as murals, and talk time for sharing units of study. The kindergarten and third-grade children also write to each other regularly.

After about 25 minutes of kite-flying attempts, the group returns the kites and goes inside the school. (There were no mishaps with the kites, and I'm happy to report that they were still in perfect condition.) As the buddies separate and leave each other to go to their respective classrooms, many hugs and warm farewells are exchanged.

Back in their own classroom, the third-graders immediately have a class meeting about their feelings of frustration and their lack of much success with the kite

flying. As they take turns expressing something important about the experience, I hear the following comments:

"My buddy ran away from me and I couldn't find her. Then I didn't have much time to fly the kite."

"I really tried but it just wouldn't stay up for very long."

"I helped a lot of people fly their kites."

"I even helped a teacher fly a kite."

When Arture takes his turn, he speaks in Spanish. His teacher translates his message: "I told Joe not to cuss in front of the little kids."

I can sense the relief and the easing of tension as children express their feelings and have them accepted. (When children haven't had the chance to express such feelings in appropriate ways, negative behavior often erupts during the very next activity.)

In contrast, in the kindergarten classroom, the talk about kite flying has very little of the frustration felt by the older buddies. Their comments are mostly positive. It is obvious that even the smallest ascent of a kite is perceived as a success for these children. Now they are "writing" in their journals about the experience.

Interestingly, many of the children can write the names of their buddies as well as they can write their own names. It comes as no surprise that there are many requests for how to spell the word *kite*. Linda reminds the children that they used the word *kite* for a story that the class wrote. That seems to be all some children need and they begin writing, while others look at the story hanging on the chalkboard.

Linda, noticing that Pierre is sitting still, asks him if he needs help to get started. "Yes," he nods. Marissa jumps up from her spot on the floor and says, "I'll help him—I'll help Pierre." Unfortunately, he wants help with spelling the name of a Vietnamese food he likes, but Marissa tries to assist anyway. After having him repeat the name of his favorite food several times, she urges him to draw a picture of it. Pierre seems satisfied and begins his sketch.

Another child says aloud, "Now I remember the word I was working on—*leprechaun*." Several minutes later, I notice that five of the children have added leprechauns to their kite pictures and narratives. I hear another child say to Linda, "Look, teacher, I wrote all these words—I write too much." She ends up giggling as she finishes making her claim.

As other children finish, they bring their journals to their teacher and read them to her. They are encouraged to find a partner and read the journal to him or her. As I listen, I hear frequent mention of "my buddy" and "flying kites," as would be expected. As children finish reading to a partner, they are able to get a variety of board games from a shelf and play with one or more friends. This happens easily and the games involve friendly exchange.

Vignette #2: How to Be a Good Partner

In a bilingual second-grade classroom, the children are gathering for a literacy experience. As they get ready, I look around the room and notice interesting displays. There is a graph of "Who Was Your Teacher Last Year?" with the names of the first-grade teachers across the top. The second-graders have drawn photos of themselves on the graph in the appropriate column. A class quilt hangs on another wall—a colorful blanket of personal squares about each child. One sign really holds my attention:

Partner Rules

Remember to listen to what your partner is saying.

Be fair to your partner.
Cooperate.

The second-graders are getting ready for a partner activity, so I will have the opportunity to see the degree to which those partner rules are observed. Penny, their teacher, has gathered the children on a rug in front of her and is showing the pictures in the book *Angel and the Soldier Boy* by Collington (Random House, 1987). As she slowly displays the story's illustrations, she encourages the children "to observe" and "to use your eyes." She reminds them that they will be telling their partners the story when she finishes.

At the end of the story, she gives directions for the tasks each pair of partners is to complete. She continues, "You can go anyplace in the room, but it's a good idea to sit next to each other. What are some places that would be good work spaces?"

Children suggest the following:

"In front of the cubbies."

"At a table."

"On the pillows."

In a later conversation, I learn that children are given many opportunities to use as much of the classroom as possible. This is in contrast to confining children to their desks or tables for most of the day's activities. "If the classroom belongs to all of us, then children should have many choices of where they want to work" (Davini, 1992) is the thinking of these teachers.

Penny then asks for suggestions on how to work with a partner on this particular assignment. Responses include:

"Take turns—one tells the story, and one writes the story—take turns."

"When you finish, tell each other which character in the story you would like to be."

Penny asks another question, "How do we listen to our partners?"

"We look at our partners."

"We pay attention to their words."

Penny then asks, "How can we be fair to our partners?"

"By being nice."

"By listening."

"One person isn't going to do all of it."

"If there's an extra page at the end, you could read it together."

A final question is then posed by Penny: "We're also going to cooperate, and what does that look like?"

"No fighting."

"We're not mean."

"We help our partners."

Penny asks Vanessa to show how partners use one book cooperatively, and Vanessa demonstrates holding a book with another second-grader.

The children look ready to begin, so Penny reminds them to check the partner list hanging on the chalkboard if they do not remember this month's partner. Within a minute, pairs of children are scattered around the room, and I hear them telling each other the story, some in English and some in Spanish. They use the book's illustrations and they add great expression to their storytelling:

"And she said, 'Oh no—I can't find my soldier boy.' "

"It was a dream! She was dreaming about that story."

"Donde estaba el soldado ya no esta?"

"Se esta llevando la moneda y el soldado le esta diciendo que no se la lleve."

As children are finishing their storytelling task, some of them don't remember the next part of their assignment. When Ernesto asks Penny what to do, his partner taps him on the shoulder and points to the chalkboard. Together, they read the directions and begin discussing their answers to the questions.

Penny reminds the children, "Use your brain and use your friend's brain as you answer the questions."

The rest of the work session goes smoothly. Children obviously have learned how to be a partner. What is apparent when watching and listening to them is that time has been spent teaching and learning about partner behaviors—and practicing partner behaviors. There is also regular feedback for appropriate partner interactions, and the feedback comes from both the teacher as well as the children.

Just as I was leaving this classroom, I noticed that Manuel ran to the back of the classroom to write something on one of the many charts. The heading on this chart was "Things to Praise Our Friends For." Manuel wrote, "I like the way Tony kept our group from fiteing today."

Vignette #3: Helping a New Student

In Laurie's kindergarten classroom, it's 5-year-old Ada's first day. From the very beginning of the day, children have spontaneously been offering, "I'll be your buddy," or "I'll show you where to put that," or "I'll help you do that." As the class moves through their morning routines, someone is always at Ada's side offering assistance. At one point, the teacher, Laurie, asks Julius to "show Ada where we put our journals," only to find out that someone had already done so.

When it is time to pass out reading books, Laurie says to Ada, "Since you're trying to learn everyone's names, you can pass them out." Laurie then encourages the children to raise their hands when they hear their names "to help Ada to get to know you." They begin with Laurie reading the names and Ada handing the books to individual children. In the middle of this distribution, Vien has a nosebleed and Laurie takes him aside. She hands over the remaining books to Margaret saying, "Margaret, read these names while I take care of Vien." Margaret and Ada finish passing out the books, and children begin reading to each other.

While this is happening, someone comes to the door with a message. Without being told, Esther, a kindergarten student, answers the door and takes the message for her teacher. She waits until her teacher finishes caring for Vien, then gives her the message. Laurie thanks Esther for being responsible.

Just before going home that morning, the children gather in a circle to talk about the morning. Many of the children tell how they got to know Ada or helped her:

"I made a picture with Ada—she colored this tree and I made the flowers."

"I showed Ada how to put her work in her file. I told her to make a pretty picture on the cover. She picked out a blue folder."

"Ada knows my name. I taught her and she said it."

Then Laurie asks Ada if the children could ask her questions about herself. "It would help us get to know you," adds Laurie.

Ada nods her head with confidence to this request. Laurie suggests that Ada point to the individual children and that the children say their names before taking a turn to ask a question. The children immediately raise their hands to begin asking questions.

"What kind of toys do you have?"

"What school did you come from?"

"Do you have a family?"

"Do you have a dog?"

Ada answers the questions easily and appears comfortable. After about seven or eight questions, Laurie tells the children that they might "wear out Ada," so they will ask more questions the next day.

As children get ready to leave, Laurie reminds them to bring their lunches the next day because it is their day to eat with their older buddies. Immediately, Julius asks, "What about Ada? Who will be her buddy?" Laurie assures Ada and Julius that she will meet with the third-grade teacher that afternoon to find a buddy for Ada.

As I observe Ada leaving her new classroom, my impression is that she feels welcome and cared for. My impression is also one of respect for the children and their teacher, and the kind of response a new child receives in their classroom. It is as if everyone is responsible for making Ada feel comfortable and part of the group. I continue to watch her leave, and her head is held high. She walks out hand in hand with a new friend. I follow behind them, and when she spots her mother, she runs to her and begins to chatter about the day in school. The chatter has a happy excited tone to it.

Vignette #4: Working on Social Goals and Academic Goals

In Mary Jo's second grade, there's a large poster entitled "What to Do When Someone Pesters You." The responses are obviously the children's ideas. They include:

Ignore them.

Say, "Please stop that."

Say, "How would you like it if . . . ?"

Tell the teacher.

Say, "That hurts me."

Say, "That bothers me."

Before beginning a mural about E. B. White's *Charlotte's Web* (Harper and Row, 1952), Mary Jo talks to the children about the project. They will be drawing scenes from the book on large puzzle pieces. She describes their goals for this activity: "Our social goal is to have quiet voices and to share materials. What materials are you going to share in this activity?"

Children suggest crayons, markers, colored pencils, erasers, and so on. Mary Jo asks another question: "Why do we use quiet voices to work together?"

Several children talk about how noisy it is in their room if all the groups are talking too loud:

"It makes my head ache."

"I can't work when it's too noisy."

"It hurts my ears."

"It might bother other classes."

Mary Jo introduces the academic goal of portraying the scenes of *Charlotte's Web*. When she asks why this goal is important, the responses are varied:

"It helps us remember the story."

"We think about the scenes."

"We learn to draw better."

As the groups of children begin, there is a flurry of activity and a buzz of conversation. It soon becomes a productive hum as children make decisions and sketch scenes. After five or six minutes of work, Mary Jo calls for attention by standing in the center of the room with her hand on her head. She reminds the class, "If your hand is on your head, then you are looking up here and listening for a message."

Her message is a reminder for the children to comment on each other's work. She rehearses with them what they can say about it. Suggestions for comments include:

"Your picture looks real."

"Tell me about your picture."

"You've been working on the sky and it's pretty."

The work on the scenes continues and I hear children commenting to each other about coloring and sharing. When the individual puzzle pieces are finished, each group brings its piece up to a table where the puzzle is being assembled. When complete, Mary Jo encourages all the children to stand around the table and look at the big picture. She asks, "How did we do with our mural of *Charlotte's Web?*" Children comment on the beauty of the finished puzzle and on the story it tells.

Mary Jo asks the children another question: "How did we do on our social goals?" The children's consensus, as a class, is that they did well. Mary Jo asks them to rate their voices during the activity with, "If you used a quiet voice, rate yourself with a 5." She proceeds to suggest the levels of 4 for not quite quiet, 3 for just OK, 2 for noisy, and 1 for very noisy, forgetting to be quiet. I watch as children assess themselves, then hold up a specific number of fingers to indicate their self-rating. I see many 5s, a few 4s, no 3s or 2s, and one 1. I can't help but contrast this approach with the more typical one of the adult telling the child whether he or she used a quiet voice. I make a prediction to myself that as these children experience being responsible for making this assessment decision, they will also take responsibility for the way they use their voices.

After the self-ratings, Mary Jo asks the children if they wish to talk about other experiences they had during their group activity. Lisa tells the group that she asked Misha about her picture. Mary Jo probes with, "What did Misha say when you asked her about your picture?"

Lisa responds, "She said I needed to change the face a little."

Mary Jo probes again, "How did that feel?"

Lisa responds, with some hesitance in her voice, "OK."

Mary Jo assures her and informs the rest of the class, "It's hard to hear criticism."

There is an immediate and thoughtful discussion by the children of what it's like to hear criticism, why people do it, and when it's good and bad. I hear comments from the children:

"Sometimes my dad criticizes me about my schoolwork, but then he helps me."

"My big sister criticizes me 'cause I don't clean up my room. It makes me mad, but then I clean it."

"When parents criticize us, it's because they want us to be good."

"Yeah, they really love us and that's why they do it."

"Sometimes when I get criticized, I really can do a better job."

It is an insightful conversation about a sensitive topic. I must remind myself that I'm sitting in a second-grade class, not a room full of adults.

Before leaving this classroom, I am distracted by a display of books made by the children. Interestingly, all of the books seem to have two authors. I look closer and see:

"Brown Bear" by Mom and Me
"A Happy Day" by Elizabeth and her father, Jesse Gonzales
"Morning" by Kallen and Al Akiyama

One book says it with special clarity: "The pictures are by mom, not me." I decide that these books must have been one of the family homework projects. I'm impressed and can imagine the children's pride when reading a book produced by their parents and themselves.

Vignette #5: A Classroom That Feels Like a Family

"I want you to feel like this is a family, a family in which everyone can work with everyone else" (Davini, 1992). That is a common wish heard by the children in Sandy's first-grade classroom. To her peers, Sandy expresses a similar plea, "We, as teachers, need to make this school the safest, most trusting place to be." As children arrive in her classroom, they receive a warm greeting from Sandy and from their peers. I don't see a single child who does not receive an acknowledgment by at least one other child. It is now April and I'd like to know how this family was established over the previous months.

I watch today's routines for clues. At arrival time, specific materials are set out on a table for the children—simple play materials: puzzles, cards, pattern shapes, and games. I notice that pairs of children use these materials, and I hear them approaching each other to make arrangements:

"Karim, do you want to play checkers with me?"

"Jose, want to play 'War' with me?"

"Jeannie, come on, let's get the shapes."

I also hear negotiations:

"No, I don't want to play checkers anymore. I never win."

"OK, what do you want to play?"

"I want to do puzzles. I'm good at puzzles."

"OK, we'll do puzzles today."

This example of problem solving and cooperation tells me that these children have learned to live together in this classroom.

After a short time of this play activity, cleanup is signaled and directions for the day's partner activity are given. I listen to the directions that concern today's partner interview: "Today, ask your partner his or her first and last names. Then ask your partner his or her favorite color. Be sure to find out why he or she likes that color. And see if there's anything special they want to tell you about that color."

As children begin their interviews, I see that Sandy is paired with one of the children and participating in the interviews. Her partner looks quite happy in her interactions with her teacher. I listen to one pair of children:

"What are all your names?"

"My names are Miranda Anna Ruiz."

"What is your favorite color?"

"I like purple best."

"Why do you like it?"

"It's my momma's favorite color. She has purple dresses and I do too."

"Do you have any purple toys?"

"No, only dresses and flowers."

"OK, now it's my turn."

I learn that these interviews have been a daily activity since the first of the year. In the beginning, children were directed to find a new partner every day until they had interviewed every class member. After that, they were able to choose a partner for a week or were given a week-long partner assignment by Sandy. Sandy describes the activities as "low-risk and simple" interviews designed to help children get to know and be known by every classmate. From my observations, these interviews look like they work to establish positive relationships for peers and help bond children to their classroom community.

After the partner activity, the children gather to share highlights of their interviews. "Did anyone learn something about a friend that they want to share?" Sandy asks. Several children describe a color choice and reasons for the choice.

Mignon shares, "My partner Iris and I like the same color—yellow."

Peter states, "I used to like blue but now I like black like my partner does."

After a brief sharing, children move to their tables. There are four children at each table and in the center of the table is a wooden crate of materials: pencils, crayons, scissors, paste, and other items. More often than not, I have seen each child with his or her own set of materials in other classrooms. Having a common set of supplies provides more opportunities for negotiating, sharing, and group responsibility in this classroom.

I see that on each table there is also a bowl of assorted buttons and a stack of paper cups. Two children at each table distribute the buttons and cups, and the children are soon involved in a sorting activity. They don't seem to need directions.

After a short time, I ask the children at one of the tables what they are doing. They tell me that they are finding "buttons that go together." I see that most of the children have sorted them by color. Just then, Sandy tells the children to do their group sharing routine to find out how each group member sorted their buttons. The children take turns easily in their groups. They share their classification schemes: "I put all the blue buttons together" or "I put all the big buttons together."

After barely a minute of this sharing, Sandy directs them, "Work with the person across the table from you and find new ways to put your buttons together." Some children move their chairs to another side of the table, some take their buttons and cups to the floor, and some stay in place and reach across the table.

Most partners quickly begin their new sorting. Sandy walks around the room, listening and observing. She stops by two children who cannot agree on a classification scheme. Each child has a different way to sort the buttons. Sandy reminds them that there isn't a "right way" but that both of their ideas are ways to sort the buttons.

At the end of the activity, Sandy notices that one of the children looks upset and frustrated. She sits with the child and her partner and asks, "What's happening here?" The upset child blurts out, "I don't want to do this anymore." Sandy assures her that she doesn't have to, and the child asks, "I don't have to?" with wide eyes and surprise in her voice. Sandy assures her again, and the partners pick up their materials and return to their table.

When the other children finish, Sandy's directions are for one person from each set of partners to "turn to the person on your right side and tell him or her how you sorted the buttons and what you learned." After a minute, the directions allow the other person to tell about his or her sorting. When this sharing is finished, Sandy asks the entire class, "Did anyone learn a new way of sorting from someone else?" Several children volunteer and describe "sorting by rough and smooth" and "sorting by number of holes in the button."

Again, I see a smooth routine and hear active involvement in both the sorting and sharing. Later, Sandy tells me that she realizes that sometimes children need assistance to work cooperatively with a specific partner. She would rather not wait for tension to build between partners, so she doesn't hesitate to step in and do some "coaching."

Later in the day, I stop back in Sandy's room to see the children making a class book on what they have learned about fractions. The children make a group list of "What We Learned" then add individual drawings and group murals. "These books act as a review and continue the teaching," Sandy tells me, "because the children can read them all the rest of the year."

Just before dismissal, the children gather in a circle with Sandy and talk about what they did today. Sandy role-plays, "I'm your mom and I ask you what you learned in school today." Several children respond. Sandy continues, "I'm your grandpa and I want to know what you did in school today." Several other children respond. Then

Sandy asks individual children for "one new idea you learned today." I notice that the door is open, and a number of parents are standing nearby and listening.

Sandy finishes the circle time with a sharing of her own: "I learned about Rona's favorite color today and all about her black dog." She continues, "I also have a new idea about fractions—that they help us share with friends." She reminds the children, "I learned that from you."

Vignette #6: Making Connections Between School and Families

It is 30 minutes before dismissal, but there's already a large group of parents at Longwood School. Some of them have stopped in the office for various reasons. As I listen to the conversations, I browse at a parent display table. There is an interesting newsletter called "Hayward Kids" with descriptions of activities for entire families for the month of April: a treasure hunt at the flea market; an "earth day" discovery list; and details about an Iranian Cultural Festival, an Indian Magic Show, and a Pakistani Cultural Hour.

I notice that parents pick up the "Hayward Kids" newsletter as well as copies of an attractive 3″ × 5″ card with "6 Simple Ways to Help Your Child Do Better in School." The ideas, or "simple ways," listed on the back of the card include: SHOW INTEREST: Ask your child to teach you something he learned in class today; and HAVE HIGH EXPECTATIONS: Let your child know you believe she can do it and that you expect her to do the best she's capable of doing. Although the card is published by the Education Commission of the States, the philosophy fits well with the Child Development Project approaches of the school.

Outside the office, more parents are seated at picnic tables placed on the grassy area between the two wings of classrooms. There is pleasant conversation and the principal, Jon Hassel, joins them to chat about the day. He encourages them to come to the family film night scheduled for that evening. The movie is a Dr. Seuss story, "The Lorax," and it has been selected to encourage family discussions about the values of helping and caring.

After listening to the information about the family film night, I decide to attend the event to observe the kind of connections being made with families. That evening, I arrive and the small gymnasium/auditorium is filling with people of every age. The popcorn and juice add to the festive mood. For some of the parents here tonight, this must be quite a contrast to the feelings they previously had when they visited a school.

Soon, the lights dim and the film begins. It is not a terribly long film but it is very entertaining to the crowd. Occasional laughter is heard, as well as a cheer now and then.

When the film ends, Jon Hassel asks the crowd to turn their chairs and make small circles with other families. This takes a minute or two and there is a bit of confusion. Jon moves through the crowd and hands a yellow sheet to each group that has formed. On it are "Family Discussion Starters" for the film. They include:

Why is it important to start taking care of the earth now?
Why is it important for us to do something to save the earth?
Why can't we let others do it for us?
What can our family do now to care for the earth? Draw a picture of the things we might do.

As I listen to the group discussions, it is obvious that the children have much to say about taking care of and saving the earth. I see many of the adults listening carefully to them. I also see a look of pride on the faces of these same adults. When the children finish sharing their wisdom, the adults add a few more ideas. The look of pride is now evident on children's faces.

It is a school night, as Jon Hassell reminds the families, and the evening ends early. Jon encourages the families, "Go home and make some of those decisions about what your family can do to care for the earth." He suggests making a family book or a mural, and points to materials on a table at the entrance. "Help yourselves to paper and crayons if you need them."

Reflections on the Child Development Project

When I think about the vignettes I observed at Ruus and Longwood Schools, I am struck by the level of caring I observed in the behavior of both adults and children. The spontaneous helping, the genuine affection, and the ease of cooperation shown by the youngest of children offer a sharp contrast to the events I read about in the daily newspapers. Headlines describing gang escapades, street violence, and brutal killings by unbelievably young people receive front-page treatment and public attention. Unfortunately, few journalists report on the scenes of caring like those I observed in Hayward; they're not headline material.

I am reminded of a recent experience when a panel of former gang members came to speak to one of my classes at the university. Each young person spoke eloquently of their early experiences and of what was missing in their lives. They focused on needing to belong and to be valued. They described the man who directs their rehabilitation program as someone they respect and who respects them, as someone who models the kind of nurturing they never had. They also spoke of schools as places where they didn't fit from the time they entered, as places where they had no say or control, and as places where they were not expected to succeed.

With the vignettes from Ruus and Longwood in mind, I replay their stories in my memory. As I reflect on what I saw in the Hayward schools, I can't help but try to imagine these former gang members and their families participating in the Child Development Project. I predict that their stories and their lives would be quite different. The needs they describe today are almost identical to the needs being met by the approaches used in the classrooms I visited. Awareness of the human need to belong, to be valued, to be cared about and understood, and to be responsible is not new. However, the attitudes and behaviors of caring are sometimes difficult to maintain in today's world. The Child Development Project and the educators, children, and families associated with it are powerful reminders of the kind of "caring communities" that all of us need and can have.

Questions and Issues

1. There are some who would question the extent of time spent in the buddy activities with respect to outcomes for both younger and older children. Take a stand on this issue and consider either the advantages or the disadvantages of the buddy arrangement and activities.

2. There has been some criticism of the Child Development Project's emphasis on helping others, with concerns that children won't be able to "stand up for their own rights." Some parents have expressed concerns that their children might not be independent or assertive. Respond to those concerns.

3. When fourth-, fifth-, and sixth-grade students in the Child Development Project schools were questioned about their perceptions of their classrooms and relationships with their peers, they responded more favorably than students in comparison schools. Their responses were collected by means of surveys asking if they worked together with peers on classroom problems, if the class was like a family, if their classmates really cared about each other, and if they had a "voice" in classroom decisions. If you wanted to collect such data from the young children we observed, how would you assess their perceptions? What do you predict you would learn?

4. In many ways, the Child Development Project proposes that schools provide the kind of relationships that are missing in the lives of some children. To some extent, the project asks schools to compensate for what may be missing in some families and communities. There is often a hesitancy on the part of educators to take on such a huge responsibility when they are already weighed with more demands that can be met in a school day. There is also a philosophical resistance to "stepping into a family's territory," to promote values, and to teach moral behaviors. Debate these issues.

References

Benard, B. (1993). Fostering resiliency in kids. *Educational Leadership, 51* (3), 44–48.

Berliner, D., & Casanova, U. (1989). Creating better school citizens. *Instructor, 99* (2), 24–25.

Davini, S. (1992, April). Personal communication.

DiMartino, E. (1990). The remarkable social competence of young children. *International Journal of Early Childhood, 22* (1), 23–31.

Doescher, S., & Sugawara, A. (1989). Encouraging prosocial behavior in young children. *Childhood Education, 65* (4), 213–216.

Goffin, S. (1987). Cooperative behaviors: They need our support. *Young Children, 44* (6) 75–81.

Katz, L., & McClellan, D. (1991). *The teacher's role in the social development of young children.* (ERIC Document Reproduction Service No. ED 331 642).

Kohn, A. (1990). *The brighter side of human nature.* New York: Basic Books.

McGrath, M., & Power, T. (1990). The effects of reasoning and choice on children's prosocial behavior. *International Journal of Behavioral Development, 13* (3), 245–254.

Melson, G., & Fogel, A. (1988). The development of nurturance in young children. *Young Children, 43,* 57–65.

National Association of State Boards of Education. (1991). *Caring communities: Supporting young children and families.* Alexandria, VA: National Association of State Boards of Education.

Schaps, E., & Solomon, D. (1990). Schools and classrooms as caring communities. *Educational Leadership, 48* (3), 38–42.

DENVER, COLORADO

Denver Indian Center Preschool

"The Circle Never Ends" Curriculum in a "Centered Learning" Environment

I am on Interstate 70 heading west past the perimeter of downtown Denver, and within minutes I leave the freeway and exit at Alameda. Once on Alameda Street, I am enclosed by an endless border of franchise eateries interspersed with automotive parts stores, used-car lots, body shops, and a Goodwill Thrift Store. As I turn on Morrisson Street, the scenery changes. Now I am surrounded by restaurants, food stores, and other businesses identified as either Vietnamese or Spanish. I know that I am close to the Denver Indian Center and I wonder if children from this neighborhood attend the school I am about to visit.

The Preschool Context: The Denver Indian Center

Within a few blocks, I reach the Denver Indian Center. A chain-link fence encloses the entire facility. The building's past life is obvious. Even with the addition of colorful cosmetic touches—painted Native American symbols—the building's exterior takes me back to the public schools of the 1950s. In back of the center is a settlement of about 40 Pueblo-style square houses. The houses are quite small and

I wonder if the children who attend the center live in them. The little community piques my curiosity and I make a note to ask about it.

Once inside the center, nostalgia emerges as I walk through the hallway floored with familiar beige linoleum and walled with beige tile. Even the radiators have remained. The sound of children's voices is coming from the opposite end of this hall, so I move on. As I do, I scan the information covering the walls to get a feel for more of the center's activities: an announcement of a Special Housing Repair & Fix-Up Program; a Science, Math, & Technology Conference for Girls; invitations to the Denver Museum of Natural History; and posters celebrating Native American Heritage Week. It is already clear to me that the preschool program is part of a bigger program—one of services to Native American families.

As the children's voices get louder and the preschool gets closer, the walls display children's creations and newspaper clippings about the preschool. There are the usual bright paintings, photos of field trips, a parent information board, and a display of reading and math worksheets. I'm surprised to see the worksheets. I have a strong bias against them but I hold my response until I have more information. Soon, I have arrived at the office of the preschool director.

The Energy and Commitment of the Preschool Program

My orientation to the Denver Indian Center Preschool begins when I meet the individuals who have provided leadership to the program since 1979. At first, they appear to be as unlikely a collaboration as I have ever encountered. Lisa Harjo is a wiry, confident, articulate woman of Choctaw descent. She has degrees in elementary education and child development. Her appearance is delightfully unconventional, and her conversation quickly reflects that she has continued much of the advocacy of the 1970s. Lisa is the director of the preschool program. Her partner, Irma K. Russell, brings to mind the broad-shouldered German grandmother who loved me dearly but tolerated little nonsense. She lets me know that this is her life's work and that she studied with Maria Montessori and worked with A. S. Neill at Summerhill. Her thick German accent sounds strange in the context of this Native American preschool, but I realize as I listen to her words that she is very much part of this community. Irma is the head teacher of the preschool, and teaches 4- and 5-year old children, all of whom are Native Americans.

As I get to know Lisa and Irma, I discover some of the qualities they have in common: high energy and unflinching commitment to the preschool program. I listen as they describe their multicultural curriculum model called The Circle Never Ends. The curriculum was developed by Lisa and Irma with the assistance of a grant from the Bernard van Leer Foundation, and the model earned top honors at the National Indian Education Conference in 1990. The opportunity to observe The

Circle Never Ends curriculum in use with young children is one of the motivations for visiting this Denver site.

"The Circle Never Ends" Curriculum

Lisa and Irma give me some background information about The Circle Never Ends. "American Indian legends are used as the center of the curriculum web" with the intent that this oral tradition will promote literacy and communication skills for young children while transmitting traditional knowledge and an accompanying sense of identity. The legends act as conceptual organizers for activities, and they can be adapted to other cultures. Lisa and Irma describe the curriculum with intense pride, and emphasize its sensitivity to the variation within their intertribal urban community.

Centered Learning

Before I begin to observe, Lisa and Irma want me to be especially aware of the concept of "centered learning" that also distinguishes their program. A description of the classrooms is the first step to understanding centered learning. Each classroom is a homeroom for a specific age group, but instead of having a variety of learning centers in it, each room (there are three of them) is arranged as an individual center. For example, the homeroom for 4- and 5-year old children, which I will visit, is focused on cognitive learning ("thinking skills, number awareness, fine motor development, sorting, discrimination, sequencing, language, memory, sensory explorations, and many more"). It is like one giant cognitive learning center.

The other preschool rooms are each arranged with a different learning focus. This centered learning arrangement is accompanied by unique routines. For example, during "center time," children have the freedom to move between the rooms and to interact with all the teachers. This aspect of centered learning intrigues me and I am anxious to see it "in action" along with the curriculum model.

An Unusual Beginning to the Preschool Day

There seems to be so much to talk about with Lisa and Irma, but it is time for preschool activities to begin. Lisa must get to her office, so we schedule more time to talk during the children's naps. Irma shows me to the "cafeteria" where children have been eating breakfast. Several children are finishing their cheese toast and orange juice while others are playing with hula hoops or large rubber balls in the open space next to the tables. I realize that the cafeteria is actually a combination gymnasium/auditorium with the usual stage and bleachers and basket-ball hoops.

I notice that there are several dozen packages of bakery products on the bottom row of the bleachers: hot dog and hamburger rolls, cinnamon rolls, and assorted sliced breads. I'm curious about this display but I hesitate to ask because the preschool staff are assembling children for a circle. Later I will learn that the bakery products are donated "day-old" items and are available for anyone who participates in the center's activities, including the parents of the preschool children. In the meantime, children have finished putting hula hoops on hooks and are sitting in a big circle. I am aware that this large room has become very quiet.

One of the teachers is in the middle of the circle with a shallow clay bowl of dried cedar, and another teacher is softly beating a drum. I move closer to see and hear them. Christine Payan, the assistant teacher with the 4- and 5-year-old children, reminds the children that the cedar will be burned to make smoke. She describes the smoke as a kind of blessing, and explains that the group will offer a prayer for "all my relations." Children suggest possibilities for their prayers: "for my mom and dad," "for my dog," "for my baby," and "for the trees." Once the cedar is lit, I watch as each child and adult waves a bit of smoke to themselves, taking turns as the bowl of burning cedar is passed around the circle. I hear each one say, "All my relations." Christine whispers to me, "It's a purifying act—we cleanse ourselves." She points out that parents and siblings have remained to take part in the blessing, and I note several younger brothers and sisters in the circle. I feel quite privileged to have been present during this special event.

After the "smoking ceremony" is finished, the teacher with the drum leads the children in several Native American songs: "O Great Eagle," sung in Lakota and English, and "Ala Ala," a happy song sung in Navajo. They recite some chants accompanied by the children giving sign language for various animals: buffalo, deer, horse, shark, bear, owl, and others. The final song, "Inkpata," is a Dakota love song and it is sung in Sioux and English. When the song ends, there is a feeling of warmth and closeness, even in this very spacious room. I realize that I have begun to witness The Circle Never Ends as part of the morning routine. The "smoking ceremony" and singing certainly contribute to these children's sense of identity as members of the Native American community.

Getting Acquainted

As we leave the "cafeteria," I see Irma wave to a father who is carrying a very young child. She greets him with, "Your hogan is so beautiful—I never thought of making it like that." He grins and responds, "Oh, I just used a strip of cardboard and wound it around." He grins again, obviously pleased with his contribution. As we walk to the classroom, Irma thanks him profusely for his help with this week's curriculum. I think to myself, Good, it sounds like I will learn about hogans during my visit.

I follow the children to their classroom and formally meet Irma's teaching assistant, Christine Payan. She is a parent of children who have completed the preschool program and she has spent several years volunteering and preparing for her assistant role. Her mother was a teacher in the preschool for 12 years.

I enter the classroom and quickly survey the environment for the materials and equipment I expected to find in this cognitively centered classroom. They are all here and in great abundance, but my attention is immediately diverted to the children's activity. Most of them are choosing puzzles from shelves on the wall and taking them to a large, round table nearby. I hear their conversation:

"You've got lots of pieces."

"This one's part of a big, fat tummy."

"Do you have a circle?"

Thomas discovers that his wooden puzzle piece will spin and exclaims, "Hey, this is magic." Anza disagrees, "No, it's because the table is shiny—no, it's because the table is flat." As you may have predicted, everyone at the table is soon experimenting with puzzle pieces to see if they spin.

During this time, Willow, a volunteer, has covered the other circular table with a substantial layer of newspapers and is scooping moist clay from a large pail. She expresses concern about "getting started right away so that the clay won't dry." Christine assures her that she can go ahead and not wait for the usual morning routines. Children begin to pull up chairs and watch her. I am surprised by their silence. I wonder why they're not asking their inevitable questions. Maybe they don't know Willow very well, I think to myself. Before I can determine the reason for their silence, Willow asks the children about the masks they have been studying, and I hear them respond with ease and enthusiasm:

"They're scary, but I like them."

"They have feathers and paint."

"They have lots of colors."

I suspect that the children have been learning about masks as one of the curricular activities—part of the "transmission of cultural knowledge."

"The Circle Never Ends": Mask Making

Willow tells the children that they can make masks of their own faces, and urges them to touch their faces to "see how your nose is shaped" or to "feel what your hair is like." Irma Russell joins the five children at the table and the six of them begin working with their individual mounds of clay. The table is hushed for a time. Each individual is completely absorbed by her or his manipulation of clay. As faces begin to emerge from the clay, they spark conversation. Anza points to Irma's clay face and tells her that she needs lines across her forehead. Willow points to the braids on the side of Joe's head and asks him if he has hair on top of his head. Joe decides to put a feather on top of his head instead of more hair. William asks Willow to look at his mask, and he hears, "Yes, you do have that long chin," as she points to that feature in the clay. Irma tells Summer, "Look—your sister made earrings on her mask too."

Although there are activities in other parts of the room, the clay mask creations hold my attention and I remain to listen to the continuing conversation. I watch as Thomas slowly touches his face and traces his nostrils, his eyebrows, and his tongue. Soon I see that he has made spiked hair, spiked eyebrows, and a tongue protruding from his mouth. He causes a great deal of excitement as everyone rushes to his place to see his creation. Willow shows genuine enjoyment of the face and comments to Thomas, "You have wonderful ideas."

"The Circle Never Ends": Pictures of Sheep

As children decide that their clay faces are complete, they move to the water table or to the other round table where Christine is facilitating an activity focused on sheep. I decide to investigate and I hear Christine ask the children, "Remember when we went to the stock show and saw the people shear the sheep?" I don't hear a response. I see that there are plastic models of sheep, photos of sheep, and varied art materials, including cotton, on the table. There are also sheets of white paper with a sheep outline drawn on them.

Again, Christine prompts, "Do you remember why we are making pictures of sheep?" For a few moments, no one answers, and she asks again. This time, she directs her question to September.

"The Navajo people took care of sheep," responds September, who is gluing cotton to her paper, filling in the shape of a sheep. She has colored some grass and trees around the animal.

Christine asks another question: "Why were sheep so important to the Navajo people?"

This time, Joe answers, "Because they used all the parts of the sheep."

"Yes, every part of the sheep was used by the Navajo," continues Christine.

The other children do not appear to be very involved in the conversation or the activity, and Gordon says, "I'm getting tired" halfway through his coloring on the sheet with the outline of a sheep. Christine does not insist that the children finish—only that they put their names on their papers. She remains at the table as the children leave.

By this time, it appears that those children who have indicated an interest in making a clay mask have all had a chance to make their faces. Willow asks Christine if she would like to make one. Christine goes over to the table and spends a few minutes looking at all the faces. She is joined by Gordon, and together they begin work on their own clay faces. I seize this chance to talk with Willow and explore her relationship with the children. I find that she is a scheduled volunteer who comes weekly with interest and expertise in creative arts. Willow expresses the satisfaction she gains from working with the preschool staff and the children. I think to myself, So she's not a stranger to the children. This realization causes me to wonder again, Why didn't the children ask questions while she was preparing the clay? Before I can come up with an answer, increased activity in the classroom captures my attention.

Time for Centered Learning

The children appear to be choosing their own activities again, and I notice that the sliding doors between the classrooms are being opened at this time. The three preschool classrooms become one long room. I decide to explore the other rooms as the children make their decisions to do the same.

In the next classroom, the "home center" room, are dolls, cushions, blankets, baskets, cradles, mirrors, dress-up clothes, kitchen furniture, food products, dishes and utensils, and puppets. The dolls represent different ethnic groups, as do the many pictures hung around this room. There are several small Navajo rugs, baskets, shawls, jewelry, and pottery. There are also trays (the cafeteria type) of objects used for "culturally comparative teaching." One example of this is a tray of present-day cooking utensils and some primitive wood and stone ones from one of the tribes. This room not only invites dramatic play and creativity but the materials look like they will promote the literacy and communication skills intended by the curriculum.

The next classroom is focused on art, crafts, and music. There are many rich examples of Native American crafts: rugs, baskets, beadwork, weavings, clothing, drums, and other musical instruments. There are also more traditional early childhood education items: easels, fingerpaints, crayons, scissors, pipe cleaners, many kinds of paper, fabrics, markers, paintbrushes of different sizes, beads, and natural dyes. Again, this room is decorated with many pictures and posters of the past and present Native American culture.

As I continue to browse in this room, I notice that science materials have been integrated with the art and music materials. I see the usual science materials—rocks, shells, leaves, flowers, plants, twigs, and feathers—but I also notice an emphasis on the natural environment with baskets of gravel, sand, and pebbles, as well as roots, fossils, acorns, bark, bones, furs, skins, leather pieces, and pictures of the elements of air, fire, water, and earth. I am especially intrigued by the blending of natural materials with art and music in this environment.

The Hogan Inspires Children's Artwork

As I explore this room, I notice that a model of a hogan is placed in the center of a round table in this classroom. I think to myself, This must be the hogan that the father made. I realize now that a hogan is a hexagonal dwelling made of logs and mud. On the table around the hogan are watercolor sets, brushes, and jars of poster paint. Some of the 4- and 5-year-old children from Irma's homeroom are seated with large sheets of paper in front of them.

The children's paintings reflect recent experiences and discussions about hogans. Alice finishes a bright-colored painting of a hogan with grass and trees around it, and announces that she will "make a second picture on the other side" of her paper. She is quickly offered another piece of paper by Lisa, the teacher in that room. Lisa has been observing the painting activity and occasionally pointing out aspects of the hogan's structure.

Anza announces that he has made a boat on a little lake next to his hogan. His friend, Summer, follows with an announcement of her own: "This is a picture of my sister and me by a hogan."

Lisa responds to Summer's picture and announcement with, "Yes, you and your sister went to visit your aunt who lives in a hogan. I remember seeing the photos you brought to school." Summer smiles shyly and goes to hang up her painting.

As I once again walk through the three open rooms, I can't help but notice that the 4- and 5-year-old children are spread throughout the rooms. In contrast, the younger children, ages 2 and 3 years, have settled primarily in the "home center" room or near their homeroom teachers. This raises some questions for me about this "Centered Learning" approach.

Back to Cognitively Centered Learning

With those questions in mind, I return to my starting point, the homeroom, to observe the cognitively centered learning activities. I remember the worksheets hanging in the hall display and wonder if children are using any in this room. As I begin to scan the room, I see that several of the children are using materials on a rug. I watch as Joe takes a small rug from the cart full of well-worn bathroom or kitchen rugs. He places a tray of magnifying glasses and lenses on his rug, and Thomas joins him.

I remember reading that these rugs are intended to help children define their space for activities. I can see that children have spaced their activities around the room with rugs and locations of their choice. This room is bursting with activity, but my attention remains with Joe and Thomas as they experiment with the lenses and magnifying glasses. I hear the following conversations:

"Your tongue is very big and fat."

"I see hundreds of Miss Irmas."

"Now there's two of you."

"You look different."

Joe and Thomas continue experimenting with the items on their tray and alternate different magnifying glasses and lenses to look at each other. Their experimentation is involving them with concepts and the language associated with those concepts.

I move and listen to the conversation at the water table:

"Look—I made this great thing to squirt bubbles," William exclaims as he attaches three tubes to each other. He fills the bottom one, then slowly tips the whole invention over so that the water fills the top. He repeats the procedure several times.

William asks Irma if he can color the water. She nods and gets some food coloring from a shelf. "What color do you want to start with?" she asks.

William says without hesitation, "Blue."

Irma puts blue coloring in a small container and William adds water to it. Eventually, it is poured into the water table, and Irma asks, "Can you see the color?" Several children shake their heads, and Irma asks what they can do.

Alessa asks, "Can we have green in the water?"

Once the water has both blue and green coloring in it, interesting conversation begins:

"This looks like a dinosaur ocean."

"Let's pretend that we lived a hundred days ago."

When Miriam tattles, "Thomas splashed water in my eye," she is told, "Talk to Thomas; tell the person who did it."

Near the water activity, Nikki and Delta are looking through a tray of medical equipment:

"Pretend that I'm sick, OK?"

"This is to pick up stuff that you drop or to pick up yucky stuff" (while manipulating the tongs).

"Take my blood pressure."

Irma urges Delta to use the stethoscope and Delta hesitates. Irma says "stethoscope" again, this time pointing to it and telling her she can listen to Nikki's heart.

Delta immediately picks it up, places the appropriate ends in her ears, and tells Nikki to come to have her heart checked. This is one of many language experiences I'm seeing in this classroom—and so far, no worksheets.

Alice has returned to her homeroom and has been sitting and watching Gordon and Harold. Irma approaches her and asks, "Are you a player or an observer?" Alice says, "I'm watching." "So you're an observer," Irma replies, and Alice nods.

After a few minutes, Alice wants to play and I'm immediately curious to see her strategies for joining the two boys. First, she asks and the boys refuse. She responds with, "If you don't let me play, I won't be your friend." Gordon pauses and seems to think about it, then says, "Whoever goes the fastest gets to play," and hands Alice some marbles. The two boys have constructed a kind of track with a ramp, some obstacles, and a bridge. I watch in anticipation after hearing Gordon's challenge, but it seems to be forgotten rather quickly, and soon Alice is obviously playing with the two boys. The conversation is now filled with "Take turns" and "Mine is faster." There is a great deal of negotiation, but it becomes quickly apparent that Alice is now "running the show." She is arranging the track, deciding whose turn it is, and encouraging the two boys with an enthusiastic "You did it" whenever their marbles succeed through the entire track.

A Return to Homeroom Activities

I hear Irma telling the children that it is almost cleanup time and I watch. Cleanup is a quick and uneventful process. There are obvious well-learned routines. I see the little rugs folded and piled on the cart, the trays of materials returned to shelves, and the water play accessories dried and returned to their places. I notice that the children clean up wherever they may be, no matter which classroom they are in. They then return to their homeroom. When the cleanup looks complete, the sliding doors are pulled back in place and the three classrooms are separated again.

During cleanup, children are also using the bathroom, and I hear Irma remind them to wash their hands. William says, "We already did," pointing to the water table. She nods and points him to the bathroom.

When children return from washing, they sit on the floor in a circle. Irma sits on a low chair and begins with, "Let's all reach up to the sky." Fingers wriggle in the air around her. When Nikki asks why they're having their circle at this time, Irma explains that they needed to have their mask-making activity earlier when the clay was wet and ready. They do a finger play about face parts, and Irma connects it to the faces they made in clay. She asks what season it is, and hears "Winter" from most of the children. "Last week we thought it was spring because it was so warm," she reminds them.

Then Irma shows large flashcards with numbers and objects on them, one at a time. They include 1 Hopi kachina, 2 moccasins, 3 clay pots, 4 buffalos, 5 ears of blue corn, and so on. Children count the items on each card, then write the number in the air. Irma then leads the children as they count to 10 in Sioux. She pulls out the number card with the 1 Hopi kachina and tells them, "Next week, a gentleman is going to come in and tell you a kachina story about a special fish kachina." I think to myself, Rather than counting balls or kites, these children are counting culturally relevant objects, and they're counting in their own languages. For this age group, however, I wonder if the counting might not be more meaningful if the children could count real moccasins or ears of corn.

After the counting, Irma announces with a hushed voice, "Today we are going to hear a story about hogans." I'm thrilled and I watch with anticipation as she distributes puppets to each child. There are puppets of several birds, a beaver, a spider, an ant, and an Eagle, and puppets representing a woman, a man, and a little boy. Irma has drawn a cave on the chalkboard with brown chalk and she has a bowl of shells in her lap. She proceeds to read a Navajo folk tale, "Homes for the Dine" with children's puppet participation at the appropriate times. The story tells of the Navajo's First Woman, First Man, and Little Boy's search for a better home than their cave dwellings. Their journey takes them to the Bird People, the Water People, and the Insect People to ask for their help in designing a new home. They show appreciation for the advice they receive by giving little gifts to each group—shells from the bowl in Irma's lap. The story ends with the decision to combine all the advice into a structure now known as a hogan. It is an engaging story and one that

illustrates the beauty and simplicity of the Native American legends. (For the complete legend, see the appendix at the end of this chapter.) "Homes for the Dine" is one of the many legends that are considered central to the curriculum web of The Circle Never Ends.

After the story, Irma brings out the model of the hogan that the father had built. She and the children talk about the shape of the hogan, then compare it with the pueblo previously studied. Irma allows plenty of time for the children to examine the hogan model, even when the conversation ceases. Then she shows them a large picture of the inside of a hogan. She asks, "What's different about the furniture in your home and the furniture in this home?"

"There's no TV."

"Not much furniture."

"I see Navajo rugs."

"Where are the beds?"

When the children have identified the differences that are evident from the picture, the group becomes quiet.

A Reminder of Cultural Identity

The children begin to move about, showing signs of restlessness and fatigue. Irma dismisses each child to pick out a book by asking the name of his or her tribe. Their responses are varied: Cayawa Creek, Rosebud Sioux, Ochala Sioux, Arapaho, Hidatsa Ute, and Lakota Sioux. I remember reading that there are at least 50 tribal groups represented in the children attending the Denver Indian Center Preschool, and that the center serves an intertribal community of approximately 18,200 Native Americans.

As the children choose their books, I take time to look over the overflowing bookshelf. I note several titles related to the day's activities: *Clay* by Jeannie Hull (London: Franklin Watts, 1989), *The True Book: The Navajo* by Alice Osinski (Chicago: Children's Press, 1987), and *The Village of Blue Stone* by Stephen Trimble (New York: Macmillan, 1990).

From one of the children "reading" books, I hear a chanting of "Kachina—china—china—kachina—china—china." Then I hear two other children, September and Molly, asking each other questions about the pictures in their book:

"What do you think she is riding on?"

"A horse."

"What is this stuff?"

"Rocks."

"Which one is different?"

"The scary one—that mask."

"Who makes these rugs?"

"Indian people make these rugs."

The confidence and ease with which the two children conduct this interaction tells me that it is a familiar scene. It reminds me that we adults can hear ourselves by just listening to children.

As I turn my attention from the bookshelf and children's responses to the books, I notice a sight that absolutely tickles me. Although they are supposed to be looking at books, two children have cameras and are engaged in make-believe photography of each other and their classmates. I watch as Delta stops at each activity and "takes a shot." She also pauses by individual children, kneels down in front of them and "snaps a picture" just as I have been doing all morning throughout the classroom. The scene reminds me of the influence we have as models for children.

In a short time, children are told that it is time to go to lunch. I hear Willow bid farewell to the children and to Irma and Christine. She says that she will be back the following week with the masks baked and ready for paint. Irma confers with her briefly about purchasing paint. Cleanup is followed by another bathroom stop on the way to the cafeteria.

The "Cafeteria"

There is a lot of activity occurring in this large space as we enter at noon. On the stage is a young man painting child-size picnic tables in bright primary colors. Next to the tables where the children had breakfast are three more rows of tables. At them are seated "senior citizens" who participate in programs at the center. Immediately, some of them come over to greet individual children. I'm pleased to learn later in the day that the "seniors' " involvement with the preschool takes many forms, from teaching dances, to telling legends and stories, to demonstrating native crafts. They also make items for the preschool during their activity sessions: doll clothes, puppets, sand pictures, and weavings.

Several teachers greet individual "seniors" at their tables, and I see that Irma will be eating with them. She explains that her health demands their "special diet." The children's lunch consists of turkey, corn, potatoes, salad, and pears, and this menu seems to prompt great appetites. All the children eat well, and there's an easy flow of conversation at all the tables.

When the children finish eating, they leave the table, scrape their plates, and return to the classrooms one or two at a time. It is obviously time for a rest. Children look tired and offer little resistance. Miss Christine helps them get out mats and covers, and the room is soon filled with sleeping children.

Some Questions Answered

Once it is quiet, I seize the opportunity to talk to Lisa and Irma about what I have seen so far. I have questions about the curriculum, but I'm still curious about a sight that greeted me as I arrived at the center: a community of pueblo-style houses next to the center. The explanation is that several years ago, through a federal grant, the center was able to finance the construction of these low-cost housing units for elderly and disabled residents. Some 40 percent of the population of the little community is Native American.

My questions now turn to the preschool program and centered learning. I think that I am beginning to understand the idea but I ask about other aspects of the approach. Irma clarifies the homeroom component with, "It's a place for sharing information, ideas, and topics for activities." Each homeroom has a schedule appropriate for the age group, and the curriculum concepts are woven through the activities conducted within each age group. Most of The Circle Never Ends curricular activities took place in the homeroom this morning.

As we converse, Lisa adds the important aspect of observation of children for evaluation purposes, and provides sets of checklists for the developmental areas of personal/social, gross/fine motor, cognitive, and multicultural. The checklists are designed to be used during center times as well as during homeroom activities. Teachers are encouraged to plan lessons and activities that give children opportunities to develop the skills listed in the checklists.

The multicultural checklist captures my interest because I have seen few examples of specific outcomes related to cultural awareness and identity. Throughout the morning, I observed numerous interactions that promoted the skills I see in the checklist. A section of the checklist illustrates the kind of outcomes that are expected of the 4- and 5-year old children:

- Names own tribe
- Identifies 3 tribal dwellings
- Identifies and describes Indian artifacts
- Strings beads and other cultural objects (corn, seed, shells)
- Is willing to learn sign language
- Can sign 3–5 objects
- Listens to legends and cultural stories
- Can retell the main events of a legend or a story
- Shows pride in work completed
- Describes things he/she wants to do
- Knows how to define his/her work area

Source: Harjo, L., & Russell, I. (1990). *The circle never ends.* Denver: Denver Indian Center. Used by permission.

My last question to Lisa and Irma is prompted by the display of what I have called worksheets that I noticed hanging in the hallway when I first arrived. During the morning, as I watched the children filling in the sheep form drawn on paper, I decided that it, too, was a worksheet. The paper with the sheep outline was more open ended than those displayed in the hall. Irma responds to my inquiry with a concern about the preschool children's transition to public kindergarten and primary grades. She tells me of a comprehensive follow-up study (Luellen, 1991) of children from the preschool. The study described a "culture shock" experienced by the children upon entering public kindergarten. Much of the shock was attributed to the omission of their own culture in the environment, materials, and methods used in the kindergarten classes. The children responded by being very quiet, socially withdrawn, and struggling academically.

From Irma's standpoint, the worksheets are a "readiness" strategy to help the preschool children feel more comfortable when they arrive at kindergarten. She described their use for both reading and math skills so that the 4- and 5-year-olds would have confidence and preparation for the curriculum ahead in kindergarten. She sees my mild skepticism and reiterates the importance of readiness for the children she has taught "all these years" so that they can be successful when they leave the center. Irma's concerns and experiences sound legitimate, but I'm left with questions about the use of worksheets as the best approach to the problem.

Ending the Day with Informal Work and Play

Our conversation is interrupted as children wake up from their naps. Irma returns to the homeroom and she invites those children who are awake to a game of Color Bingo. Four children play with her, and I note that even when someone wins, they keep playing the game until each child has a Bingo—it is a game where everyone wins. As they play, Irma asks them to identify their color and their shape. After two games, Gordon wants to be the caller and he is encouraged to do so. Irma becomes a player, and Gordon begins with, "Green square," soon followed with, "Blue triangle."

Alice and Summer, who are sitting in chairs facing each other, are "drilling" each other with alphabet flashcards. When Summer gets stuck on *V,* Alice can't help her. After a pause, the two girls look up at the alphabet border hanging above the chalkboard and recite the alphabet until they get to *V.* When they do, they both shout "Vee" and squeal.

After about 20 minutes, a tray of snack food is delivered: granola bars and milk. The children gradually leave their activities and eat. Once it appears that most of the children have eaten their snack, Irma announces that it will be story time in a few minutes. Some children complete their activity and put materials away while others continue their play. Irma begins the story for those who appear interested. The story is about parents, and she stops at intervals in the story to ask questions. When the book shows a picture of a child being tucked in, Irma asks, "Who tucks you in?" Children's responses include:

"My mom."

"I tuck myself in."

"I just put my head on my pillow and go to sleep."

Later in the story, when a picture appears depicting a mom showing a child how to sew, Irma tells the children that Molly's mom is teaching her how to bead. "She makes beautiful earrings out of beads," Irma mentions. "So does my auntie," adds Molly. The story finishes as parents arrive to pick up the children.

The dismissal is relaxed with a lot of conversation. Irma and Christine let parents know that the children did not go outside due to the extreme cold. Several parents nod as they bundle up their children. Christine moves about the room, straightening a few materials and shelves. Irma heads for the office to take care of some individual parent letters, and I learn that Lisa has left to present a beadwork demonstration at the art museum.

Ending the Day with Reflection and Unresolved Issues

I, too, leave the preschool and the Denver Indian Center, turning carefully back onto Morrisson Street. My head is swimming with ideas and issues. I am faced with an awareness of my very limited knowledge and understanding of the Native American culture. I feel quite uncertain about articulating my questions and concerns, but they are with me. I make a promise to myself to read the Luellen (1991) study that Irma described, to better comprehend the concerns I heard expressed. I also commit myself to developing sensitivity to the needs of Native American children by seeking both literature and conversation. I intend to return to my questions and concerns once I have a broader understanding of the issues of educating Native American children.

I leave the Denver Indian Center impressed by the communitywide approach so energetically undertaken by the individuals I encountered today. I am comforted by the exchanges between young children and the "senior citizens." I am inspired by the "smoking ceremony" and the legends that make up The Circle Never Ends curriculum. I am also feeling changed by my entrance into another world—a world where I was the minority. Today was a powerful experience—one that will remain in my mind and heart for a long time.

Questions and Issues

1. Discuss the physical arrangement of classrooms for "centered learning." What are the advantages and disadvantages?
2. Explore the issue of "centered learning" from the standpoint of the mixed age grouping of 2-, 3-, and 4- and 5-year-olds. If you support the approach, suggest some strategies for helping the younger children use a greater variety of materials.
3. With The Circle Never Ends as a curricular model, what aspects of the "cultural oral tradition and knowledge" of your community would be incorporated in curriculum for young children?
4. Consider the problems of "culture shock" faced by the children from the Denver Indian Center preschool upon entering the public schools for kindergarten (as described by Irma on page 00). What approach would you take to prepare children for the transition?
5. Discuss the "worksheet" approach to the transition. Examine it from the perspectives of children, parents, the community, and the changing emphasis on worksheets in many public schools.
6. Review the sample items from the multicultural checklist and suggest how they can be integrated into *developmentally appropriate curriculum*—that is, "curriculum providing meaningful contexts rather than focusing on isolated skill acquisition, with a wide range of activities related to children's direct firsthand experience" (Bredekamp, 1987). Find examples of those activities in the day's events at the Denver Indian Center Preschool.

References

Note: This reference list is more extensive than those in other chapters, and it extends to native cultures in Canada and other countries. It includes theoretical work, research studies, and "how-to" application materials. It represents my own exploration of the issues of educating Native American children.

Billman, J. (1992). The Native American curriculum: Attempting alternatives to tepees and headbands. *Young Children, 47* (6), 22–25.

Brady, P. (1992). Columbus and the quincentennial myths: Another side of the story. *Young Children, 47* (6), 4–14.

Bredekamp, S. (Ed.). (1987). *Developmentally appropriate practice in early childhood education programs serving children birth through age 8.* Washington, DC: NAEYC.

Britsch, S. (1989). Research currents: The contribution of the preschool to a Native American community. *Language Arts, 66* (1), 52–57.

Cadiente, R. (1986). *Juneau Indian studies elementary curriculum guide, grades K–5.* Juneau, AL: Juneau School District, Indian Studies Program.

Cardwell, G. (1990). *Cultural lessons for teachers of American Indians, Alaska Natives, and Canadian First Nations.* Norman, OK: American Indian Institute, Oklahoma University. ED340525.

Dupuis, V. L., & Walker, M. W. (1988). The Circle of Learning at Kickapoo. *Journal of American Indian Education, 28* (1), 27–33.

Dyson, D. S. (1983). *Parents' roles and responsibilities in Indian education.* Las Cruces, NM: Office of Ed Research & Improvement. ERIC ED286704.

Harvey, K. D. (1990). *Native American recipes for the classroom.* Denver: Circle of Learning Preschool Program.

Harvey, K. D. (1991). *Native American games for the classroom.* Denver: Circle of Learning Preschool Program.

Harvey, K. D., & Harjo, L. (1993). *Indian country: A history of native people in America.* Golden, CO: North American Press.

Kasten, W. C. (1992). Bridging the horizon: American Indian beliefs and whole language learning. *Anthropology and Education Quarterly, 23* (2), 108–119.

Leavitt, R. M. (1991). Language and cultural content in native education. *The Canadian Modern Language Review, 47* (2), 266–279.

Light, H. K., & Martin, R. E. (1985). Guidance of American Indian children. *Journal of American Indian Education, 25* (1), 42–46.

Little Soldier, L. (1992). Working with Native American children. *Young Children, 47* (6), 15–21.

Luellen, J. E. (1991). *A study of the Native American early childhood education curriculum "The Circle Never Ends."* Denver: University of Denver, Dissertation Abstracts.

Matiasz, S. (1989). Aboriginal children and early childhood education. *Early Child Development and Care, 52,* 81–91.

National Association for the Education of Young Children. (1993). Educating yourself about diverse cultural groups in our country by reading. *Young Children,* 48 (3), 13–16.

Paul, A. S. (1991). *Early childhood education in American Indian and Alaskan native communities.* Washington, DC: Department of Education, Indian Nations At Risk Task Force.

Reyhner, J. (1988). *Teaching the Indian child.* Billings, MT: Bilingual Education Program, Eastern Montana College.

Reyhner, J. (1992). American Indian cultures and school success. *Journal of American Indian Education, 32* (1), 30–39.

Skinner, L. (1991). *Teaching through traditions: Incorporating native languages and cultures into curricula.* Washington, DC: Department of Education, Indian Nations At Risk Task Force.

Slapin, B., & Seale, D. (Eds.). (1991). *Through Indian eyes: The Native experience in books for children.* Berkeley, CA: OYATE.

Stairs, A. (1991). Learning processes and teaching roles in native education: Cultural base and cultural brokerage. *The Canadian Modern Language Review, 47* (2), 280–294.

United Indians of All Tribes Foundation. (1983). *Organizing and operating an Indian preschool.* Seattle, WA: United Indians of All Tribes Foundation. ERIC Document Reproduction Service No. ED 232 839.

Williamson, K. J. (1987). Consequences of schooling: Discontinuity amongst the Intuit. *Canadian Journal of Native Education, 14* (2), 60–69.

Appendix

Homes for the Dine (A Navajo Folk Tale)

How the Bird People, the Water People, and the Insect People taught the Navajos how to build the hogan. *Dine* means "The People" in the Navajo language.

Long Ago

Long ago the Navajos lived in caves. First Woman, First Man, and Little Boy lived in a cave.

The cave was dark. Sometimes it was damp. In the winter it was filled with campfire smoke.

Little Boy said, "I don't like this cave. It's too dark."

First Man said, "I don't like this cave. It's too cold."

First Woman said, "Let's go and visit the Bird People. They know how to build good homes. Maybe they can help us."

Eagle's Home

They saw Eagle.

His home was up on a mountain.

Eagle said, "Look at my home. It is round like the sun. It is made of logs."

"Your home is too high for us," said First Woman, "But it has good, strong walls. We'll remember your good, strong walls when we build our home."

"Good-bye," said First Woman, First Man, and Little Boy. "Here are some white shell beads for you."

Oriole's Home

They saw Oriole.

His home was in a tree. It was like a basket.

"It's a good home," said Oriole. "The wind can't blow it away."

First Woman said, "We can't live in the top of a tree. But you've taught us how to weave baskets."

Little Boy said, "Thank you, Oriole," and he gave him some orange beads.

They said good-bye and went on their way.

Woodpecker's Home

Then they heard a sound. It was a drum sound. They saw Woodpecker. He was high in a tree.

"Where's your home?" asked Little Boy.

"In a hole! In a hole!" said Woodpecker.

"Navajos can't live in a tree," said Little Boy, "but please make that sound again."

Woodpecker made the drum sound again.

"Thank you, Woodpecker," said Little Boy. "You've taught us how to make the drum sound."

"Good-bye. Here are some red feathers for you."

Cliff Swallow's Home

Cliff Swallow's home was high on a canyon wall. It was under a ledge.

First Woman said, "Hello, Cliff Swallow. Please show us how you made your home."

Cliff Swallow flew down to the river. He came back with some mud. "This is how I did it," said Cliff Swallow. I made it of mud."

"Thank you," said First Woman. "When we build our home we'll plaster it with mud. Here are some black beads for you."

Beaver's Home

"Who is that?" said Little Boy.

It was Beaver. He was sitting on top of his home. His home was in the water. It had a round roof. There was a hole in the top to let the sunshine in.

First Woman said, "Hello Beaver. We like your home. It has a good roof. We'll remember your good roof when we build our home."

They gave Beaver some pretty white shells and said good-bye.

Spider Woman's Home

Spider Woman's home was in the ground. She was doing something.

"What are you doing?" asked First Woman.

"I'm weaving," said Spider Woman. "Didn't you know I'm the best weaver in the world?"

She taught First Woman to weave.

"Thank you," said First Woman. "Now I can weave a blanket for the door of our new home."

They said good-bye and gave Spider Woman some red berries to dye her yarn.

Red Ant's Home

First Man said, "I see a little hill over there."

"Someone lives in the little hill," said Little Boy. "I think it's Red Ant."

"Come down! Come down the ladder," said Red Ant.

First Woman, First Man, and Little Boy liked Red Ant's home. It had an opening at the top, and a door on the side where the sun shines in the morning.

And from far away Red Ant's home looked just like the earth around it.

They gave Red Ant some pretty rocks to scatter on his roof, and said good-bye.

The New Home

First Woman said, "Now let's go back to our mountains and build our new home."

"We'll call our home a hogan. It will have good, strong walls in a circle, like Eagle's home."

"It will have a roof like Beaver's roof. It will have an opening at the top, and a door at the side like Red Ant's home."

"It will have a blanket at the door to keep the cold out, as Spider Woman taught us."

"It will have plaster mud over the walls and roof, as Cliff Swallow taught us. It will be warm in winter and cool in summer."

So this is the way Navajo hogans are built to this day.

Source: Harjo, L., & Russell, I. (1990). *The circle never ends.* Denver: Denver Indian Center. Used by permission.

5

Riley School

Respect for Children as the Source of Curriculum

Have you ever said to yourself, If I had my own school, I could teach the way I believe, and I know I could reach each child. About 20 years ago, Glenna Plaisted followed her beliefs about meeting individual needs and abilities and founded Riley School. Her own home is part of the campus and her vision is energetically implemented in a program that "is designed to encompass the intellectual, artistic, and practical sides of each individual child." Today, Riley School enrolls 50 children, ages 4 through 14 years old, and each one of them has an individual program that flexes with his or her changing interests, needs, and capabilities.

A Preview

With more than 20 years of successfully meeting children's individual needs, I wondered what Glenna's secrets were. I had to ask, "What advice do you have for those who want to provide the kind of education you've achieved here at Riley?" She was quick to respond, "You've got to have a faculty that's committed to the whole child." She described her teachers as a family: "They're connected to the whole school, not just a class."

Another strength of Riley School, from Glenna's standpoint, is structure. "You've got to have a structure but it has to be broad. It's got to support children."

Anticipating my question, Glenna added, "Children are not handpicked for our school. They are a cross-section of what you would find in any school."

When you read the descriptions of Riley School that Glenna and her staff have developed, you begin to anticipate what you will see in the classrooms. It's a place "where the ground rules are courtesy and laughter, and where children are the subject of learning, not the object." It is the kind of language that entices most of us to want to see for ourselves—and so we will. Come with me as I depart for Glen Cove, Maine, and Riley School.

Approaching Riley School

I head for Riley School by traveling on Route 1 past picturesque harbor towns and endless miles of coastal beauty. Glen Cove itself is a collection of country roads, scattered houses, and a few commercial buildings. It is an area where people are either very successful with their thriving businesses and large fine homes, or struggling to survive the area's lagging economy.

The highway through the area is fenced by signs describing every possible tourist service, but I can't miss the distinctive green and gold Riley School sign. An arrow directs me down a side road at the water's edge. After five or six modest frame houses, Warrenton Road is edged by open fields and occasional groves of trees. On the right appears a large distinctive stone carved with the school name, and a gravel drive that takes me through the trees.

Once out of the forest cluster, I face Riley School and am struck by the stunning quality of its architecture and its prominence in the setting. There are two school buildings: a large grey cedar building with steeply slanted roofs over two wings, and a new wood and glass structure of contemporary design that houses the library. The Riley School buildings and the rambling house and barn that Glenna Plaisted calls home are surrounded by 45 acres of meadows, ponds, and forest beauty.

A Welcoming Environment

As I enter the main building, I pause to admire a beautiful ceramic collage representing the natural resources of Maine hung above a massive carved wood credenza. It feels like I am entering a home. Next to the credenza is an overflowing basket of children's shoes that causes me to wonder. As children pass, I observe that they are in socks or slippers, moving about in pairs or small groups, chatting comfortably. I also observe children walking in the fields and on the pathways between this building and the library or the director's house, with the difference being that they are wearing shoes. I look around for my destination, the Lower School, and am directed to the right from the entry hall.

Before I enter the Lower School, I pause to consider the aesthetics of the Riley School environment. There is a simplicity and a sense of order around me. Not only does it feel welcoming but it also communicates a message of respect for children.

Exploring the Lower School

The Lower School is a classroom area as well as a group of 11 students ranging in age from 4 to 7. The classroom is a large square room with a loft built over a third of the space. Below the loft is a carpeted area reserved for block play with shelves of blocks and accessories enclosing the space. The classroom is bright and open with large windows on three sides. There is an oversized faded stuffed chair and several bookshelves across the room from where I enter. I notice that there are science materials in most parts of the room: plants, watering can, potting soil, and planting equipment on one counter; a rock collection, shells, and scales on another; bones on the window sill; and magnifying glasses, magnets, a compass, and science books on a shelf. Near the sink are two paint easels.

Adjacent to where I am entering are individual cubbies for children's belongings. There is a listening center with a tape recorder and earphones on a small table. In the center of the room are three tables that accommodate 12 chairs. The walls are only minimally covered: two oil paintings of Maine seascapes, two small bulletin boards, the tiniest of calendars with only the day's date showing, and a few children's drawings obviously hung by the individual artists.

Sharing Insights and Reflections

Janeen Hamel Chin is the teacher for the Lower School. At our first meeting earlier this morning, I was struck by her quiet assurance. I learned that she has 12 years of teaching experience and has been at Riley for 6 years. In one of her most enthusiastic descriptions of her work at Riley, Janeen talked about her daily journal writing and the ability to have a head teacher respond to her thoughts. "It's like we're having a dialogue about teaching, about my children and my classroom. It gives me incredible feedback, raises issues and questions, and helps me see things with so much more perspective."

As Janeen and I wait for the children to arrive, I take time to read her journal, which she shares with me. I want to get to know her better so that I can understand what I observe in her interactions with children. Janeen began writing this year's journal during the week before the start of school, so I am able to hear her thoughts about her class and her teaching as she prepares for the school year. I read the previous days' pages:

> *September—crisp, clear, blue-skied, ever-changing, muted leaf colored, hopeful of new beginnings—ahhh, September!*
>
> *During September I relish each warm sunny day, as if summer will never return. I soak up the sun to save for the cold dark days of winter. I'm energetic, productive and optimistic. I look forward to investigating outdoors with children, catching insects, watching butterflies, and running during tag games. Then there's the chance to wear warm wool sweaters and pants welcomed after months of sweating. Children begin the month so very hopeful and excited . . . and we adults can make all the difference in whether the child remains enthusiastic and hopeful, or becomes discouraged.*

Sept. 5th

> *As I unpack the boxes of new supplies, I find myself particularly excited about the science materials. What a tremendous gift! I'm looking forward to studying science with the children, learning for myself, discovering together, watching the fascination in their eyes, and listening to their many questions. We have a microscope, a wonderful new microscope, "eyewitness" books, an ant farm, a hermit crab habitat, a crystal growing kit, planting supplies, a flower press kit. No wonder teaching children keeps me young and playful and alive with wonder! I want the children to have a variety of experiences that are rich and deep, and capitalize on their preferred interests, and I see no reason that young children can't study with depth and detail. The "eyewitness books" are for adults and children alike. They do not oversimplify and insult a young child's intelligence. That aspect is very important to me. Children are at different developmental stages, but they are not less intelligent because they are children. Sometimes, they are treated that way. There are many children who are more intelligent than I am, but I can do some things that they cannot do because of experience or training or development.*
>
> *Children need more respect in society for all they know and can do, for all that they see and intuit, and for their general thought processes. As I plan the arrangement of the room and all its materials, I'm aware of how much more is offered here than in a traditional classroom for young children. It is a very exciting place for all the children and adults who are involved.*

The excitement and personal philosophy expressed in Janeen's journal heightens my anticipation of the teaching and learning setting before me. I feel as eager and hopeful as she sounds when I enter the Lower School at Riley.

It is the first day of school! During the previous week, the children and their parents visited and participated in "getting-acquainted" activities for those new to the school and those who had attended the previous year. In this Lower School class, 2 of the 11 students are really experiencing a "first day" at Riley: Hannah and Leo.

Individual Explorations in Science

It is now 9:00 A.M. and most of the children have arrived. At two of the tables are children already engaged in science activities. Janeen informs me, "We have science first in the morning because there is such high interest, and then so much of the day's activities comes out of science." At one table Reggie is poking through his rock collection, occasionally looking at a sample with a magnifying glass. "Look— frozen quartz—look at these crystals," he says to Robert. Robert picks up a sample and asks, "I wonder if this one floats." The two boys go off to the sink to check. At the same table, Jon and Brook are examining a snake, and Monty is drawing it. The boys talk about gardens after Jon tells them he found the snake in his garden. He begins to give advice about how to find snakes, ". . . and then you look under the plants but be quiet."

At the other table, Leo, Hannah, and Samantha are preparing to plant cuttings with the help of Leo's dad. I notice that Leo is sitting as close to his dad as he possibly can. He looks like he wishes the other children weren't there and that he

had his dad all to himself. I see Janeen also observing this scene, and she approaches the table. She chats about planting with Leo's dad and gets the group started filling pots with dirt. She gives Leo instructions about where the watering cans are kept and asks him to be in charge of filling the cans with water. The activity is accompanied by curiosity and ideas.

"What if the plant isn't OK?"

"We could ask a gardener."

"How about if we put these outside in the summer and bring them in during the winter?"

"I can hear the roots growing."

Janeen stands back from the table and observes. Later, she asks, "Why do you think we call it a spider plant?" Samantha responds, "Because it looks like its hanging from its web." In response to another question about the need for soil, children argue a bit then turn to Leo's dad. He offers, "I've seen a pansy grow right through my driveway. Actually, it grew between the base of the foundation of our house and the driveway. Do you think that it needed dirt?"

No one answers, but by this time Samantha is paging through one of the books about plants and Hannah begins to do the same. It becomes obvious that these children can already read. I hear Samantha say, "Look, this is about dirt." She reads, "Plants need a place to put down their roots and grow. . . . Plants use food in the soil" (*The Young Child's Encyclopedia,* 1988). Lively discussion follows about the food in the soil as children skim the pages about plants, "Look at this sandy place—only one plant—like the beach." I notice that Samantha places a slip of paper in the encyclopedia to mark her place.

At the end of the same table, Keenan and Matthew Thomas have a box of bones and drawing materials. Matthew Thomas offers, "I'm trying to draw dinosaur teeth. I like to look at these." Keenan proceeds to draw a "great white shark" and points out that "Mine is longer than yours" and "He has a fin here." At a small corner table, Monty demonstrates to Morgan and Brook how to use the microscope, saying, "What the microscope does is make things look bigger—it helps our eyes." The boys examine flower petals and seeds as the assistant teacher, Barbara, observes. The three boys ask her to look through the microscope whenever they get excited about what they see.

A Gentle, Respectful Pace

As children begin to tire of their activities, Janeen encourages them to put materials away and wash their hands for a snack. She asks Jon what he needs to make a cover for the can in which he brought the snake. Together they decide on waxed paper and tape. Children are already at the other tables selecting snacks from their lunch boxes and bags: yogurt, fruit, carrot sticks, and cheese and crackers. I am impressed by the nutritious quality of the snacks and ask about them. Janeen replies, "We've communicated quite a bit with the parents about snacks and lunches, even made suggestions of appropriate foods." She adds, "Of course, we've discussed the same ideas with the children during the year." I can see that both parents and children responded very well.

Janeen joins the children at the table and sips a cup of tea that she made for herself. She describes the morning's activities and adds, "Samantha, please walk with Leo and his dad and show them how to get to the French class after you finish your snack."

As children finish eating and putting lunches back in cubbies, Janine leaves to teach math to a group of Upper School students. This is a new procedure for the entire school this year. The teachers are teaching their curriculum specialty or interest to children of all ages, and Janeen's specialty is math. I overheard the teachers talking about this change with great enthusiasm as I arrived. Glenna's words about faculty "connected to the whole school, not just a class" come to mind. This teaching arrangement really contributes to those connections.

Children Pursue Their Interests

After Janeen leaves, I watch as two of the children walk across the field to the house for photography lessons, and five others walk to the library for French lessons. Two of the Lower School children run to catch up with Janeen, apparently to join others for math. Dan, a fifth-grader, arrives to lead a drama activity.

Only Hannah and Matthew Thomas have chosen to work on drama. Dan begins with, "We'll pick out a book, then we'll look at it and I'll read it to you, then we'll pick characters and act it out." Hannah selects Eric Carle's *The Grouchy Ladybug* (Crowell, 1977). Dan reads the book with great expression, and the two young children become more obviously interested as the story proceeds. Dan stops, "Would you like to act it out? There are two of you and two ladybugs." Hannah and Matthew Thomas seem unsure and don't answer. Dan tries again, "Shall I keep reading and we'll see?" This time, both children say yes with certainty.

At the end of the story, Dan asks, "Now would you like to do part of this book as a play?" Matthew Thomas responds, "All of it." Dan begins, "Well I don't think we can" but then stops midsentence and says, "We'll try." He continues, "Now, you have to use a lot of motion with your hands when you act." Dan looks at the two children and asks enthusiastically, "Who would like to be the grouchy ladybug and who would like to be the friendly ladybug?"

He proceeds to take them through the pages, giving them lines to say from the story and he acts as the narrator. At one point, he stops to teach them "stage left" and "stage right." Occasionally, he stops with, "This is a long page—look at all the words—this will be a hard page to do."

When Hannah expresses fatigue, she leaves to choose something else to do. Matthew Thomas, however, is insistent on continuing. Dan asks him, "Do you want to do it again with me as the other ladybug?" He hears a definite "yes" and responds with, "You know that actors rehearse and rehearse until they get it perfect." He adds, "That's what we are doing." After five more pages of rehearsing, he looks at his watch, saying, "I've got to go to my next class but I'll see you on Wednesday." Matthew Thomas sits and pages through *The Grouchy Ladybug* as Dan gets ready to leave.

Dan's ease and enthusiasm for this drama activity prompts me to talk with him before he leaves. When I ask about why he chooses to engage in drama activities with young children, he responds with, "Oh, my mom used to have a day-care center, so I know how to work with young children and dress-up clothes." He continues, "Sometimes we put on plays in the loft or the barn." I also learn that Dan directed the Lower School children in *Peter and the Wolf* the previous year.

Matthew Thomas listens to our conversation and adds, "I was the bird in it." He tells Dan, "I've been practicing 'Man overboard' for a play about ships. I can't do very well at home because my sister is too little to do plays. She messes up."

At the same time that Dan, Hannah, and Matthew Thomas begin to dramatize their story, other children from the Lower School go to the library. There, the French teacher, Marian, greets the five children and Leo's dad on the deck with "Bonjour." She chats with them about speaking French as a little girl in Switzerland, then introduces herself to each with a handshake and a greeting using his or her name. Within minutes, children are responding to, "Levez-vous, s'il vous plait" (Stand up, please), "Tournez" (Turn), "Marchez" (March), "Touchez la tete" (Touch the head), and "Touchez le nez" (Touch the nose). All of the phrases involve movement, and Leo and his dad watch and imitate those who learned the phrases last year. Marian then points to colors on children's clothing and pronounces "rouge," "vert," "blanc," and "bleu," with children repeating after her. Soon, children are excitedly shouting color words independently as she holds up color cards.

As Leo's dad gets up to leave, Marian moves to sit next to Leo and immediately places her arm around his shoulders when he becomes upset. By the end of the third French song, one complete with lively movements, Leo looks more comfortable and participates with his peers. Several children hug Marian as they depart from the deck to walk back to the main building. I am touched by the warmth and affection of the adults thus far. The interactions truly communicate the feelings of family.

I am curious about the photography class that I heard two of the children talking about. They went to the class, so I hurry to the porch of Glenna's rambling house, where a group of eight are gathered on the steps reviewing the "dos and don'ts" of using a camera. When Reggie volunteers a rule for camera use, he is handed a camera and asked to demonstrate the rule he offers. Children ranging in age from 5 to 14 role-play using a camera and urge each other to remember some rules:

"Always wear the camera strap around your neck."
"Hold the camera still."
"Check for film inside."
"Never put your finger on the lens."

Some of the children say that they have used a camera before and others indicate no experience. They are asked, "Have you done photograms? Pin-Hole cameras?" As children respond to the questions about previous experiences, Reggie appears to have some background in photography, but Morgan's responses indicate no camera experiences. When the time is up, Reggie runs through the fields, and I struggle to keep up with him. I can tell that he's bothered about something, and I want to hear about it.

Responding to Individual Needs

Reggie runs into the room, looks about, and heads for Janeen, who is also just returning to the classroom. He bursts out with, "I don't want to go to photography anymore." Janeen sits down at a table and motions to him to do the same. She leans forward to be close to him and gets him talking about his reasons. She encourages him to stay with photography "a few more times" and promises a conference with him the following week to plan his schedule if he wants to change to another class. I observe her writing in a notebook immediately after this conversation before moving through the room to observe children's activities.

Other children are arriving and going to an activity list to make selections. Their choices include puppets, clay, dramatic play, blocks, games, drawing and construction, and listening center. They take turns placing a clothespin that has each child's name on it next to the type of activity they choose. Barbara, the assistant teacher, supervises the selection and becomes involved in a discussion with Morgan and Brook of how clothespins work. Robert asks, "How do they make them?" and the three boys examine the pins for answers. Barbara asks, "What would you use if you wanted to make a clothespin?" and the boys decide that they could use wood and rubber bands. Morgan heads to the construction center to see if he can make clothespins, and the other boys follow.

In the meantime, Samantha helps Hannah select an activity and put her clothespin in the right slot, then goes off to the puppet theatre. She manipulates a puppet on each hand and uses two different voices. After a few minutes, she looks around the room and calls to Barbara and Hannah to come watch her show. I wonder how often Samantha has given puppet shows, and if this activity was a favorite of hers last year.

During this time, two of the boys go to the block area and begin to gather a large number of blocks from the shelves. They spend the first 10 minutes negotiating what they will build and how to use the spaces. In the "good junk" construction area, Robert is making a "moving van because I've moved a lot." He informs Jon, "I'm putting tape all over it so it won't be all blue—so it will look old."

Jon asks, "Whose tape is this?"

Robert answers, "It belongs to the school."

They ask Janeen and she responds, "It belongs to the class—all of us."

Janeen's response that the tape belongs to the class continues the communication of respect for the children in the Lower School. The routines and the environment send the same message that I observed this morning.

Respecting Children: Supporting Their Decisions

It seems that all the children are involved in an activity of their choice except Leo. He begins to look teary, looks around the room, and goes to his cubby. He gets out his stuffed dog and stands near the game shelf. Janeen approaches him and asks if he would like to play a game. He nods and together they browse the game selections. When Janeen suggests that they could play Candyland, Leo gives an enthusiastic yes and begins to tell his teacher how to play.

Barbara, the assistant teacher, approaches Brook and Monty, who are wandering around the room, and reminds them, "You have 10 minutes left—how are you going to spend it?" They choose drawing materials and begin to work intently. Brook wants to sharpen a pencil for his drawing and Barbara spends time reviewing with him how to use the sharpener. She encourages him to find a second pencil and to practice using the sharpener.

After making excited comments about cars and pointing out the varied tires in their drawings, Monty asks, "How much time do we have before math?" When told that he has five minutes, he confides, "I don't want to be late for math—I like math" and begins clearing up his materials.

Completing the Morning

Children are individually encouraged to clean up and choose a math activity. Soon, they are busy with geoboards, large decks of cards, Mankala (an African stone game), shapes, and materials for drawing. Two older students from the Upper School have arrived and immediately join children in their activities.

Several children are reminded that it is math time, and Leo asks, "What is math?" Janeen responds, "Math is about figuring things out. It's about numbers, games, or puzzles." Children are heard counting objects, describing how they made designs and patterns, and referring to squares and rectangles. The older students ask questions as they play with the Lower School children. An older boy and two younger boys are at a table giving each other problems to do. I hear, "I'm going to think of a hard one this time," and soon after, "That was too easy." The hum of excited involvement is maintained for over 30 minutes.

After math activities, children go outside. Some play on the deck just outside the classroom, some in the sandbox, and some on the play equipment in the adjoining field. On the deck are crab nets, an anchor, and old wooden crates. In the field are a climbing structure and slide, swings, and a tree house, and at the edge of a field is a large and very inviting net strung in the trees.

John brings his snake outside and a small group joins him watching it in the sandbox. After a few minutes, he takes it out to a grassy area. The rest of the children stay in the sandbox with Barbara. Samantha expresses a wish to go outside more, and Monty chimes in with, "Me, too." Barbara responds with, "Maybe if we got cleaned up and got our stuff together faster we could have more time to play out here. I'm new at these routines so I'm just learning. I'll get faster, too."

Lunch Time: Relaxed and Social

Children have a choice of eating lunch on the grass or on picnic tables. Janeen asks several children to take Hannah and Leo and show them the tables to help get them started. Most children sit on the grass to eat and are joined by children from other classes. The scene is one of a comfortable, family-like meal with lots of conversation about food, last night's activities, younger siblings, and pets. Matthew Thomas and Jon are overheard:

"Matthew Thomas, why do you like boats so much?"

"I just love boats. My dad builds them and I'm going to build my own. We went sailing last night with Mr. Horsten and we had a fast ride. His boat is new."

"You know a lot about boats."

"Yeah, Russian ships are my favorites. I saw the stern of a Russian ship a few days ago. That's probably what I'm going to have when I build a ship."

I listen to their conversation as we eat lunch together. Brook and Samantha are with us, and it's been much like a meal with friends. When I finish, Matthew Thomas asks if he can have my avocado pit to plant. With my "yes," he takes off to wash it and "get it ready for planting."

After eating, several children from the Lower School (Reggie, Jon, Morgan, Monty, and Keenan) join a game of soccer on the open lawn in front of Glenna's house. Two of the Upper School teachers watch the game and act as referees when the need arises. The game stops with the announcement that it is time to go to the next class, and of course, there is a bit of a groan over stopping the soccer. The children depart with "good-byes" to each other and I am again reminded of the family quality of Riley.

Children's Choices Direct Afternoon's Activities

The children from the Lower School head to the library where Janeen awaits them. With the children, I enter the cool calm of this setting surrounded by glass and softened by foliage indoors and out. Earlier, I learned that the library design was developed with the input of all the children in the school. They contributed draw-ings, ideas, and suggestions, and were actively involved in the arrangement of the books.

On this first afternoon of the school year, Janeen guides Hannah and Leo through some of the sections of the library while the other children browse through various parts on their own. Morgan, Samantha, and Jon are soon at a table reading, while Reggie and Monty are selecting from a shelf of books on dinosaurs. I notice that Samantha's choice is a book about plants, and Jon is reading about snakes. Dan is also there, selecting books for his research project on drama. He smiles and warmly greets the Lower School children.

After 20 minutes of quiet reading, Janeen moves about the library, letting children know that she is ready to go back to the classroom. As children arrive there, she encourages them to get their individual file boxes of words for writing. Matthew Thomas proudly shows me his word cards. It is not surprising that they all relate to ships. Jon permits me to look through his cards and I see the following: *red streak, battle toads, Donatello, Raphael, humpback whales, my little snake, sky,* and *rocks.* I also see that he has begun a story about his snake and is intensely involved. It occurs to me that Jon's interest in snakes has directed many of his learning activities today. This is also true for Samantha and her curiosities about plants, and Matthew Thomas with his box of words about ships.

Communicating Respect for Children's Needs and Feelings

While children continue to use their word cards in a variety of ways, Janeen works with each child individually. She approaches Keenan and asks, "Is this a good time to listen to your words?" and he nods affirmatively. Again, her message in this simple question is one of respect for the child. I feel certain that if Keenan had said "No," Janeen would have asked him to suggest a good time.

Other children are seen writing, illustrating, and reading their writing to each other. Leo says, "I think I know how to read" as he selects a book and begins looking at the pages and mouthing words. When she's free, Janeen goes to him and listens to his "reading."

Hannah has just a few word cards in her box (developed at the previous week's visiting day), but she rehearses them over and over. I hear her proclaim, "I'm getting so good at words that I can't remember my name."

During this time, Keenan comes to Janeen and asks to rest. She offers the choices of going to the library, moving to the rug in the other part of the room, or listening to a story with a headset.

He leaves and goes to the library. Children aren't usually offered so much freedom in their choices, but here at Riley School offering alternatives is consistent with the child-centered approach.

Children's Curricular Input

Janeen begins to read with Morgan, who has gathered some science magazines. When they come to an article about shearing sheep and making wool for sweaters, Morgan asks, "What is shearing?" and "What are they doing to the sheep?" Janeen rubs the back of Morgan's neck and asks if the barber uses an electric razor to cut his hair on the back of his neck. When Morgan nods his head, she responds, "That's what it's like to shear sheep." At the end of the article, Janeen asks Morgan if he would like to see what the wool looks like. He is immediately enthusiastic, and they talk about going into town to a wool shop. I learned earlier that off-campus learning is valued at Riley, and that these children had previously participated in boat building, factory production lines, farm chores, and work with a local sculptor.

Literacy activities continue and I notice that Morgan has made three new word cards for his file: *sheep, wood,* and *shear.* He shows them to Janeen and she suggests that he try to use them in a story. During this time, I observe that two children are in the overstuffed chair reading a book, and that Brook and Reggie are working on a mural of an airport with extensive detail and dialogue. Samantha and Monty are discussing their names at the chalkboard:

"If you just use my nickname, it's three letters, but my whole name is eight letters. How long is your name? Want to see me write my name real big?"

I didn't notice but two students from the Upper School slipped into the room and have been sitting and reading with individual children. One of them reads a story to Matthew Thomas with elaborate expression and frequent, "What do you think is going to happen next?" The other Upper School student listens intently to Hannah read a simple story.

Nearby, Leo is "reading" Brian Wildsmith's books of pictures (*The Trunk, Whose Shoes?* and *The Nest*) and occasionally stops to show someone a page. Janeen moves from child to child, listening to each one read from a book of his choice or from her own writing. During this routine, Hannah approaches Janeen and begins to interrupt. She is told, "Hannah, when I'm reading with someone, I want you to wait." Hannah steps back and listens to Morgan read. Again, the message of respect is clear.

During this time, I notice that Reggie is beginning to move around the room somewhat "wound up" and I watch to see how the situation will be handled. When Janeen also notices, she faces Reggie to say, "We can't handle your energy in here. Either slow down or go outside and run it off." He returns to the mural where Brook is hard at work adding detail to the airport. Reggie watches and then begins to draw in another corner of the large sheet, talking to himself as he works. I hear, "Just work on the picture—just work on the picture."

Robert and Keenan have both written several pages and are busily making a book. Keenan says, "I'm going to teach you how to make the book. When you make a book, you've got to tape it like this." To me, he says, "We're making this wicked, scary book and no one will want to buy it." The boys excitedly describe how the cat lost its eye in their drawings.

Later, children clean up their writing and drawing materials and gather around Janeen, who reminds them of rules for outside play. "When I am not with you outside, you may only go to certain places. The net and the woods are off limits. That's because I'm not there to assist you with problems." She adds, "You will have 10 minutes to play before reflection time." Hannah asks, "What is reflections?" and Jon answers, "It's when we tell about our day." Hannah nods knowingly and heads for the basket of shoes. Other children remain near Janeen as she passes around a box of cards and each child selects one. The cards have classroom cleanup tasks written on them: *water plants, wash tables, vacuum, straighten cabinets, put up chairs,* and so on.

Within a few minutes, only Reggie and Brook are left in the room. Reggie vacuums vigorously and Brook sets chairs up on the tables. Outside, all of the remaining children are in the sandbox with Janeen and Keenan's mother. An animated discussion is occurring in one corner about ants and crickets. After 10 minutes, Janeen leads the group to the deck nearby. Only Robert remains in the yard, climbing on a rope swing. Janeen urges him to join and reminds him that he has "choices to make." He plays a few more minutes and then joins the group.

Reflections

On the deck, the children sit in a circle with their teacher and begin "reflection time." Janeen waits until it is quiet, then tells the children that they can now share their reflections.

Keenan begins without any urging, "I liked my day, especially when I was drawing with Robert."

Hannah quickly adds, "I liked it when we went outside."

Janeen responds, "You enjoyed being outside. What was good about it for you?"

Hannah answers, "I like the sandbox when we all sit together."

"I liked showing my snake and reading snake books," says Jon.

Janeen adds, "Did you notice how everyone was interested in your snake? We were glad you brought it."

Jon grins.

Brook says, "I used the microscope and taught Robert and Monty how to see in it."

Janeen replies, "Yes, you really helped your friends use our new microscope carefully."

"I liked it when we were at the soccer field," exclaims Reggie.

Matthew Thomas adds, "I got an avocado seed and we're going to plant it."

"I liked planting a spider plant and seeds," comments Samantha.

Janeen adds, "It sounds like planting went well for several of you. It does feel good to plant something. Now, did the day not go well for someone? Is there anything you want to talk about that wasn't good for you?"

Leo quickly contributes, "I didn't like it when my dad left."

Janeen nods and notes, "Yes, that was a sad time for you."

Monty remarks, "I want to say one thing. The book I read today, it was a kind of baby book. It went 'Big Bear, Little Bear'—baby stuff" in a voice full of disgust.

Janeen agrees with his impression and suggests that maybe it would be a good idea to read the book to Keenan's little brother or Samantha's little sister when they come to visit. "You will be very good at reading it to them." Monty nods and lets go of his annoyance.

A message comes for the group, "Reggie's mother will be a little late." Reggie grins and says emphatically, "Yes." Other children begin leaving as they spot a parent or a group gathering for their carpool. The first day of school winds down with a gentle and gradual end.

Reflections About the Day

As I review my observations of today's visit, I am curious once again to hear Janeen's thoughts. She shares her journal of that first day just as generously as she shared her classroom.

Sept. 6th

The first day is complete, and not without joy, satisfaction, and hopeful-ness. There's an interesting group dynamic between new and returning students, and between four-, five-, six-, and seven-year-olds. There's in-

credible energy and enthusiasm. During our reflections, the common thread that ran through many descriptions of the day was an enthusiasm for science. I anticipate many more science activities outdoors—natural science. The microscope was used extensively by Brook and Reggie, and others looked at their "finds" from the fields. They are very careful and fascinated by what they see.

As I reflect upon six and a half hours together today, I'm amazed that so much about children is apparent in such a short time, if one can only see. The children enter the classroom and proceed in their activities and interactions in the way that they see the world. The essence of the child is there to be seen and remembered. Information that the child gives us so early about her/himself can be put to powerful use in planning the child's schedule, bringing content to the curriculum, approaching the child, creating a positive dynamic community with all children playing active roles, communicating to the child and parents . . . the list goes on. Although I have noted these observations for years and applied the knowledge to my teaching, I've never realized just how quickly they show themselves, just how much an observer can gain in one day, two days, one month. And the exciting aspect of using observation to plan is that it takes away the guesswork and makes this work so much easier. Listening, observing, being open, and setting high expectations are key ingredients to a successful year together.

I want to spend a lot more time with Monty and Reggie. This is their last year in the Lower School and I worry about meeting their needs and challenging them. Hannah seemed to slip right in our routines and handled transitions easily. I need to find out more about her interests. Leo, on the other hand, will need more time to get comfortable with us. I'll ask Robert to do some activities with him tomorrow. I'll alert the other teachers at our morning meeting—he's going to need some extra support.

I finish the day's journal entry and feel hopeful for the year ahead at Riley School. Like Janeen, I also learned so much about the children in the Lower School in this first day. If children are truly going to be the source of curriculum, Janeen's role demands the careful and consistent "kid watching" she practices. Additionally, as more and more programs move to mixed-age grouping, the experiences of Janeen and the children of the Lower School provide great insights for educators and parents.

I am filled with a strong desire to share this story as I leave the comfort of the Lower School classroom and the wonder of walking through the fields to the library. In the years ahead, when school begins in September each year, I will think of Riley School and reminisce about this first day with fond memories and inspiration.

Questions and Issues

1. Think about the many first days of school you have experienced as a teacher and as a student and compare them with this first day at Riley School. What implications emerge for the mixed-age arrangement of the Lower School?
2. What kind of connections do you find between Janeen's journal reflections and her teaching role and approaches observed in the classroom?
3. If Riley School were not private, what curricular concerns would be voiced about the individualized approach?
4. Some have expressed concern that these children would experience significant difficulties if they should move or transfer to another school. If they came to your classroom or neighborhood school, would they face many transitional problems? If so, what changes would they have to make? What problems would the children encounter? What would be comfortable for them?
5. Analyze the first-day experience for Hannah and Leo from their perspectives. If you were Janeen, what would you have done differently?
6. Analyze the teaching role in the Lower School. Consider the most important instructional approaches Janeen uses as she works with children.
7. Predict what Janeen's plan book might look like for this day we observed. What kind of entries would you expect to find in her plan?

References

Amonashvili, S. (1989). Non-directive teaching and the humanization of the educational process. *Prospects, 19* (4), 581–590.

Cartwright, S. (1991). Interview at a small Maine school. *Young Children, 46* (3), 7–11.

Castle, K. (1989). Child-centered teaching: Through children's eyes. *Childhood Education, 65* (4), 209–212.

Evans, T., Corsini, R., & Gazda, G. (1990). Individual education and the 4R's. *Educational Leadership, 48* (1), 52–56.

Glines, D., & Long, K. (1992). Transitioning toward educational futures. *Phi Delta Kappan, 73,* (7), 557–560.

Goodlad, J., & Anderson, R. H. (1987). *The non-graded elementary school.* New York: Teachers College Press.

Holly, M. L. (1989). Reflective writing and the spirit of inquiry. *Cambridge Journal of Education, 19* (1), 71–80.

McCutcheon, G. (1992). Facilitating teacher personal theorizing. In E. W. Ross, J. W. Cornett, & G. McCutcheon, (Eds.), *Teacher personal theorizing.* Albany: State University of New York Press.

Wassermann, S. (1990). *Serious players in the primary classroom* (Chapter 1). New York: Teachers College Press.

Wiersma, W. (1986). *Individually guided education: An alternative form of schooling.* Paper presented at the annual meeting of the American Educational Research Association, San Francisco.

6

Rogers Elementary School
A Dynamic Teacher Team and an
Individualized Assessment Approach

In 1991, Mary Nall and Wendy Payne decided it was time for a change. Both women had been teachers for many years and worked together early in their careers. It was 1979 when they taught in the same school and became close personal and professional colleagues. After they began teaching in different schools, they regretted that they hadn't stayed in touch with each other very well.

At about this same time in 1991, Trevor Calkins, a principal, was asked to start a new school, Rogers School, and to handpick a staff committed to innovation. When he began staff recruitment, Mary and Wendy were interested. The time was right. Their families were grown and they felt that they had the energy and freedom to experiment and make changes in their professional lives. The attraction of a futuristic educational environment called to them. Just as compelling was their desire to team teach in a school culture that would support their efforts. Rogers School not only offered a building designed for team teaching but Trevor Calkins made it clear that collaboration was part of the environment for which he was hiring.

Mary Nall and Wendy Payne applied for the new teaching positions as a team, and insisted on being interviewed as a team. The two teachers described their desire to experiment with mixed-age grouping, integrated curriculum, and assessment approaches. They used every argument they had to convince Trevor Calkins that

89

they were the ones to hire. "We even told him that he wouldn't have to worry about us having children or staying home with little ones," Mary adds when she retells the story. They were convincing and they got the jobs.

Before the School Doors Open: Beginnings of Change

Mary and Wendy were part of the school staff that met monthly with parents and community members in the summer before Rogers officially opened its doors for students. The major purpose for the meetings was to develop a policy for assessment, evaluation, and reporting procedures. "To grade or not to grade" became the most critical issue. Initially, parents supported the idea of personalized education but they didn't want to give up letter grades. Trevor Calkins describes the concerns of the parents: "When asked what they wanted to see in their children's reports, parents responded that they wanted to know what their child could do including his or her strengths and weaknesses. They wanted the reports to be personal and individualized and they wanted to know where their child stood in relation to other children of the same age. The task was daunting" (1992, p. 12).

Trevor also describes the concerns of the teachers: "The staff soon realized individualization and personalization of instruction are difficult to implement—especially if we gave letter grades. Strengths and weaknesses are evident through letter grades, but personal action-plans to resolve weaknesses are difficult to set in a rank-ordered system. Everyone cannot be at the top of the class" (1992, p. 12).

The dilemma for the Rogers School staff was intensified by their commitment to the kind of changes being called for by the British Columbia Ministry of Education plan for reform called "Year 2000." A major portion of that reform agenda focused on the same issues being discussed by teachers, and parents at Rogers School. In a document published by the Ministry of Education for British Columbia, when assessment and evaluation were described, parents, teachers, and children are talked about as "contributors" to the process of studying a child's development. The 1992 document describes assessment and evaluation "based on *what* and *how* the child *thinks, knows, feels,* and *can do.*" That description sounded like the personalized and individualized assessment being discussed at the meetings at Rogers School. The language in the Ministry of Education document was different but the concept of assessment was similar to what the teachers and parents wanted for their children at Rogers. As the document described the changes in assessment and in reporting, one phrase caught my attention: "Building a bridge from home to school." The series of meetings being held by the staff and parents of Rogers School were certainly constructing a foundation for such a bridge.

Focusing the Observations

As I read the series of documents released by the Ministry of Education (1991, 1992) and the Rogers School Assessment, Evaluation, and Reporting Policy, the questions of How to do it? became more intense. How do teachers truly personalize assessment practices? How do they measure and record what each child thinks, knows, feels, and can do? I was ready to see the changes and the policy in action. I wanted to be able to present a case description in which assessment was truly personalized and individualized, and so I planned to focus my observations on that aspect of the program at Rogers School. I think that many teachers and parents are working toward such assessment and would like to see the concept at work. I was also intrigued with the team teaching proposed by Mary Nall and Wendy Payne, and so I would observe these teachers to see how the team arrangement works. I had questions. What are the advantages? Are there disadvantages? What is it like for children? How is it connected to the assessment process?

To get these and other questions answered, I scheduled a visit with Trevor Calkins, Mary Nall, and Wendy Payne at Rogers School in Victoria, British Columbia. I would arrive the first day after their vacation break. The spring weather directed my travel plans and I chose to use the large comfortable ferries to get to Vancouver Island and the city of Victoria.

Seeing Both Sides of Victoria

Like most tourists who arrive by ferry, I begin my drive through Victoria at her magnificent harbor with its historic tourist attractions. It is a breath-taking place to start. There are magnificent coastline hotels reflected in the water, a complex of stately Parliament buildings, and lush parks with beds of vibrant colors and green velvet lawns.

As I continue through Victoria, I reach a downtown area that looks a bit like home—a real mix of old and new office buildings, department stores, restaurants, and apartments. Downtown Victoria is an easy drive, and now the suburbs appear. These neighborhoods look much like those in which many of us live. I leave Route 17 at Rogers Road and see the elementary school on top of a picturesque hill overlooking the highway. To get there, I drive through two sections of the surrounding community. The first is a sleepy little neighborhood of homes built in the 1950s—modest bungalows with single-car garages. Beyond this is a neighborhood of larger split-level homes with double-car garages and obvious amenities such as color-matched lampposts, fountains, and sculptured landscaping. My impression of this neighborhood tells me that most of the children at Rogers School live comfortably. The neighborhood looks fairly traditional, so the community culture may not easily accommodate educational changes. My impressions confirm that the innovations at Rogers School needed to be developed with parent and community involvement in order to be successful.

The area immediately surrounding the school is a surprising contrast to the neighborhoods just beyond. On two sides are lush pastures with at least two dozen cows and their calves, and beyond are several modern and picture-perfect grey and white farm buildings. There is a definite look of prosperity. Adjacent to the farm is a panorama of hilly terrain thick with trees. Later, I learn that this is the Christmas Hill Nature Sanctuary. I can't help but think about the resources for learning that abound in the acreage surrounding Rogers School—such as field trips and natural materials.

Arriving at Rogers School

I am surrounded by children and parents also headed for Rogers School, so I turn my attention to my driving instead of the surroundings. As I turn into the school parking lot, I notice many cars pulling up to the entrance and dropping children off at the front door. The school is an impressive contemporary structure of wood and glass with several atrium-like areas between classrooms. As I enter the front door, there is a now familiar routine in place. Everyone—children, parents, and teachers—is removing "outside" shoes and putting on soft "inside" shoes. There is a basket of "extras," soft slippers, at the door for people like me, who should know better by now.

I receive a friendly greeting from the school secretary and immediately meet the principal, Trevor Calkins. My conversations with him prior to my arrival in Victoria told me that he is intensely involved in the classroom life at Rogers. As we walk through the school, he supports my decision to observe Mary and Wendy's team-teaching arrangement: "Mary and Wendy blend their teaching styles and professional strengths into an exciting team—they're a dynamic duo."

As Trevor Calkins walks me to their rooms, I notice that the school is a maze of very wide hallways and that children use those spaces for all kinds of activities. I see children reading, writing and drawing, socializing, and working on group projects on the floor throughout the halls. Trevor tells me that the reason for changing shoes is to keep the carpets and floors free of dirt so that the children can use these as clean "work spaces." "In fact, this was suggested by the children when we opened the school," he adds. As we proceed to Mary and Wendy's rooms, we pass a spacious and inviting library adjacent to where we are headed.

"The Dynamic Duo" and Their Classroom Settings

When Trevor and I arrive at Mary and Wendy's classrooms, I am immediately intrigued by the physical arrangement and the vitality of these rooms where I will be spending the next few days. There are two bright open rooms connected by a wide work area with sinks and shelves of materials. In addition, the classroom design has several interesting spaces that invite small groups of children to play and work within. In one of the rooms is a loft, and the wide hallway outside the rooms appears well used for additional activities. Describing all of the features of these classrooms would take several pages and may not allow you to see it clearly, so I have sketched a floorplan for you (Figure 6–1).

As you can see from my sketch of the classrooms, the physical arrangement really supports the team teaching that Mary and Wendy enjoy. Both teachers and children move easily back and forth between the rooms, and so do I as I observe this bustling scene. I am especially interested in seeing how these two teachers coordinate their roles for a team approach to their work. A total of 21 first-graders are in the two rooms this morning, and they will be joined by an almost equal number of kindergartners in the afternoon. This particular blend of ages intrigues me, and I look forward to seeing how Mary and Wendy work with the first grade/kindergarten combination of children.

As I get ready to observe, I reflect on the descriptions of assessment approaches and the evaluation process of the British Columbia schools, and renew my interest in seeing such practices in action. The assessment emphasis for young children is on observational data and narrative reporting. Such an evaluation approach is

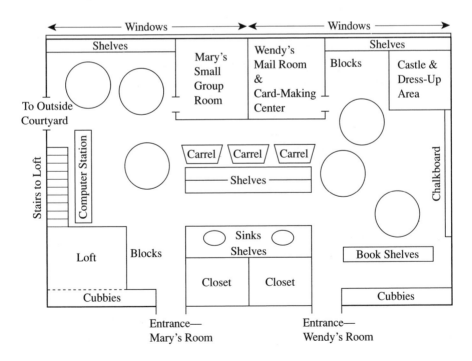

FIGURE 6–1

philosophically comfortable for so many teachers, but the question always follows, How do I find the time to do so? I anticipate some answers in my observations of these two teachers.

The Morning Begins

It is 8:40 A.M. and the children arrive one or two at a time. Several students, who are obviously not in first grade, arrive and explain to me that they are sixth-graders and that they spend their first 20 minutes in activities with a younger "buddy." "We usually read stories or play games," one sixth-grader adds. As we talk, another teacher enters to borrow all the "babies" Mary and Wendy can spare. I'm puzzled. "Babies?" My confusion ends when I see her leave with an arm full of dolls.

Many of the first-graders arrive with books and want to talk about them with their teachers. I hear one of the teachers say, "*Long Ago in A Castle*—Where did you get this great book? You could do a book report on this." Wendy listens as Henry tells of going to a bookstore with his mom to find a book on castles. He shows her the bookmark he got at the store. She asks if they can show the book to the class later in the day, and he grins in response.

Marshall approaches Mary with a book he has found in the classroom and says, "I think that I should actually take this home—it has directions for making a castle—can I do it?" Mary responds, "Yes, write me a note that you're taking it home overnight." Marshall goes off to do so and Mary turns to me to explain, "We started studying castles weeks ago and they don't want to stop." She acts a bit embarrassed about the castle theme and goes on to say that she and Wendy wanted to study spring or plants or something "that feels more appropriate," but the children took off with the topic of castles. She shows me the drawbridge and castle entrance that the children had made out of paper at the stairway leading to the loft. We chuckle over their sign proclaiming castle rules:

Castle Rules:

- No play fiting in the castle
- No bosing anyone around
- Have to have fun
- Wate til the bridge is up
- No throwing banana's
- No eating play fruit

Mary leaves me to continue her greeting of children and taking care of needs, and I move about the room to see how children are spending this "free choice" time.

The first thing I notice is that Marshall has been joined in his enthusiasm over the *Build Your Own Castles* book by another boy, Sam. They browse through the

pages, and before long they are at Mary's side with a request. "Do you have any big pieces of cardboard? We want to make flags and people for our castle." Mary encourages them to use this early time to make lists of what they need" and to save their construction for "centre time." The boys go back to their carrel with paper and a pencil box and begin their list. Another boy, Jonah, joins them and they rearrange the carrel by moving other equipment out of the way and adding a chair. I think to myself, These children are in charge of their environment—making it work for them. I continue to watch the three boys and hear their delight at working together:

"How about one castle for the three of us?"

"How about three castles in three days?"

Laughter follows this second question, and then they begin the list. "Kitchen knife—that's important. Spell it." They continue, "Matches, coins, toothpicks. . . ."

I continue past the threesome through the work area to Wendy's room where several children are rearranging word cards in a pocket chart with the heading "Once

Upon a Time." Some of the words on cards are *queen, troll, castle, moat, dragon, spell, wishes, magic,* and *beast.* There are empty cards that the children use for writing verbs and prepositions as they compose sentences.

Near the pocket chart activity, I glance over to the row of computers and watch Mandy write about "The Castles."

> In castles have taoers (towers). And in castles have a gat (gate) and they have fels (fields). And in castles they have bedrooms. And in castles they have canapea bed in ther rooms. And they have a dek (deck).

She offers to read it to me and is obviously pleased with her work. Her oral version assists me with words like *taoers.* I watch as she prints her story and notice that she makes two copies. When I ask, "Why did you make two copies?" Mandy tells me that one is for her teacher and one is to take home. I watch as she places one copy in her cubby and one copy in a file folder on a nearby shelf. Mandy's story is certainly the kind of work that informs individualized assessment reports. I wonder what else is collected for assessment.

Many of the children are taking turns reading to their sixth-grade buddies, and I notice that Wendy is moving around the room, taking notes just as I am. Just then, Mary comes in the room asking, "How are the children in your room doing?" Wendy responds with, "Fine—anytime now." Mary agrees and suggests that they get ready. I hear both teachers announcing, "Boys and girls, finish up what you're doing and come together for board messages." As I watch the children complete activities, I realize that the children have been free to spend their time in either room, not confined to a "homeroom" arrangement.

Morning Routines

Soon, all the first-graders are gathered in Wendy's room on the floor in front of the large chalkboard. Just then, two older students come to the door and introduce the two teachers to a new student, Yolanda, from their class. Wendy asks, "Where did you come from?" and the student responds, "Edmunton." Mary follows with, "Is it cold there?" and the student responds, "Yes, but it's not snowing anymore." Wendy urges the first-graders to greet Yolanda and there are shouts of "Hi." Both Mary and Wendy warmly extend a welcome to the student with, "We're glad to have you at Rogers."

When the visitors leave, Wendy focuses attention on the chalkboard where there is a message with letters missing in the words:

TODAY W- ARE BACK IN SC-OOL
WE CA- DO AN-T-ING
IT WIL- BE FU B-CAUSE IT IS SPR-NG

Rudy is appointed "teacher" to lead the "board message" activity. He gets a glittery wand and he very dramatically scans the group to see if he has attention. Wendy sits by his side, coaching him when he needs help. Mary, on the other hand, sits off to the side of the children and takes notes during this large group activity. At the front of the group, Rudy calls on children to fill in the missing letters, and they complete most words with ease. When Julie can't supply the *Y* in *ANYTHING,* she chooses a friend to help her. Her friend whispers the letter and Julie fills in the missing space.

As the message is close to being completed, the group becomes impatient with Arthur, who is taking a turn filling in a missing letter. Wendy quiets the group with, "Remember what Mr. Calkins said about keeping your thoughts to yourself so that the person at the board can think his or her thoughts clearly." The group is hushed and Arthur fills in the last letter of the board message.

Now Wendy takes over the chalkboard and Rudy sits with the group. She calls attention to the *ING* in *SPRING* and asks, "Can you think of other words with *ing?*" Their list includes *inning, thing, coming, king, ping, sing, wing,* and *cling.* During the entire "board message" activity, Mary has been taking notes and occasionally comments on children's ideas. At one point, Wendy directs her to "make note of that—there's still some problem with the silent *h.*" Later, I learn that Mary's notes, anecdotal data, are used when she and Wendy review the day and the week, and ultimately when they prepare narrative reports to parents.

From the *ing* focus, Wendy then leads the children to a discussion of spring with, "Look around the room and find signs of spring." The room has been set up well for this question. There are vases of flowers around the room, large pictures of trees in bloom, and a display of artificial trees, plants, and flowers. Mary interrupts to say, "Mrs. Payne certainly made the room beautiful today, didn't she?" After a series of comments about the many flowers children were seeing in their neighborhoods, Wendy prompts the discussion with, "You know what I saw buzzing overhead this morning?" The response, "Bees," aroused an immediate hubbub of talk about bees.

When the buzz over bees quiets, Wendy comments, "Boys and girls, it seems like you have a lot to talk about—all the signs of spring—and many of you are excited about what you did on your break." She continues, "I think that you need to get to your journals and write some of that." There's a cheer from the children and a rush to get journals. There is no hesitation to begin writing. Children spread over the two classrooms and some chat with friends while writing. Others write quietly by themselves. Mary and Wendy move about, observing and interacting with the children.

As the children finish, they approach one of the teachers to read their journal entries. There does not seem to be any differentiation as to whose class children are in. They approach whichever teacher is free at the moment. Some of the children read independently and some read with their teacher. When a child finishes, Mary or Wendy asks questions that require the child to add more information or detail. For example, when Gigi writes about going to the science fair during her school break, Wendy asks her to "write about something you enjoyed at the fair." Sometimes, Mary writes a question at the end of the journal entry. Adam's writing offers an example. In his journal is written:

We went to a wedding.
I was a flowber boy.
We bot a new car from Honda City.
We had fun.

Mary writes to Adam, "What does a flower boy do?" He writes back, "I carid the ring." As I listen to the interactions and hear the content of the children's journals, I am reminded of the description of assessment I read earlier. That description emphasized "what and how the child thinks, knows, feels, and can do." This journal writing time certainly provides opportunity to observe and collect samples of that kind of information about children.

As the children finish their journal writing, Wendy announces, "We have a set of 'easy-to-read' fairy tales here. They are all very different from any fairy tales you have ever seen. You'll like them. Pick a book and get your reading log. You can do a web or a map or a book report."

As the children select the fairy tales they wish to read, both Mary and Wendy continue to interact with children about their journal entries. I hear, "You put an exclamation mark here. You did think fishing was exciting." Another child's vacation description is followed with, "Did you stay in a hotel or a cabin?" At the same time that children are sharing their journals with their teachers, they also share with each other. I hear children commenting on each other's journals much like I have heard their teachers do. The journal writing experience provides rich assessment information about the children, and it is also a social occasion.

Soon, all the children are reading fairy tales and I note that there is an unusually unique and extensive collection of the tales, so children have many choices. At this point, I am startled as Mary and Wendy leave the room "for a break" and I hesitate as I follow them to the teachers' lounge. I keep looking back at the two classes and wonder about the children. When we arrive at the lounge, I see that all the other teachers are here, too. I can't stand it, so I ask, "What about the children?" I'm told that there are several teaching assistants roaming the school checking on all the classes, and that the children are quite independent.

Teacher Talk in the Lounge

The sixth-grade teacher who had collected Mary and Wendy's dolls announces to the group in the lounge that her class is beginning a unit of study called Family Life Curriculum. She requests, "If you see my children hauling babies around, please note how they're treating them and give them some feedback about their child care." To the librarian she adds, "Watch that they don't leave them in the library."

Trevor Calkins, the principal, informally reports on his visit to schools in Alberta during the break. He describes how he showed samples of the Rogers School narrative progress reports and heard comments such as, "These are so clear," "These are specific," and "These are what we've been looking for." He expresses his appreciation to the staff for their work on the narrative reports that are ready to go home in the afternoon. He wants to give the teachers recognition for all their work on the reports and says, "This is a message I want children to hear." He asks for 10 minutes at the end of the day, and a very brief assembly is scheduled.

The remainder of the break is spent discussing how to schedule parent conferences. There is a major concern among the staff to be sure that schedules accommodate those families with more than one child in the school. The teachers decide to spend half of their lunch time on the following day together working on a school-wide calendar of conferences.

This kind of middle-of-the-day break is unique, like so much at Rogers School. Decisions that are made as a result of these brief informal staff meetings usually are relegated to a once-a-week meeting or are made by the administrator. This daily practice certainly communicates the collaboration that is valued at Rogers.

Back in the Classrooms

When we return to the classroom, children are recording their work in their folders titled "My Reading Log" (Figure 6–2). Children place a variety of assignments in the folder: drawings with labels, short book reports, story maps, and webs of characters and events. I take note of the different forms for the children's choices. One is a story web form from Ginn and Company. One is an original form for a brief book report that calls for the title, author, what the story is about, how it ended, and a description of the child's favorite part.

As children place their work in their reading logs, Mary and Wendy encourage them to form a group with three friends and talk about the book they read. I hear, "Remember that if you really liked your book, you want to encourage your friends to read it too" and "Be sure to give some interesting details from your story." I am amazed at the smoothness of the routine, as children gather in groups of four and immediately begin taking turns telling about their book. Again, I observe Mary and Wendy moving from group to group, listening to the interactions. After a few minutes, they look through the reading log folders and jot a few notes. The folders are portfolios of children's literacy work and reviewed weekly by the teachers. Much like the anecdotal data from observations and the journals, the folders provide a look at what and how children *think, feel, know,* and *can do.* Even the choice of how to communicate his or her book report—a web, or a picture, or a story map—provides information about how a child thinks or how he or she can do a report.

My Reading Log

Books I've Read	Date	My Comments

FIGURE 6–2

Source: Rogers School. Reprinted by permission.

Centre Time and More Choices

As the small groups finish their reporting activity, they are reminded that it is "centre time." I watch as children spread through the two rooms and all the little niches to work in an interesting variety of "centres" (their spelling). The computers are popular, and the four chairs in front of them are full immediately. Wendy requests help from Julie at the computers with, "George needs help getting started

on the computer. Can you help him?" Julie turns to George, gives him directions to begin, and watches until he is able to work independently. Again, I notice that children feel free to pull up extra chairs next to friends, so that the computer work becomes a social activity.

In the dramatic play corner, Kim, Lulu, and Meredith are dressing up in what is clearly "prince and princess" attire. Lulu and Meredith wear long dresses, filmy scarves, jewelry, and crowns. Kim has a crown, a full-sleeved shirt, and a wide belt with metalwork on the front. The three children are very involved in selecting their clothing and looking at themselves in the mirror.

In one of the niches to the side of Wendy's classroom is Paula with a mailbag on her shoulder. She's sorting envelopes into boxes and is very seriously "getting ready to deliver the mail." On a table in this room are materials for making greeting cards: construction paper, old cards, scissors, markers and pencils, glue, and bits of decorating material. I watch as children use old cards with the former greetings removed and make new insides for their own greetings. Several of them are busy making birthday cards.

On a large open space on the floor is a giant neighborhood map with address cards and transportation vehicles. Three children are on the floor with plastic cars. One of them has a flattened paper bag that is a ferry boat. I listen to the conversation:

"I'll show you where Vancouver is. Get on the ferry now."

"Here we go. (Lots of automobile sounds) You can get on now."

"Move to the back. Keep in the lines. We're ready to leave now. Now we're out in the water."

Outside in the hall are three children sitting in front of a puppet theater. Behind the puppet stage are two children with a variety of puppets. The story seems to be about the dog who lives at the castle and the princess who needs help. Soon after the story begins, one of the puppeteers directs the audience to get chairs to sit on and not to get too close. He gives an ultimatum, "If you want to watch, you have to move back." Wendy joins this group and supervises when needed. At one point, she reminds the puppeteers to use loud voices so that the audience can hear. Children come and go throughout the production. Fortunately the "improv" quality of the story makes it easy to transition in and out of the audience.

Back in the classrooms, I spot the prince and princesses up in the castle (the loft) rearranging the furniture. I hear Kim, Lulu, and Meredith working through their negotiations and I hear an occasional command:

"Let's make this our living room, OK?"

"We can put the chairs over here and the table here."

"We need this here to protect from our enemies."

I've climbed halfway up the stair to listen and the children occasionally look my way with stares that aren't welcoming. I may have broken one of the castle rules, so I return to the classrooms to note other centre-time activity.

I observe that there is extensive block building in both classrooms, and that Marshall, Sam, and Jonah are still enthusiastically working on gathering materials listed in the *Build Your Own Castle* book. After a little more than an hour, I hear both teachers asking, "Children, could you tidy up what you're doing now?" They remind the children that it is almost time for lunch.

A Second-Grade Expert and More Castles

The cleanup is calm and fairly swift. As children finish, they join Wendy on the floor in her room and sing "I Know a Castle in the Clouds." A slightly older student is waiting at the front of the group with a beautiful model of a castle. He is a second-grader who made his own castle and he has come to show it to the two classes of children. When most of the children are seated, Wendy asks him to tell about his castle. He proceeds with a verbal tour of the model:

"This is where everyone lives—the keep. These are the towers. They shoot arrows from here. This is the portcullis—the gate (he lifts it). There are loopholes in real castles because the walls are so thick, but I didn't make any. Here's a wallwalk just above the gate, and a moat to keep the enemies from coming in."

Wendy encourages children to ask questions, and most are curious about what he used to build the castle. He points to different towers and identifies the size milk carton he used. He talks about his mom's glue gun and how she helped him secure a chain in place on the drawbridge. Mary asks, "Can we keep your castle for a brief time while we study castles so that we can look at it?" He responds with a question, "How long?" Mary suggests that they return the castle to him on

Friday before he goes home, and he agrees. She asks him, "What are you studying in your class?" and he responds, "Vegetables," but doesn't sound very enthusiastic.

Lunch Time and a Time for Team Planning

As the castle builder leaves, children get their lunch boxes and gather in groups at tables throughout the two rooms. When the weather is good, they eat outside, but today it is raining. Mary and Wendy supervise the children for a few minutes, then two sixth graders come in to each classroom to "take care" of the children. Wendy asks the older children, "What do you have planned for today?" They respond, "Hangman."

I follow the two teachers to the lounge again and listen to their planning conversation:

Mary: We really need to start our beans. It would be awfully nice to do the bean planting with our older buddies. Do you think so?

Wendy: Sure. I'll take responsibility for scheduling it for one morning this week with the sixth-grade class.

Mary: What else do we need? Let's see—cups, soil, and beans. I'll pick those up.

Wendy: Before planting, let's have time for them to examine the beans, to take them apart maybe, and then to draw what they see. Then later, they can plant them.

Mary: Let's plan a form for them to record their observations, something like, "The first day, my bean plant looked like _____."

Wendy: Yes, and let's have space for them to draw their observations, and then continue with, "The next day, my bean plant looked like _____."

Mary: During the day, we can read that contemporary version of "Jack and the Beanstalk." There's good language in it—lots to write about. It will help connect the activities.

Wendy: In that book, the giant writes a letter to Jack. We could have them write a letter to the giant for their journal writing activity.

They agree to the plans for letter writing and bean planting and prepare to leave the lounge. Mary heads back to the classrooms to check on the children and the Hangman games. Wendy has her guitar with her and she heads to the large set of stairs near the school entrance. She sets up a music stand and tunes her guitar. As she's doing so, children from the first, second, and third grades around the school file in and sit on the stairs in front of her.

Aesthetic and Artistic Development

As soon as most children are assembled on the stairs, Wendy warms them up with a "Do re mi fa so la ti do." Children use their hands to move up an imaginary scale as they sing the notes following Wendy's lead. After a few minutes of this warm-up, a child from an upper grade plays a clarinet solo. Afterwards, Wendy has several children try to make a sound to demonstrate the difficulty of playing clarinet.

Now Wendy strums her guitar and children sing rounds of "Fish and Chips and Vinegar." She stops once and reminds the children to hold their heads up while singing. The children cheer when she announces that they will sing "Rufus Rustis Johnson Brown." They sing it through, then split it into two parts, then switch parts and sing it again. Wendy then works on a new song with the children, and I notice that when she plays a note or a series of notes, the children can easily replicate it with their voices. Wendy congratulates a new child for succeeding in singing all of the songs with the group. When it is time to return to classrooms, I feel wistful. Listening to the music and the singing was such a beautiful experience, and I notice that a number of the teachers have been sitting, listening, and sharing my enjoyment.

I do a quick count of the children before they leave. There are about 96 first-, second-, and third-grade students. I am very impressed by the level of skill they demonstrate. I learn that they rehearse twice a week and am again impressed by the commitment of teachers and children to this musical experience.

The Kindergartners Arrive

As Wendy and the children return to the classroom, I join them and find that Mary is already finishing a book with the kindergarten children. She has read the poem, *Mommy Slept Late and Daddy Fixed Breakfast* by John Ciardi. The children are intrigued with the term "manhole cover" and discuss what it is and what it's made of. Mary asks, "Can women go down in the manhole?" and some of the children say, "No." Then, Vanessa says, "No, my mom would be scared." Monty says, "Not a pregnant woman, but other women could." Mary chuckles and responds, "Yes, women can go down in the manhole." She follows this with telling the group that it is time for the afternoon circles.

As the group of kindergarten children separate into two groups, I count 22 children gathering in Mary's room and 24 in Wendy's room. Both teachers begin their afternoon circle with a discussion of spring break. I hear Wendy ask, "How many of you went away for spring break?" Children raise their hands, and then Wendy asks, "How many of you stayed here?" She shows her group the spring vocabulary that remains on the chalkboard in her room, and discussion of spring begins again. After a few minutes, Wendy instructs, "Find a partner to share your spring break with. Talk about what happened last week when you didn't come to school. Tell about what you did when you went away or when you stayed here."

Once again, I witness a smooth routine as children join with a partner. I note that first-grade and kindergarten children mix well in this activity, and I am even more impressed as I listen to the verbal interactions of the partners:

Nathan announces, "It was my birthday and you know where I went?
Julie guesses, "To the circus? To the park? I don't know."
Nathan replies, "I went to a farm and we saw goats. I got to milk a goat."
Julie then asks, "How did you do that? Did you drink the milk?

This conversation continues with intensity as I move to listen to another set of partners. I hear Adam again describing the wedding and his role as a flower boy. He has brought a large photograph and points to the wedding participants, "This is the bride." His partner asks, "Is that your mother?" "No, that's my aunt," Adam responds. He names the participants in the photo, and his partner listens intently.

Both kindergarten and first-grade children again demonstrate the independence I have observed in the morning session. Their conversations are expressive. They appear to be listening well to each other. It is obvious that they have had lots of practice and experience. I am certain of the importance of these independent routines for children's development, but also for Mary and Wendy's observational practices. As I watch and listen to the partners, I realize how much I am learning about these children's language development, their social skills, and their experiential background. Their conversations are another rich source of personalized assessment data for Mary and Wendy.

How Children Feel about School

After the partners finish sharing, Mary calls the children back to her circle, "Let me just give you an idea of what we're doing this afternoon." She continues, "We have an assembly at the end of our day, so our schedule is full. During our time this afternoon we will be working on a castle-building activity with Mrs. Payne's children, and we will do two activities on our own—a self-assessment form that talks about what you like to do in school and a surprise activity that you've never done before. We're going to do this form first because I want to 'pop' these into your report cards to go home today."

Mary begins with a brainstorm of all the activities the children like to do in school. On the large sheet of butcher paper, she writes their suggestions: *buddies, playground, writing, board messages, centres,* and so on. When children run out of ideas, Mary adds a few more words to the sheet and says, "You can use this list when you fill out your form about what you like at school."

Children take their forms to a variety of places in the room: the floor, tables, the loft, carrels. I observe children thinking hard about their choices and filling in the blanks on the form. They use the words on the butcher paper to indicate their favorite activities, activities in which they do well, and activities in which they can help others. It takes only a short time for children to do this task, but their teacher is once again learning about *how* and *what* they *feel* and *think*. Within minutes, the forms are completed and Wendy's children are entering the room for a large group activity—group castle building.

Castle Activity with Prior Planning

Mary and Wendy both present directions for the castle-building activity: The children will be assigned to groups and to a particular kind of block. Each group is to build a castle cooperatively, sketch it when finished, and then complete a worksheet on how many of each shape and size block was used in the building.

The advantages of team planning are evident in the smoothness of this activity. It is obvious that the two teachers have developed the group lists beforehand and identified a captain for each group. It is also obvious that they have planned the specific kind of blocks and made sure that there are 10 sets of blocks available for the activity. I watch as children form groups and begin building with multiple sets of Legos, wooden unit blocks, cardboard brick blocks, small colored blocks, and boxes covered with adhesive backing. There's a bit of frenzy as children begin, but it eases considerably as groups begin to talk about "planning," "deciding," and "drawing."

Of the 10 castle-building groups, only 2 do not seem to be functioning well. In one of those groups, the children split into two work teams after a struggle to begin. Soon, two girls are building their own castle and two boys are building their own castle. Mary informs me that one of the boys has difficulty playing and working with girls. The other group with problems can't agree on their direction, so Wendy sits with them to facilitate their work. I hear her suggest, "Let's let each person tell what he or she has in mind for the castle, so you get to hear all the ideas before deciding." Before long, that group is building together but they need occasional adult guidance.

During this time, I observe once more that the teachers are taking notes. "You certainly see the leaders emerge in this task," Wendy comments to Mary. "Oh, definitely," Mary agrees, "And do you notice how some of these children can visualize really well?" Once again, these teachers are learning "what and how their children think, know, and can do."

After most groups have completed their building tasks and sketched their castles, Mary and Wendy remind them of their tally sheet (Figure 6–3). To complete the sheet, children simply draw the shape in the box and count the number of that shape used in the castle. Then they draw another shape and count the number of that shape, and so on. It is intriguing to see the different ways that the groups go about counting their blocks. Members of two of the groups leave their castles intact and each group member counts the number of a specific shape block. In other groups, the castles have been knocked down and children sort the blocks into groups of same shape blocks and then count the blocks in each group. One of the groups not only

Make a block castle.

How many ⬜ ? _____

How many ⬜ ? _____

How many ⬜ ? _____

How many ⬜ ? _____

How many ⬜ ? _____

How many blocks did you use?

_____

FIGURE 6–3

Source: Rogers School. Reprinted by permission.

sorts into groups but sorts each individual group into tens and ones. Each group then comes up with a total.

The children all come together to compare results. Mary asks, "Did anyone use more than 100 blocks?" Lulu and her group members raise their hands, and Lulu volunteers, "We used 125—that's how old Canada is." One other group used more than 100, and Mary raises the question of why these two groups used so many blocks. Children quickly reason that there were more of the small Lego blocks than any other kind of block.

When the discussion of castle building finishes, Mary and Wendy hold up cards of children's addresses. When individual children see their own address, they proceed to a centre. As children become involved in centres similar to those I observed this morning, I overhear the two teachers sharing information about individual children in the castle-building activity. The information focuses on two distinct areas of development: ability to cooperate and function as a group member and ability to participate in the sorting and counting aspects of the activity. Most of their comments focus on what children *can* do and the variation in how they do it.

Centre time is shortened because of the end-of-the-day assembly, but children are very involved for their brief time. Again, I find it difficult to tell which children are in first grade and which children are in kindergarten. It is also difficult to tell which children are in Mary's room and which children are in Wendy's room. It's one very large group of children involved with materials of interest and with friends of similar interest. They move back and forth through the work space to either room, and their teachers do the same. This team-teaching arrangement gives children flexibility, an expanded environment, and opportunities for interaction with two adults.

One More Chance to Assess While Children Learn

When centre time ends, the children gather in their own classrooms for one final activity before assembly and dismissal. Mary's class sits on the floor and she begins, "I've been observing many of you measuring lately. You've been measuring your castles and measuring yourselves on our growth chart. We're going to start using all kinds of measuring in the next few weeks. So we have an activity today that will get you started. I want you to see if you can form a line all together with the smallest child on this end and the tallest child on that end. You can do this anyway you want."

The children immediately begin with ideas:

"If you're not sure, you can stand back to back to measure."

"Start with the smallest ones."

"Start with three people and then get two more."

For the next 10 minutes, three different children try organizing the children into a line. They succeed in arranging only four children. Then, one of the kindergarten children, a very petite girl named Sandy, loudly says, "I know what to do." The group allows her to take over and she begins adding children to the line of four children already arranged. I watch spellbound as the children follow her directions and stand still in their places. Sandy gets lots of coaching from the other children while she estimates the "right spot," measures with her hand on heads, and steps back to verify her placements for each child. She succeeds in completing the line of children, then places herself at the end as the shortest child, which she is. Mary claps with delight, "You did it all by yourselves." She grabs a camera and takes several pictures, then encourages the children to talk about their experience among themselves. Throughout this entire activity, Mary takes notes and expresses her surprise at Sandy's leadership. She comments, "I learn something new about these children every time I watch them."

The Day Ends and Report Cards Go Home

Children gather their belongings after discussing their measuring activity, and the day ends with the distribution of report cards. As she passes out the envelopes, I hear Wendy reminding the children, "These are your report cards. Each of you has met with me about what I wrote in these. Remember—I described your favorite book, talked about what you do well, and planned what we will work on the next few months. During the break, Mr. Calkins read your reports and wrote his note on them, too. You will enjoy reading them with your parents."

Report cards in hand, children go off to the brief assembly with their teachers. There, Trevor Calkins tells the children of his and their teachers' pride in their work and learning over the previous months. He describes for the children how important the reports are for them and their parents, "They help you and your parents see all the hard work and effort you've been putting in at school." He encourages children to sit with their families and look at the reports together.

The assembly ends with Trevor describing his appreciation to the teachers for all the hours and labor that went into the report cards. "Each of your teachers gathered information for months, then studied that information to write reports on every one of you," he explains to the children. He applauds the teachers and the children join in. The assembly closes and the children head home on a festive note.

After they leave, I browse through copies of the report cards for the children in Mary and Wendy's room (with their permission, of course). As I read the descriptions of "Observations and Growth," and the "Focus for Next Term," I reflect on the opportunities for data gathering I observed as I watched the two teachers today. As I read the reports, I had a picture of *what* and *how* the children *think, know, feel,* and *can do.* Specific details supported the statements about each child's development and learning. Even when it is obvious that there have been problems or concerns, the report describes those in terms of what is happening, without many labels.

I find myself thinking of the children and their families as they review the report cards. Since the children are familiar with the reports, I can imagine them adding comments or explaining certain items in the narratives. I can hear parents or older siblings asking questions. The scene is compatible with the kind of support and encouragement I witnessed for children in the classroom today. An example of one narrative report card is a final demonstration of the individualized assessment at Rogers School (Figure 6–4).

Name: _____ Birthdate: _____

Greater Victoria School District #61

Second Report

March 1993

OBSERVATIONS AND GROWTH:

Marshall

- continues to be an enthusiastic member of our class and is becoming a self-directed learner.
- is becoming a fluent and confident reader and is enthusiastic about many new books. He especially enjoys books by Shirley Hughes, *The Big Cement Mixer* being his favorite! He often reads books to his friends at buddy reading time.
- is becoming more interested in writing, especially if it's connected to a project he's working on. He often makes lists or writes directions, and has started to notice standard spelling.
- Occasionally he uses punctuation and demonstrates a beginning understanding of its use. He likes to copy pages of books on the computer.
- is especially challenged by opportunities for problem solving. In our recent science and math construction unit, he identified problems that most of use didn't anticipate, and delighted in solving them. His plan for displaying our work showed evidence of complex thinking and sensitivity to his classmates.
- has a good understanding of numeration to 100. He uses manipulatives to perform addition and subtraction and can generalize these concepts to situations that occur in our classroom life. He's very interested in measurement and used good skills in our bridge construction project. His bridge building was impressive.
- has an amazing memory. This is particularly noticeable when he needs directions for the computer. He only needs to be shown a procedure once. He actually helps other children a great deal with the computers. He takes great pride in his computer skills.
- has made real efforts to improve his classroom and outdoor behavior especially during the past month. He appears to be more patient with the other children, and is realizing that he can't always be in charge. He is better able to describe what he feels during times when he's frustrated.
- is a good athlete and an eager participant in our floor hockey games.

FOCUS FOR NEXT TERM:

- to continue to support his developing understanding of addition and subtraction.
- to encourage him to find more uses for writing and punctuation.
- to support his efforts to get along with his classmates and express his feelings.

_____   _____

Teacher's signature   Principal's signature

This report demonstrates impressive growth in reading, writing, math, thinking, and social skills. WOW!   T. C.

FIGURE 6–4

Source: Rogers School Staff. Reprinted by permission.

Questions and Issues

1. When Trevor Calkins hired Mary and Wendy, there were definite advantages in that they knew each other well, had worked together, and desired to team teach. Without these advantages, what kinds of struggles could teachers face in a team arrangement? What could individual teachers do to foresee potential problems and to begin team building?
2. What if Mary and Wendy had been given classrooms at opposite ends of the same hallway? How might they have carried on a different form of team teaching?
3. Consider the variety of assessment practices you have observed in other early childhood settings. Critique them using the following criterion: Did they provide information on *what* and *how* children *think, know, feel,* and *can do?*
4. Recommend individualized assessment practices that you did not see in the team teaching in Mary and Wendy's classrooms.
5. With all of the opportunities that exist in Mary and Wendy's classrooms for recording anecdotes about individual children, the issue becomes one of organization for record keeping and recording. Devise or construct several approaches to organizing the anecdotal data that the two teachers collected.
6. The Ministry of Education document suggested that parents, children, and teachers are all "contributors" to the evaluation process. Although it is impossible to observe every practice in use during a one-day visit, predict how parents and children might be involved in the Rogers School assessment practices on other days.

References

Bredekamp, S., & Rosegrant, T. (1992). *Reaching potentials: Appropriate curriculum and assessment for young children.* Washington, DC: National Association for the Education of Young Children.

Calkins, T. (1992). Off the track: Children thrive in ungraded primary schools. *The School Administrator, 49* (5), 8–15.

Davies, A., Cameron, C., Politano, C., & Gregory, K. (1992). *Together is better: Collaborative assessment, evaluation, & reporting.* Winnipeg, Canada: Peguis Publishers.

Leavitt, R., & Eheart, B. (1991). Assessment in early childhood programs. *Young Children, 46* (5), 4–9.

Lightburn, B. (1992). Working smarter . . . not harder: Anecdotal report writing. *Prime Areas, 35* (2), 68–70.

Ministry of Education. (1991). *Primary program: Foundation document.* Province of British Columbia: Ministry of Education.

Ministry of Education and Ministry Responsible for Multiculturalism and Human Rights. (1992). *Supporting learning: Understanding and assessing the progress of children in the primary program.* Province of British Columbia: Ministry of Education.

Picciotto, L. P. (1992). *Evaluation: A team effort.* Ontario, Canada: Scholastic Canada Ltd.

Van De Weghe, R. (1992). What teachers learn from "kid watching." *Educational Leadership, 49* (7), 49–52.

Wisnia, L., & Rutherford, S. (1992). Assessment and evaluation for some areas in a primary classroom. *Prime Areas, 35* (2), 20–28.

7

Poe Cooperative Nursery School

Parent Involvement: Building Community for Children and Parents

Poe Cooperative Nursery School is housed in Poe Elementary School in Houston, Texas. The neighborhood surrounding Poe is a revealing microcosm of Houston's life, representing the city's diverse population and socioeconomic structure.

In one direction are picture-perfect streets lined with houses that look like they came straight out of *Architectural Digest*. The lawns are manicured and the front entrances are adorned with seasonal displays. At 8:00 A.M., just before Poe opens its doors, a stream of women depart from city buses and disperse down the streets. They each enter a home for the day's work of child care or cleaning and other household tasks.

Across from Poe is an apartment complex that appears to be past its prime. A few blocks farther is a major street with side-by-side franchise eateries and very small and worn-looking businesses. Street corners in this area are inhabited by men, young and old, who appear to be "hanging out." Nearby are inexpensive homes with untended yards, and occasional abandoned autos in the driveways and streets.

A Preview

A history of Poe Cooperative Nursery School offers some insights to the contrasts in the neighborhood and helps you predict the student and parent population of the school:

> *In the early 1970s, enrollment at Poe Elementary School declined dramatically in response to the court-ordered racial integration of the Houston Independent School District. Poe parents approached the superintendent with their concern about declining enrollment and the loss of neighborhood children to private schools. Their discussions resulted in the founding of a preschool as a way of attracting community families to Poe. (Hansen, 1992)*

The school district provided space, utilities, and nominal maintenance, while parents coordinated administrative details and participated as classroom assistants. Two preschool classes were opened and almost immediately were filled. Enrollment at Poe Elementary soon began to rise. On numerous occasions, Poe-Co (as the children and adults refer to it) has been credited with being the magnet that changed the enrollment and parent involvement pattern of the elementary school.

The years since 1974 have seen Poe-Co children and parents move in and out of locations within or connected to the elementary school until the construction of a new wing specifically for the nursery school was completed. In 1991, Poe-Co became the first parent cooperative preschool to achieve the nationally recognized (NAEYC) National Association for the Education of Young Children accreditation. Today, there is a waiting list of children and parents wanting to be part of Poe, and scholarships are available to ensure the intended diversity within the program.

Today's Program Intentions: A Framework for Observing

The goals of Poe-Co reveal the unique concept of this program we are about to observe. First, "Poe will offer a quality preschool program for children ages 3 to 5, and as a parent cooperative, the program will offer growth experiences for both children and their parents." The second goal is not often recorded for early childhood education programs: "Poe-Co will function as part of the overall program at Poe Elementary School. The nursery school will give families an opportunity to become familiar with Poe Elementary School and to participate in the public school program" (Hansen, 1992). The goals of Poe-Co will give me a framework for observing this program. I am interested in seeing how these parents are involved and how connections are made with the elementary school. It's time to see this successful collaboration in action, so let's proceed to Poe Cooperative Nursery School in Houston, Texas.

Getting Acquainted

As I walk up the well-worn sidewalk to Poe-Co, I am faced with a large, rectangular, traditional-looking, brick elementary school with a fenced playground off to the side. I pause, intrigued by another sight. "That's Mr. Okiyama, a neighbor of the school," I'm informed with a casualness that tells me that this scene is a regular occurrence. Mr. Okiyama, oblivious to the massive arrival of children and parents, is immersed in his Tai Chi at one end of the playground. I seem to be the only one on the sidewalk watching him. Parents and children make their way to either the elementary school entrance or the Poe-Co entrance. I hear last-minute conversations and wishes for the day. There is a community feel to the activity outside the school.

Opening the large wooden door of Poe-Co releases a burst of conversation and activity. The entry is tiny and full of parents and children either entering or departing. Many parents stop and consult the large bulletin board for parents to see who is scheduled to work in the classroom that day or to be reminded of their own upcoming turn. There are notices of classroom activities and resource needs, plus news clips and announcements of community events. The NAEYC accreditation certificate is proudly displayed in the center of all these communication artifacts. When checking the books on the shelf below the bulletin board, I note *Workjobs, The Hurried Child,* and *Eager To Learn,* along with other books of interest to parents.

The crowded entry area opens to two spacious classrooms, one on the right and one on the left. At first glance, it looks like there are as many adults as there are children. As I walk in and listen, I realize that most of the adults are parents lingering to talk to children, to the teachers, or to each other. There is such a relaxed atmosphere that Poe-Co immediately feels welcoming. I listen to the conversations:

"What's in the water table this week? It's so soft. The kids are going to love it, but you're in for quite a mess."

"Stay a minute and watch Ronny with the nutcracker. Yesterday he spent half the morning cracking walnuts. He was so determined."

"Daddy, come do the computer with me."

"Jennie is so excited to wear a coat today. She may want to keep it on all morning."

The conversation and movement back and forth between the two rooms is so lively that I can't tell which children are in which class. The class lists hanging on the doors indicate that there are 16 4-year-olds in the room on the right. Their teacher is Miss Silvina, a bilingual teacher from Colombia, South America. Her co-teacher is Miss Suni, a former Poe-Co parent. In the classroom on the left are 16

3-year-olds. Their teacher is Miss Nancy, who also is the director of Poe-Co. Her assistant is a teacher who is new to Poe—Miss Carina.

About 10 minutes after my arrival, most of the parents have left or are saying good-bye to children and teachers. It is delightful to notice that many parents are hugged by more than their own child. The room of 4-year-olds beckons with inviting activity in every corner, and I enter the classroom.

The Morning at Poe-Co: Relaxed and Involving

On this day, November 3rd, Miss Silvina is on a colorful Navajo blanket under the loft with Meredith, Andy, and Eric. The children are arranging pumpkins, Indian corn, and several varieties of squash in baskets. Miss Silvina shows them pottery made of clay from South America, telling them, "Indians used these for buckets to carry this food." Nearby at a small, round table, Mary, a parent, and Nicole and Ralph are weaving strips of colored paper and talking about the cold weather. In the background, I hear a tape playing soft, mesmerizing tones of Native American chants.

Back under the loft, Meredith discovers that the kernels will fall off the cob if she taps the ears of corn. She and Eric accumulate a pile of corn kernels, then attempt to pound them in the *metate* that Miss Silvina showed them earlier. They don't talk to each other; all their energy seems to be directed to freeing as many corn kernels as possible and crushing them. Eric gets a cooking pot from the adjacent dramatic play center and begins to fill it with the kernels. There continues to be no conversation, but an easy passing back and forth of the pot to be filled with the kernels. I wonder if anyone will be bothered by their activity.

At the sand table on the opposite side of the room, three 4-year-old girls—Jennie, Kerth, and Linda—are filling measuring cups from the mound of flour in the table. As they pour it on their hands, I hear an occasional low squeal accompanying, "This feels soft," and "Now my hands are white." After a time of "messing about," Miss Silvina approaches and asks if they are ready to make playdough. Without hesitation, the three girls express their interest and move all the flour to one side of the sand table.

Next, they measure the flour with cups, counting with Miss Silvina and responding to, "Is there more on this side or this side?" Then she asks, "Do you think we will have enough?" Linda assures her as she counts the last cup needed for the mixture. Kerth fills her cup with salt and joins in with, "Now we have *two* cups, now *three* cups, now *four* cups," in a sing-song chant with her friends and teacher. Oil and water are added and the contents of the sand table are now the beginnings of playdough. The girls are mixing with their hands and conversation focuses on how the mixture feels. When Douglas arrives, Jennie reminds him to get his smock on.

Parents Are Well Prepared for Their Roles

Across the room on the floor, Elizabeth, a parent, sits with Jonas and Teddy, who take turns holding a guinea pig. Kelly walks to the edge of their small group and expresses, "I wish I had a guinea pig." She sits next to the others and observes Jonas and Teddy stroking the animal. Kelly tries again, saying, "It's so soft. I like him so much." In a minute, Jonas passes the animal to Kelly. She smiles and snuggles her head to the guinea pig. This scene is a good reminder to trust children to work things out in their own way.

Teddy announces loudly, "I have an idea. Let's try this—we could build him a house out of blocks, then we wouldn't have to put him back in his cage." Kelly doesn't think it will work, saying, "No, he will be scared," snuggling the guinea pig a little tighter.

The parent, Elizabeth, doesn't comment but moves closer to Kelly and touches her on the arm. No conversation seems to be necessary. I am impressed by this gentle nonverbal approach. I remember reading about an orientation for parents on the subject of children's behavior and appropriate guidance strategies. The handbook information for parents also encourages parents to use the kind of approach I just witnessed Elizabeth using (see the appendix at the end of this chapter).

The guinea pig is now relaxed in Kelly's lap again, and she pets it gently. She continues to watch the two boys closely as they begin to take blocks off the nearby shelf. As they gather blocks, Jonas and Teddy discuss how to build the guinea pig structure. "We need to make it this big," says Jonas. He indicates size by stepping out the area he is describing. Teddy glances his way, but stays absorbed in gathering blocks from the shelf.

Curiosity about activities in other parts of the room nudges me to move from the block area. I make a mental reminder to get back to see Jonas and Teddy's construction and check on the guinea pig's well-being. I notice that Miss Suni has been sitting for most of this time at one of the long tables in the center of the room. She has been joined from time to time by individual children and I observe her writing as they dictate.

Four-Year-Old Authors Are Encouraged

Meredith, who is with Miss Suni, is asking her to write Meredith's name. When she finishes, Miss Suni prompts, "Now I will wait for your story."

Meredith responds, " 'The Garfield at Home.' "

"Is that your title?" Miss Suni asks and Meredith nods.

After the title is written, Meredith continues, "The Garfield went to watch TV and then he saw us on TV." She pauses to watch the transcription taking place, then goes on, "Then he ride the bike. Then he stopped riding his bike. And then he went home."

Miss Suni finishes writing and encourages, "Now let's read the whole thing. This is a good story, Meredith."

They read together.

Meredith begins dictating more, "Then he went in the forest at night, and he runned from a big ghost."

As Miss Suni writes, she sums up, "Now Meredith, in this story, we have Garfield and a big ghost."

Meredith wants to read it again, so they read it together.

Douglas stands nearby, listening to the story.

Meredith expresses, "I want to make a play."

Suni responds, "Your story would make a good play. What character do you want to be?"

She responds, "Garfield." Just then, she sees Douglas listening and asks, "Be the ghost?"

He shakes his head fiercely to tell her "no" and walks away quickly. Meredith's gaze and attention follow him as he wanders to the activity beginning at the next table. She abandons Miss Suni to check out what is happening there.

I wonder, Will Meredith's teacher call her back, try to attract her to the Garfield play? No; instead, I see her observing Meredith in her next activity.

Activities Involve the Children and Adults

Like Meredith, I also become distracted and begin to look about the room. Eric catches my attention and I realize that it has been 45 minutes and, incredibly, he is still under the loft, crushing corn and filling his pot. Every so often, he puts the

pot on the stove nearby and stirs the contents. His involvement in the activity is intense and he seldom looks about the room or turns to the voices of children and adults. I can't help but think, And they say that young children have a short attention span.

Now I want to see what interested Meredith. She is standing next to four children who are making beads from the playdough. Meredith doesn't interact with them—she just watches. Miss Silvina has displayed several strings of colorful and interestingly shaped beads in the center of the table, and the children examine them with much fingering of the shapes. Three of the children make beads of differing shapes and sizes, using craft sticks to poke holes through their beads.

Earlier, Douglas joined the three girls at the table and he is also working with the playdough. His only participation (repeatedly patting a large mound of dough) prompts enormous teacher encouragement and enthusiasm. I am told by Miss Suni, "Douglas hasn't touched many materials—he shies away from most tactile experiences." With hand motions, Douglas now lets his teacher know that he needs more playdough for the bead he has in mind. He tries to describe a tubular shape with hand motions. He leaves the table and gets himself some empty toilet tissue tubes from a nearby shelf. After working with his newly enlarged mound of playdough and the tubes for a few minutes, he decides to make binoculars out of the tubes instead. He gets himself some tape and works on connecting the tubes, smiling to himself. Once connected, Douglas moves about the room, showing the binoculars to anyone who will look.

Hints of Curriculum: Thanksgiving Already?

The bead making continues as I again roam the room observing other activities. A small table set up with a display of magazines and photographs is so attractive that I can't help but browse through a copy of the Fall 1992 *Native Peoples* (published quarterly by Media Concepts Group, Inc., in affiliation with the National Museum of the American Indian at the Smithsonian). Before moving on, I note the name of the tape that continues to soften the activity noises of the room: "Honor the Earth Pow Wow: Songs of the Great Lakes Indians" and Native American Flute Music by R. Carlos Nakai from Canyon Records.

When I look into the next-door classroom of 3-year-olds, I see them painting an enormous box with brown paint and hear talk of their "log cabin." Later, I will hear this same class talk about the Pilgrims and Thanksgiving. I begin to wonder if this holiday focus is the reason for all the Native American artifacts, music, and related activities (bead making and weaving) in the 4-year-olds' classroom. I decide to ask and my suspicions are confirmed. When I hear that Thanksgiving is indeed the focus for all the children, I carefully question starting the curriculum so early in the month. I am told: "We have lots of wonderful activities for these three weeks and the parents and children just love them." I learn that the weeks of activities culminate in a large feast at the school for parents and children. For now, I put aside my feelings about holiday curriculum and return to my observations. I remember to return to the blocks and see what is happening.

Back to the Block Area

Back in the block area, Jonas and Teddy continue their intense building efforts. Their structure is now almost as high as they are, with a floor area of about 3′ × 5′, and featuring tower-like arrangements here and there. When I listen to their conversation, it becomes clear that the guinea pig is now forgotten. In fact, I see it back in its cage, probably relieved not to be surrounded by piles of blocks. Instead, there is talk of "race cars and police and Batman" as the block play continues. Meredith comes by and slips into the building cooperative.

Teddy watches her add height to one corner of the structure and asks, "Are you a girl, Meredith?"

She responds, "Yes."

He frowns and snaps, "No, you're not."

"OK," she says, "I'm a boy, I only play with boys."

The three are quiet and the building activity picks up momentum as they compete for the remaining blocks. The negotiations are surprisingly calm and quiet, and I get the impression that these three children play together often.

Parent/Teacher Interactions: Guidance and Understanding

Back at the bead-making table, Candace, a child who arrived only a few minutes ago, stands hesitantly and watches the activity. Miss Silvina takes her by the hand to an empty chair and talks softly to her as she hands her the colorful beads. After a minute, I hear her ask, "Would you like to make some beads?" Candace nods and immediately gets her own modeling dough and stick. She works quietly amidst the buzz of conversation.

Miss Silvina moves to the entry hall where Candace's mother has been waiting and watching her daughter. I hear her say to the teacher, "We've had a very difficult morning. She becomes quite determined and resists everything—breakfast, getting dressed, being hugged, talking, coming to school. I've been sending her to her room when she gets in those bad moods. She just stays there and comes out when she feels better. I'm trying some minerals for her. What do you think?"

Miss Silvina asks questions and listens carefully to Candace's mom. They discuss a health food store in the neighborhood and the quality of its organically grown produce. I hear, "We've been buying only sugar-free foods and it seems to be helping."

During the last 20 minutes, Andy and Kelly have been quietly assembling puzzles at a long table. The puzzles represent a range of difficulty, but both children appear able to put all of them together with ease. The only conversation I hear is when Miss Suni sits at the table to observe, and Kelly asks about Consuela.

"Consuela isn't here."

"Where is she?"

Miss Suni responds, "I don't know, but maybe she'll be back tomorrow."

Kelly nods with, "I hope so. I love Consuela, you know."

"You do?" asks Miss Suni.

"Yes, I told you, I do," says Kelly.

Miss Suni watches the puzzle making and makes notes on her folder. She comments to Miss Silvina who is nearby, "We need to bring out more complex puzzles. Keep a few of these on the shelf but add more difficult ones."

Concluding the Morning's Activities

Miss Suni now moves around the room, stopping at each activity and group of children saying, "It's almost time to clean up—five more minutes." She then sits in the block area and observes the three children who are now negotiating changes in their structure. Meredith moves blocks around while the two boys begin to argue. Miss Suni asks them to tell her about their building, and they compete for her attention as they point out details. Teddy asks in a whisper, "Can we knock it down?" Miss Suni motions to all three children to come close to her and asks, "If we knock blocks down, what do we pay attention to?"

Teddy responds, "People hafta stand back so they don't get hurt" and nudges Meredith to the side. He begins knocking the towers down gleefully. Jonas does the same on the other side of the structure, and Meredith inches away to watch. Soon the blocks are a massive pile on the rug, and Miss Suni challenges them with, "Let's see what good block cleaners you are." Meredith and Jonas begin placing blocks on the shelves, while Teddy watches. I think to myself, What a familiar scene.

At the bead-making table, a parent is helping children place their playdough creations on small sheets of aluminum foil. There is a high level of involvement in the cleanup process here—scrubbing the table, gathering playdough bits into a plastic container, hanging plastic smocks, and washing the sticks at a sink just a few feet away. Somehow, no one has to be reminded or coaxed to scrub a table or wash the sticks. The children seem to love doing "adult" work.

Soon, Linda, Candace, Kerth, Jennie, and Douglas are getting coats and jackets from their cubbies. There is a real excitement about this because it's the first cold day of the season and an unusual occurrence for Houston. Miss Silvina acknowledges this with, "You're so excited about wearing jackets, aren't you?" Children nod and take turns showing her their clothing. Some even have hats and mittens.

Back in the block area, Miss Suni is tactfully trying to get Teddy to pick up so that "we can go outside with our friends." She offers to help him and he gets more interested in the cleaning process. They work together, and the area is soon block free. She tells me that the classroom is used in the afternoon for a bilingual

kindergarten, part of the elementary school, and regrets that block structures cannot be left standing.

Outside on the playground some of the children are climbing on a wooden structure and others are swinging. Miss Silvina is playing a guitar, singing a melody from South America, and leading a line of dancing children. A parent joins in and more children get in the line. There is a kind of free-form singing and dancing activity for the next 10 minutes. A class of kindergarten children arrive and spread out on the playground. The space is large enough to prevent a feel of crowdedness. I hear and see parents and teachers conversing across programs, and children soon melt into one community of play. The familiarity is apparent and I am convinced of the potential for easy transition for Poe-Co children and parents to the elementary school.

More Insights about Poe-Co

While most of the children are outside, Andy and Kelly have remained inside with a parent and are setting the two long tables with napkins, cups, and plastic knives. One of today's parent volunteers, Elizabeth, is filling baskets with bagel halves and setting cream cheese containers on the tables. There is an easy interaction between the parent and the two children. Kelly asks, "Why isn't Kerth helping you?" Elizabeth, who is Kerth's mom, responds with, "She really wanted to play outside. I'm glad you and Andy are here. It gives us a chance to be together, and you two are great helpers." I can't miss the grins on the children's faces.

When finished, Kelly and Andy put their jackets on and dash outside. It gives me an opportunity to ask the parent, "Do many of the Poe-Co parents work outside of the home?" She responds, "Most of them do." (The exact number of working parents is 85 percent, and 25 percent are single parents).

"I'm an editor of a journal at Rice University, which is just a few blocks from here," she tells me.

"How do you do it?" I ask.

She describes a routine of putting extra hours in at the job on other days to compensate for her volunteer time at Poe-Co. "My boss knows that this is my priority and is flexible with the arrangement." She provides an additional insight to Poe-Co's success and appeal:

"We haven't been here very long. We moved from the East Coast. There's a comfort in knowing that you have this little village—people who know what's going on in your family and can provide support. It's especially important in a city like Houston. It's big and it can be a very alienating place, especially if you're new."

I can't help but think about all the reasons I have heard for not seeking parent volunteers because they work all day. It sounds like parents can be creative about balancing full-time employment and spending time at their children's school.

Back outside, the children are preparing to come in. I see them sitting on the old cement steps, very involved in an activity. I move closer to see what is happening. Four children are brushing the bottom of their shoes with small plastic brushes. When asked about this, they proudly announce almost in unison, "This helps keep our classroom clean." Douglas struggles with the brush and shows each shoe as he finishes, insistent that I admire his success. Linda seeks my attention too and demonstrates how the brush gets sand from the ridges in her shoes. The two children go inside, reminding each other to wash their hands for snack. Other children take up the brushes and soon the entire group is inside. They flow easily through the bathroom into the classroom and to the tables set with snacks.

Snack time is comfortable and very relaxed. Two adults are at each table and there are many requests to "please pass the cream cheese" (or the juice). Kelly asks Miss Suni, "Remember when I was sad about Consuela?" and Miss Suni responds, "Yes, you told me you loved Consuela." She asks of the two parents, "Does anyone know if Consuela is ill?" One parent assures her that the absent child has had a cold and is probably staying home on such a cold day to stay well. Miss Suni then assures Kelly that Consuela is all right and will be coming back.

At the table with Miss Silvina I hear a discussion of what everyone ate for breakfast: oatmeal and chocolate chips, oranges and cereal, French toast, chocolate milk, nothing, and coffee and muffin. Miss Silvina poses, "You know what some people have for breakfast? Fish! Once I lived in a village where everyone ate fish for breakfast." Miss Silvina adds a few details to her story, emphasizing that people live differently in other places. Several children comment that they wouldn't like to eat fish for breakfast, and Elizabeth, the parent, asks if they think there are people who might not like bagels for breakfast. The conversation gets lively as most of the children comment on this idea.

During the entire snack time, Douglas is painstakingly spreading cream cheese on the bottom side of his bagel half, checking regularly for approval from one of the adults. He shows no interest in eating it, and at the end of snack time, he wraps it in his napkin to take home. He places it in his cubby, looking quite pleased with himself. As children clean up their individual spaces at the table, Miss Suni reminds them to come to the rug for Circle Time.

The Morning Ends with Song and Cuisine

Circle Time begins with several rounds of a rousing song about Poe-Co:

Slap bang here we are again,
Here we are again, here we are again,
Jolly friends at Poe-Co Nursery School.

I notice that Kerth's father has arrived. He hugs his wife and daughter and sits next to Kerth in the circle. Miss Suni introduces a new song about paddling a canoe. She asks, "What is a canoe?" Children shout descriptions, which include "a boat" and "you row it." She also asks about the word *paddle,* and several children make a paddling motion. She sings the song once, and then slowly, line by line, has the children follow her.

After several times, she asks, "Where are we going in our canoe?"

I hear, "Africa," "Mexico," "Maine," the children respond.

Jennie suggests, "We can sing 'Row Row Row Your Boat,' " and children begin singing without any direction from the adults.

After a few more songs, Miss Silvina calls the children's attention to a book by asking, "Can you tell what kind of book this is?"

"Yes, it's a cookbook," shouts Andy.

"Tomorrow we're going to make cornbread with a recipe from this book. I've copied the recipe on our chart here so that it will be easier to follow. What do you think we will need first to make cornbread?"

Eric proudly shouts, "A microwave."

His answer is accepted with adult smiles and "Yes, we will use a microwave here in the classroom."

When the question is asked again, someone else answers "corn," and Miss Silvina points to the cornmeal ingredient on the large rebus recipe. She adds, "Eric was making cornmeal all morning in the housekeeping area." Eric goes and gets the pot of corn and proudly describes how he pounded it. Children clamor to look in the pot.

After a time, Miss Silvina points to another ingredient and asks, "What is shortening?"

Again, Eric shouts, "It makes you short."

This tickles Miss Silvina and she responds with a grin, "I don't think so, Eric." She continues, "It's like butter and we put it in cookies and pies and other things that we bake. It makes them taste good."

After reviewing the entire recipe, Miss Silvina sums up with, "We will be making cornbread tomorrow and Eric's mom will help us."

Miss Silvina brings out colorful woolen socks and gloves from Argentina. She passes them around the circle and describes how they were made by the Indians there. She thinks aloud, "We have very little time left so we will have to hold our story for tomorrow." She shows the children *The Popcorn Book,* and tells them, "We'll read this book tomorrow."

As the children leave the circle, I notice that Kerth's dad is taking his suit coat off and rolling up his sleeves. Once the room is empty, he gets a vacuum cleaner from the closet and moves chairs out of his path. As he vacuums the carpeted areas, his wife sweeps the floors and Kerth washes the tables. A quick question reveals that this is standard procedure for the day's parent volunteers. "In fact, we voted not to hire someone to clean the classrooms each day. We think it's important for the children and the community—and for our own involvement—that we do this our-selves."

Again, I think to myself, This is a surprising commitment in this world of dual careers, busy lives, and multiple responsibilities for parents. I am also stunned that the morning is over. The time passed so quickly and I actually began to feel part of Miss Silvina and Miss Suni's room. It was much like being with a contented family for three hours. Months after my visit, I heard from one of the parents, and her words sum up my impression of the morning at Poe-Co:

> *There are days when I consider that little school to be such a sane and gentle place that I really can't believe it is real. All the children appear to be thriving and the classrooms seem to be operating with a nice, smooth energy. Sometimes I wonder if a lot of our kids go home to TV or video games and use Poe-Co to kind of decompress and enter inward to that quiet creative place that every child has but doesn't access unless they're left alone. It's also important to us parents. I've learned a lot but I also feel support for what I do as a parent. (Mary Flood Nugent, parent. Personal communication, February 17, 1993. Used by permission.)*

I leave Poe-Co that morning with a few questions unanswered. However, I'm fortunate to be invited to the parent board of directors meeting this evening. I look forward to learning more about how parent participation is maintained so fully at Poe-Co and about the connections with Poe Elementary.

The Poe-Co Board Meeting

At 7:00 P.M., seven parents and the teacher/director, Nancy, gather at the home of Elizabeth, that day's parent volunteer, for the monthly board meeting. The meeting is called to order at 7:20 and the minutes are reviewed and approved for the previous meeting.

The first order of business is a review of "special jobs" parents do to contribute to the running of Poe-Co. It is reported that one parent had reviewed the school's insurance policies and recommended an increase in coverage. Another parent had donated a Polaroid camera and generous supply of film. In addition, it is noted that another parent has been opening the building, making a security check of the outside area, and setting up the movable playground equipment each morning as his contribution to the nursery school. I can't help but think that this type of individualized parent involvement must contribute to Poe-Co's success.

The next topic of discussion is the school carnival that was held the previous week as a fund-raiser by Poe Elementary School. There is a tradition that Poe-Co parents participate in this total school event by babysitting for carnival workers and by working in one activity booth. At the recent carnival, Poe-Co parents worked at a booth where children could change their hair color and get their faces painted. Tonight there is a great deal of discussion about the use of hair sprays. Many of these parents feel that the sprays are environmentally hazardous and, more importantly, not healthy for children. The discussion is intense and full of concern. The politics of the issue are made complex by the fact that the booth was popular and financially very successful. The group decides to express their concern to the carnival committee and to focus their future efforts on the babysitting service only.

Mary, one of the parents, asks the group to consider the problems encountered when children take messages or announcements home from school. Several parents give examples of items that they missed. Mary suggests, "It might be helpful to put a sample copy of what gets sent home in the new space on the parent bulletin board. That way, we can check to see if we've received it." Others agree, and Nancy assures them that the suggestion will be put into action.

A tradition at Poe-Co, "lunch bunches," hasn't been followed this year and several parents want to discuss the possibility of resuming them. The tradition was one of parents getting together once a month for both lunch and informational presentations. Mary expresses her opinion, "Once a month was just right; we had a chance to talk and to hear ideas that help us as parents."

The idea doesn't need much discussion other than when to get started. It is agreed that the practice will be resumed with a December parent lunch and a workshop on stress. A yoga instructor, who will be a Poe-Co parent next year, will be asked to provide an informal workshop.

Nancy reports that the state agency for licensing is revising the minimum standards for preschools. The discussion that follows makes it obvious that the Poe-Co parents and staff consider involvement in such matters their responsibility. Two parents volunteer to work with Nancy to review the new standards. They also make plans to attend a public forum about the revisions. Nancy reminds the group that Poe-Co was recently visited and found to be in compliance with the old standards.

Nancy makes several quick announcements:

The flooding around the jungle gym is a result of a plumbing leak. She is working with the elementary school principal to get a work order in for repair.

The parent of a new student at Poe-Co is having difficulty with her volunteer time due to the arrival of a new baby and her nursing schedule. She asks that she be excused for several months and promises to double her schedule after January.

The board is asked to donate several large cans of coffee to the teachers' lounge in Poe Elementary School to encourage the nursery school staff to join the elementary school teachers in the lounge for an occasional break.

Teachers are having some difficulty in arranging a visit to the new Children's Museum. Several parents volunteer to begin working on this.

The meeting adjourns at 9:15 P.M., but the group stays to chat. Most conversation is about children and an upcoming parent social event. Again, the feeling of a family group is evident. When individuals do leave, there are hugs and promises to get together. Even out in the street, conversations continue as parents walk home or get in their cars. It's 9:40 P.M.

I leave the Poe-Co neighborhood that evening convinced of the commitment of these families to the nursery school. I am impressed by the breadth of their involvement. The kind of decisions and participation they maintain in the nursery school is generally handled by professional staff in other programs. As I watched and listened today, I could see why the level of parent involvement maintains as the children proceed to the elementary school. These parents feel valued, influential, and confident.

Poe-Co has gone beyond the usual structure of a parent cooperative and has extended to the outcomes described in the handbook: "All parents, when they participate in or out of the classroom, add to their child-rearing skills and find a sense of community through shared experiences with other parents."

Questions and Issues

1. The philosophy of Poe-Co is simply stated: "Poe-Co offers every child a learning environment designed to foster *creativity, confidence,* and *independence.* Children are encouraged to *select their own activities, express themselves,* and *explore materials and situations* as they are ready." Consider the morning session observed with 4-year-olds and find evidence of the philosophy being maintained or not maintained.
2. Comment on the information for parents found in the appendix at the end of this chapter, "For Parent Helpers: Classroom Atmosphere At Poe-CO." Consider how this material might relate to parents volunteering to assist with your classroom or your local school. There is the possibility that the handbook information is relevant only for this particular group of parents in Houston. If so, describe communities for which the handbook would not be appropriate.
3. Poe-Co has a guideline that is adhered to very strictly: Other relatives or friends or housekeepers may not replace parents on their volunteer days. Debate this guideline with reference to your community.
4. Parents who have chosen not to participate in the Poe-Co Nursery have often referred to the lack of academic preparation. Those parents who have chosen the nursery assert that there is academic preparation. Respond to both groups of parents.
5. Discuss your sentiments and beliefs regarding the holiday curriculum issue of this chapter.

References

Berger, E. H. (1990). Parent involvement: Yesterday and today. *The Elementary School Journal, 91* (3), 209–219.

Comer, J., & Haynes, N. (191). Parent involvement in schools: An ecological approach. *The Elementary School Journal, 91* (3), 271–278.

Greenwood, G., & Hickman, C. (1991). Research and practice in parent involvement: Implications for teacher education. *The Elementary School Journal, 91* (3), 279–289.

Hansen, M. M. (1992). *Poe Cooperative Nursery School: Handbook for parents*. Houston, TX: Poe Cooperative Nursery School.

Jackson, B., & Cooper, B. (1989). Parent choice and empowerment: New roles for parents. *Urban Education, 24* (3), 263–286.

Mitchell, A. (1989). Kindergarten programs that are good for children and for parents. *Principal, 68* (5), 17–20.

Moore, S. (1992). *The role of parents in the development of peer group competence*. Urbana, IL: ERIC Clearinghouse on Elementary and Early Childhood Education.

Powell, D. (1991). How schools support families: Critical policy tensions. *The Elementary School Journal, 91* (3), 307–331.

Stanic, G., & Secada, W. (1989). Parent involvement in a time of changing demographics. *Arithmetic Teacher, 3* (4), 33–35.

Wlodkowski, R., & Jaynes, J. (1990). *Eager to learn: Helping children become motivated and love learning*. San Francisco: Jossey-Bass.

Appendix

*For Parent Helpers: Classroom Atmosphere at Poe-Co**

Poe-Co is a child's place. It is a place where each child is free to initiate her own activities and follow through with her ideas. The teachers and parent-helpers are extenders of a child's thoughts and experiences; their goal is to provide an atmosphere in which a child can develop a positive feeling about herself and her abilities.

Remember: EACH CHILD IS UNIQUE. Her talents, interests, and stage of development are different from every other child's. The following guidelines may help you as you work with the children.

Children need boundaries or acceptable limits for behavior. The nursery school has three behavior guidelines within which the children are free to make decisions. They are the following:

- Children may not engage in any activity that endangers their physical safety.
- Children may not hurt other children.
- Children may not inflict damage on any materials or equipment.

Your child will be very excited to have you as a parent-helper. Your work day is your special time together. If she stays with you, let her. When she has made sure that the other children know you are her parent, she will probably leave your side for other activities.

On your work day, your lap belongs to your child. Sitting on your lap is special to her and it need not be shared. Every child knows her lap turn will come.

Your child will probably turn to you first if she is hurt or disturbed. This is natural. Comfort her and talk with her.

*Source: Hansen, M. M. (1975). *Handbook for parents: Poe Cooperative Nursery*. Houston, TX: Poe Cooperative Nursery. Used by permission.

Ask the teacher for help or advice if there is a situation you are not prepared to handle.

If your child is a disruption, feel free to let the teacher or another parent handle the situation. Continue with your own activity.

Enjoy your work day. No one is judging you or your child. It is your time together.

The nursery program is not project oriented; a child does not need to produce a completed recognizable project. She is learning simply by dripping sand in free form patterns at the sandbox or manipulating clay at the art table. Such activities are her project.

Allow children to initiate their own activities. Observe them carefully to see when they may need a suggestion or some assistance.

Encourage a child to participate. When preparing the snack, let him set out the cups and napkins and help serve. He can then take pride in his accomplishment.

If a child needs help directing his attention to an activity, help him by inviting him to join you in a game or puzzle. However, if she is actively engaged in watching, let her. Watching is a form of participation and learning.

Don't discourage activities that may take many minutes of cleaning up. A castle built of many blocks is an absorbing creative task.

Do not clean up after children. Firmly state that the materials and equipment need to be put back in their proper places. If the task of cleaning up appears enormous to the child, say, "Let's clean this up together," and then join in.

When speaking with children, use a soft voice; talk under the noise level. Your replies to them should be thoughtful. Converse with a child; don't talk down to her.

State directions positively. Say, "Try turning the puzzle piece around," rather than, "Don't put it that way."

Use both children's and teachers' names often.

When talking to a child, sit down or kneel to his height.

When a child masters a tricycle, she is learning. Reinforce her accomplishment by saying, "You really ride that tricycle well."

Give a child a choice only when you mean to give a choice. Say, "Sand is not for throwing; sand is for digging or building," rather than, "Will you stop throwing sand?"

All class sessions follow a routine. Say, "It's time to join the group for a story," rather than asking, "Do you want to join the group for a story?"

When you need to correct behavior, be fair and consistent. State what you want positively. When a child has an object in her hand and is on the climber, say, "I will hold the shovel while you are on the climber. You need both hands when you are climbing."

8

Sabin Elementary School

Independent Learners in a Mixed-Age Classroom

In contrast to all of the teachers in this book, Bob Tourtillott is a neophyte. He came into the early childhood education profession very recently from an elementary education background. Due to circumstances and a "willingness to take the risk," Bob initiated a mixed-age class for kindergarten, first-, and second-grade children in one of Portland's public schools. Since making this decision to experiment and become a learner himself, Bob has been taking courses, working with a team of teachers, and committed to intense reflection about his work. And, in case you haven't noticed, Bob offers another contrast to all of the other teachers in this book—he's the only male.

What's Different?

Prior to this case description, you and I visited two other mixed-age classrooms: one at Riley School in Glen Cove, Maine, and another at Rogers School in Victoria, British Columbia. What is different about this mixed-age classroom of Bob Tourtillott's? In contrast to Janeen Hamel Chin's small class of 11 at Riley, a private school, there are 22 children in this public school classroom. In contrast to the two classrooms at Rogers with a mix of first grade and kindergarten, here we have *three* grade levels represented.

A final distinction—and one that influences many of Bob's teaching decisions—is the difference in the backgrounds of the children in Bob's class compared to the children in both of the other schools. The children attending Sabin Elementary School come from a lower socioeconomic community and they live in an urban setting.

Another Form of Team Teaching

Like Wendy Payne and Mary Nall at Rogers School, Bob works as part of a teacher team for purposes of planning, some instructional collaboration, and professional development activities. The teaming looks very different from that observed at Rogers School due to a number of factors. Bob's classroom is not located near those of his teammates, and the environments of the three classrooms are completely different, reflecting the individual style, interests, and talents of the teachers. Bob's classroom has a major area devoted to ceramics because of his interest and expertise. He also has a piano in his classroom. In addition, he has more computers than you will find in the other two rooms. His teammate Ann has a large sensory center and a dramatic play area, which you won't find in Bob's room. One of their teaming arrangements is for children to be able to move between the classrooms to meet individual interests and needs. "For example, if someone in my class wants to sew, he or she can go to Ann's room," explained Bob.

Another Reason to Visit

Prior to visiting Bob Tourtillot's class at Sabin School, I observed and listened to his interactions with other teachers. His reflection was so completely centered on the children with whom he works that I felt like he belonged in this book. Several practicum students visited his classroom for observational assignments and always returned with ideas, issues, and enthusiasm. Those qualities sounded like what I wanted for you, the reader, so the decision was made. I set out to visit a mixed-age classroom at Sabin Elementary School located in the city of Portland, Oregon.

As I prepare to observe Bob Tourtillott's class, I have questions about the mixed-age classroom, especially for those teachers who anticipate teaching in this arrangement. How does one begin? There must be quite a transition from teaching one grade level to teaching three grade levels at once, even for the teacher who works with children as individuals. With the potential for an even greater span of abilities, how does Bob accommodate those individual needs in varied curriculum areas? How does this affect assessment? And finally, in a public school setting, often with a designated curriculum or district goals, how does a teacher balance children's needs and remain accountable to his or her district? With so many questions in mind, I decide to arrive early for my visit to Bob Tourtillott's class at Sabin.

The Sabin Neighborhood: Portland's Urban Community

The elementary school is an impressive old brick structure, massive to the extent that it dominates several blocks of the neighborhood. There are expansive play areas—some asphalt and some grass. The homes immediately surrounding the school are modest. Many were originally "saltbox" style and were later extended with extra bedrooms. Within about six blocks of the school are several busy thoroughfares. Along these streets are a number of stores and businesses now abandoned and boarded up—victims of hard economic times and changes in the neighborhood. You will also find a number of massive churches, several dark bars, and discount stores.

At 8:15 A.M., there is a large crowd of children playing outside of the school, waiting for the bell to invite them inside. Bob's room is open, and he's sipping coffee while looking over his plans for the day. I notice that his clothing is a little strange: two different shoes and a shirt that doesn't look quite right with his pants. Personal habits? A message to the children? I don't know what to think, but I decide to hold my comments.

Meeting Individual Needs

The children begin streaming in the door in small groups, and I notice that they, too, are dressed in strange ways. I see a lot of mismatched shoes and socks. When I hear one of the children mention "Mismatch Day," I understand—and feel out of place with my coordinated attire.

I also notice that as children arrive, they go immediately to one of the computers, use the keyboard briefly, and then leave it. I sneak over to check this out and find that they are recording their own attendance and lunch requests. After their computerized check-in, children hang up their jackets and sweaters and store other possessions in their cubbies. Bob is sitting directly in their path as they leave the cubbie area, and I see him receive and give lots of hugs. He greets children in a variety of individual ways—questions about a sibling or a parent, notice of a hairstyle, and anticipation of a specific activity for the day. One child, Pauletta, comes up behind Bob and hugs his back. She is wearing one purple sock and one pink sock and shows her mismatch to him, then laughs at his. I am impressed by the relaxed and individual welcome children receive.

By this time, most of the children are writing in their journals, which take a variety of forms. Some children are writing on unlined manila sheets, some on lined

notebook paper, and some in actual notebooks. I am intrigued with the choice of several children—a sheet with a picture of a wedding, a bride, and a groom from Beverly Cleary's *Ramona Forever* (Morrow, 1984). I can't fathom why they have chosen this form of journal writing, but I expect that my observations will eventually reveal the answer. Just then, I hear Bob ask for the children's attention:

"I need your attention please. Today's the day your writing goes into your portfolios. Remember to put your first and last name on your work and the date. It's June 4, 1993. Do it right now so you won't have to worry about it."

After a pause, Bob asks the children to list the options that they have when they need help with a word. Children offer:

"Guess and go."

"Ask a friend."

"Sound it out."

"Use the dictionary."

Bob confirms the options as appropriate, and adds, "We're about 10 minutes into our writing time, and you have 20 minutes left."

I notice that many children use the dictionaries. They are large and colorful (*My Picture Dictionary* [Silver Burdett & Ginn, 1986]). I watch as Jasmine dances back to her table with one of the dictionaries. She chants as she moves, "My pictionary—uh huh, my pictionary—yeah, yeah, yeah."

As I observe these writers, I hear them use the other alternatives for getting help with a word. JoJo asks Tyrone how to spell *cool,* and after Tyrone provides a spelling, he asks, "What are you writing?" JoJo reads to him, "School is cool."

I also hear Tanya spell four different words for the children at her table. She begins to look hassled and refuses to spell any more words. I hear her say, "I'm tired of spelling everyone else's words—I've got to do my own work." I'm impressed by her ability to express these sentiments and to make a decision to take care of herself. One of the concerns about a mixed-age classroom has been that children might take advantage of the more mature or the academically advanced children. Katz, Evangelou, and Hartman and (1991) have urged teachers who work in mixed-age settings to help children learn how to refuse requests when they don't really want to help or when they need to do their own work, just as Tanya did.

As the children continue their various writing entries, I see that Bob has called three children up to the small chalkboard at one end of the room. He says to them, "You three have been using a lot of words like this lately, so I wanted to show you this word family." On the chalkboard he has written *same, lame,* and *tame.* Together they read the words. Then Bob erases the *s, l,* and *t,* and adds *g, n,* and *f.* The three children read *game, name,* and *fame,* thus receiving practice in reading the VCE (vowel-consonant-final e) vowel pattern.

Within this first 20 minutes, I have just begun to find answers to my concerns about meeting the wide range of needs and abilities in a mixed-age classroom. Certainly, the children's journal choices, and the complexity of their entries, accommodate their varied interests, abilities, and needs. In addition, Bob's small group teaching and tutoring must also be responding to those differences.

Meeting a Range of Individual Needs

For the next few minutes, Bob moves about the room, observing and responding to children's, "Can I read my writing to you?" I watch as he rubs a back while reading a journal. He comments on the writing, "You've used several new words today."

A few minutes later, I notice that Bob is watching Pauletta. He goes to the back of the room, picks up the telephone, and speaks very softly into the receiver. I'm curious, but no one else seems to notice. In less than a minute, someone is at the door delivering a large safety pin. Bob calls Pauletta over and adjusts a very large waistband with the pin, so that she won't have to keep tugging her pants to keep them up.

I move around the classroom to see what these children are writing about. One example reads:

I'm in a bad mood today because my mom made
me get dressed so I wouldn't be late for school.

Another reads:

My mom be mene to me. Do not be mene to me.

One child, Ron, has begun a story called *Space Fox Named Star Fox*. Ron is browsing through a book about space and locating space vocabulary to help with his spelling. His sentences are long and complex and his entry is well on its way to being several paragraphs.

Another child, Lisa, asks Bob for help in looking up *leopard* in the encyclopedia. She has used the "guess and go" strategy for her spelling and has written a story titled *Laprd*. Lisa's writing contains mature content with detailed sentences and punctuation. Now she wants to illustrate it and needs a picture for ideas. Together, she and Bob browse the *International Wildlife Encyclopedia* for a picture. When they find it, Lisa and several children around her look with intense interest at the photos and read some of the description. I hear their comments:

"Looks like they live in Africa."

"They're not as big as I thought."

"They look scary to me."

After a few minutes of browsing the encyclopedia and talking about the information, the other children return to their writing and Lisa begins sketching a leopard.

Pauletta is making a birthday card for her uncle. She has written *happy* by herself, then looked up *birthday* and *uncle*. Out of frustration, she approaches Bob for help with the word *Kevin*. He helps her, saying, "Names are hard to locate, so I'll help you with this." He adds, "You've got a good start on this birthday card." In contrast to Ron and Lisa's writing, Pauletta appears to be struggling with two- and three-word phrases. What is important and noticeable is that all three children are comfortable with their written expression.

Promoting Independence

Ronald brings a new box of colored pencils to show his teacher, and Bob reminds him of a class rule: "Either put them in a class box for everyone to use or take them home this afternoon." Bob adds, "You have a choice and you have all day to decide. Ronald returns to the table where he was working and puts the new pencils in his lap under the table. He subtly takes out one at a time, but children notice. Almost immediately, Tanya asks,"Can I use the purple?" Soon, three children at the table are using the colored pens. Ronald reminds them that he's taking them home today. He says to himself, "I've made my decision."

At the same time that Ronald is deciding what to do about his pens, Pauletta and her classmate Tiranna come to Bob to complain. Pauletta says, "She said she doesn't like me."

Tiranna interrupts with, "She said that she's not my friend."

Bob doesn't say a word. He watches as the two girls go back and forth with accusations about not liking the other. When there's a pause in the girls' talk, Bob asks Pauletta, "Do you think that Tiranna can convince you to like her?" She shakes her head to indicate that she does not think so. Then Bob asks Tiranna, "Do you think that Pauletta can convince you to like her?" She also indicates "no." Bob then says, "I'm not the one to decide anything here." He continues, "You two are in charge of this situation and the decisions are yours." The girls leave and return to their writing. Later, I notice that they are talking as if none of this happened.

Continuing to Meet Individual Needs

When the journal writing time is over, Bob signals the children by playing the theme song from the television show "Jeopardy" on the piano. This is the first of a number of times I will hear this tune played. Children respond to the signal, stop talking, and put their writing samples in their cubbies. I remember Bob's announcement about writing samples going in the portfolios and wonder if everyone has forgotten. I hold my question and listen as Bob talks with the children about their free-choice routines. He begins with an acknowledgment of their needs:

"I noticed that some people looked a little disappointed that they had to stop their writing. I'm sorry that I had to interrupt you. You can definitely continue writing during free-choice time. Some of you were ready to stop, so you have other choices. I have some reminders for you: You need to plant your avocado seeds and you need to glaze your ceramics. Today the computers are all available. Yesterday they weren't. Does anyone remember why?"

A raised hand is acknowledged and Tyrone answers, "Because someone moved stuff around from other people's files." Several other children chime in about the harm done to people's work and about people being more careful. Bob affirms their comments with, "Yes, we are all going to be more careful to respect other people's work and computer files." Then, Bob adds one more direction for this free-choice time:

"I think that it worked out better when we began the cleanup for the paint and block areas a little earlier than for the rest of the activities. How about five minutes before everyone else starts?"

The children nod their heads, and Bob begins dismissing them to make their choices of activities. I hear:

"If you are wearing two different shoes, you can get started. If you are wearing braids, you can get started."

"If you are wearing stripes, you can get started."

"If you are wearing plaid, you can get started."

Almost instantly, the classroom is full of activity. I notice that several children return to their journals and continue their writing. The block area is full of building and conversation, and the piano is in use. Mitchell is playing, "Deck the Halls" over and over on the piano. I learn that he has been teaching himself various songs ever since the beginning of the school year, and that the piano is his choice for this time period almost daily.

I move to the block area and watch a rocket being built and a parking structure being planned. Three boys are working together. Suddenly they stop building and talk seriously among themselves. I hear:

Boy 1:   Do you believe in the tooth fairy?

Boy 2:   I do believe because one time I got $5. 00.

Boy 3:   I got $10. 00.

Boy 2:   I got $50. 00.

Boy 1:   No, it's your mom and dad that give you money.

Boy 3:   It's my grandma who gives me the dollars.

Boy 2:   No it's the tooth fairy. I know because I slept with my eyes open and my arms spread across my pillow. And in the morning, there was $25.00.

The dispute about the tooth fairy's existence ends and the building commences. The parking structure becomes an airport, and the boys get small plastic airplanes and helicopters from a nearby shelf. They fly them around the block structure with a variety of sounds and their version of "pilot talk."

At a table away from most of the activity, two boys are playing chess. Solomon asks me if I know how to play, and when I tell him that I can't remember the rules, he gives me a quick explanation. He follows this with, "Games are good training for the brain—that's why we play so many games in here." Then he goes back to his turn and he and his partner again become involved in the intricacies of chess.

There's no question in my mind that this free-choice time responds to individual needs and abilities. The diversity of children's choices reflect that response. The difficulty for many teachers comes from reconciling such use of time with meeting district goals. This is definitely a question to pose to Bob later today.

The Teacher's Role During Free-Choice Time

At the opposite end of the room, five children are painting with watercolors. Two of them are working on a mural and the others are working individually. "I love you" is

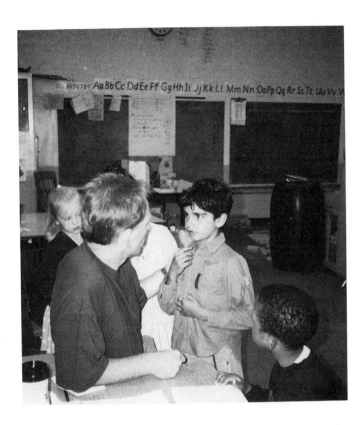

written in paint on most of the papers. As children finish, Bob assists them in hanging their work in the hallway. I notice that he is spending much of his time watching the children and writing notes on small yellow "stick-on" notes on a clipboard. Later, I learn that he files these anecdotes on sheets in the children's files. They are a critical source of assessment data about their development. In this mixed-age classroom, anecdotes are probably the most appropriate way of gathering data.

When he talks about using the stick-on notes, Bob shares his frustration about "keeping track of it all" and "finding the time." He confesses, "I'm always wrestling with myself: Should I spend the next few minutes writing this down—seize the moment as a recorder—or maintain my role as a learning partner." He admits there is a struggle between the responsibility for assessment and his own enthusiasm and need to be a "learning partner." I can relate to his dilemma when he says, "Some days I go home and I've had a powerful learning day but recorded no observations." He continues, "Then I go in the next day, stand off from the activities, and record a day's worth of anecdotes. It's like I'm a different person." He causes me to reflect with him when he adds, "I wonder what it feels like for children—it may be like having two different teachers."

Free Choice and the Diversity of Needs and Interests

Bob's question stays with me as I continue to roam the room, observing children's free-choice activities. I see a large water/sand table full of birdseed. When I ask the children why there is birdseed in the table, they tell me that the birdseed was Mitchell's idea. They also make sure that I know that *they* decide what goes in the table. Later, I learn from Bob that Mitchell researched where to buy birdseed, made phone calls, and eventually got some donated. He chuckles as he tells of Mitchell's attempt to grow birds with the seeds. "He did grow sunflowers and millet eventually." The birdseed table became so popular that Mitchell had to develop a system for taking turns at the table.

"It was a powerful learning experience for Mitchell," Bob says, "And an opportunity for him to be in charge, in control." Bob tells me that, in his work in the classroom, he looks for as many opportunities as possible to "empower these children as learners." He knows that many of the children have no control over their lives and he wants school to provide that difference.

I return to scanning the room and continue to see the diversity of children's needs and interests displayed through the wide range of activities. Four children—three girls and one boy—are standing together doing a hand jive rhyme, "Rockin' Robin." It is a fast-paced rhyme with an intricate pattern of hand clapping across the eight hands. They repeat it a few times, then individual children leave the group and are replaced by others who have been waiting to join in. In another area, two children are using a hole punch to make tiny dots to glue on paper. They're making greeting cards with messages. Nearby, three boys are looking at the day's newspaper, pointing to pictures and talking about them. And Mitchell is now playing "America the Beautiful" (over and over).

What impresses me as I consider the diversity of children's choices is the independent learning that is occurring. Some of these children are learning social concepts, some are continuing to develop their literacy skills, and Mitchell is becoming a musician.

Management Routines and Independent Learning

I see Bob ask the three boys to return to the blocks for cleanup and ask three other children to begin washing the paintbrushes. The art area suddenly receives a lot of cleanup attention. Many children offer to help wash the brushes and scrub the tables. In the block area, I notice that the boys are picking up the loose blocks but not the structures.

After a few minutes, I hear the "Jeopardy" theme again and see children stop their play. Bob announces, "We need to take the block structures down today so we can vacuum." He asks, "Who remembers how we take structures down in the block area?" He hears several answers:

"We take out one block at a time. We don't knock them down."

"You don't take down someone else's building."

"If someone says you can take their building down, then you can do it."

Cleanup is fairly smooth and efficient. One child has a large dustpan and a hand-broom and is cleaning the floor of small paper scraps from the art projects. There are four recycle bins nearby, labeled *Newsprint, White Paper, Colored Scraps,* and *Mixed.* Several children are placing large paper scraps gathered from the floor in the appropriate bins. It appears that many of the management routines in this classroom are designed to be learning experiences. I learn that many of these children come from homes in which there is no order or organization, so even the management routines work toward important goals for these children.

Bob and most of the children are gathering in the center of the room. Several children are finishing the blocks. I notice that the children have brought their writing samples with them as they come and sit with Bob. Now maybe they will put them in their portfolios, I think to myself.

Journal Sharing

As soon as everyone has gathered, Bob points to about 10 children and sends them to the other end of the classroom. During this time, Judine's mother arrives and waits at the far end of the room where half of the children have gathered. The children have made two circles and now begin their journal sharing. Bob joins one of the circles and the parent joins the other. In each of the circles, one of the children reminds the others, "Each writer can take two questions and then pick another writer." Bob adds, "Remember, questions are answered in full sentences." I wonder to myself, Is this teaching natural communication? Pauletta begins by reading the birthday card for her uncle. The questions posed to her include:

"How old is your uncle?"

"Why do you miss him?"

Another child, Julio, reads, "I will come back to my mom's house because she is alone. It is a nice house. I like it."

Julio is asked, "Why is your mom alone?"

He answers, "She's alone because she and my dad live apart."

Bob responds to Julio's answer with, "Good formal language," and I realize that this is his goal in this particular setting. As I listen to the children's writings, and their questions and responses, I see and hear a great diversity in their language development. This small-circle sharing accommodates that diversity and everyone seems to be learning the concept of "complete sentence." I remember seeing this same routine at Rogers School in Victoria.

When all of the children have had a turn, Bob asks his group if they notice how little they needed him. He elaborates, "You used formal language, you raised your hands quietly for a turn, you really listened to each other, and I didn't do much because you handled it." As they begin to talk about their independence, the other group and Judine's mother join them.

When the group is back together, Bob props up a large chart for the children to see. On it is a rhyme that the class has been working on for several days. Bob urges the children to read it quietly to themselves first and then they will talk about it. After a minute of quiet, Tiranna says, "I think we need an *I* in the first line."

Bob says, "Let's read it and see."

The children read in unison, "On Monday go to school."

Tiranna says that it should read, "On Monday I go to school."

Other children agree, so the *I* is added to the sentence. The class reads the line again, and Bob urges them to read the whole rhyme together. The rhyme ends with the lines:

On Friday I've got to say.
On Saturday I'm out to play.
On Sunday I do the cha cha cha, cha cha cha.

As children chant the rhyme, these last lines get an extra bit of enthusiasm. After the rhyme has been read again, Bob plays a tune on his guitar and the class sings the rhyme with him. Afterwards, Bob asks, "Can anyone change one of our lines but remember to keep the rhyme?"

After a long pause, Tanya suggests, "On Friday it's a happy day," and gets a cheer from the class. Bob writes her suggestion on a paper strip and places it on top of the appropriate line. The class reads the rhyme again with the new Friday line. When no more suggestions come, Bob encourages the children to be thinking about ideas so that they can make new lines on Monday.

Literacy and Learning about the Community

After he puts aside the chart stand, Bob holds up the front page of the Portland's daily newspaper, *The Oregonian.* Children immediately begin to talk about the Rose Festival and the big carnival on the waterfront. Bob waits, and when it's quiet again, he tells the children, "Jane [his wife] is going to the coast this weekend with her women friends. You remember that I told you she belongs to a women's group. So Ben and Laura and I will stay home together. Ben wants to go to the Rose Festival carnival, but I don't want to go to the carnival. So we've made a deal. I'll go to the carnival with him, and he'll go with me to tour the old tugboat that we read about in yesterday's paper. How many of you have weekend plans?"

There's a deluge of plans, especially related to the festival activities:

"Right after school I get to go to the carnival."

"Last year my cousin was the Rose Festival princess."

"There's big boats in the water by the carnival, and I get to go on them."

As the comments continue, Bob shows the appropriate pictures on the front page of the paper. After children have described their weekend plans and comments about the Rose Festival, Bob draws their attention to a photo of three teenage boys. "This is about three students in our school district who help the Meals on Wheels program," Bob tells the children. "They're volunteers—do you know what that means?" he asks. A discussion of helping those less fortunate follows until one of the children, Tyrone, says that he thinks one of the boys is his cousin. Bob suggests that they look for the names of the boys to find out. He hands the paper to Tyrone and Damien, and they skim for the names.

Damien shouts, "Here's the names—here's the names. I can't read them. Can you read them for us?"

Bob reads the three names and Tyrone says that one of them *is* his cousin. He's quite excited and tells everyone around him. Bob encourages the children to "be proud of the teenagers in our neighborhood."

I am delighted by Bob's use of the newspaper with the children. It is a relevant extension of their literacy activities and a way to bring their urban community into the classroom.

Recess, Quiet Reading, and Lunch

It is recess time and the children are reminded to place their writing in their portfolios waiting on a nearby shelf. As the children wait at the door to go outside, Bob talks to them about their playground behavior. He says, "We've been having some problems outside, and today's your first day with free run of the whole playground. I know you want to be able to use the whole playground, so let's review what to do if it looks like you could get in trouble. What will you do?"

Bob hears a shout of, "Get out of there!"

He responds, "Yes, that's right, get out of there."

The children are quite ready and they burst from the room through the adjacent outside door to the playground. I hear one of them say to another, "'Shut up' isn't nice; 'Be quiet' is nice."

This recess time and the lunch schedule have been coordinated by Bob and his teacher teammates so that the only classes on the playground at this time are the three mixed-age primary classes. The teachers think that this arrangement is good for the children because they get to know a consistent group of peers. "It creates a larger mixed-age group of children." This also helps facilitate children's movement between classes for varied activities because the children get to know each other. And it gives the teachers time together to check details and make arrangements for the week's activities. As I meet the other two teachers, I learn that this particular week is an especially busy one with the end of school approaching, so the children are remaining in their own classrooms.

Outside, I see that a large group (about 12 children), with children from each of the three classrooms, has formed a circle and are continuing the hand jive to "Rockin' Robin" and another rhyme, "Little Sally Walker" in which individual children take turns performing in the middle of the circle. Nearby one of the other teachers is playing jump rope with a group of children. Another group is spread all over the climbing equipment—hanging from bars, swinging from poles, and chatting busily while doing so. There is a lot of energy being released in this outdoor setting, but the recess is smooth and free from problems today.

When the children come in, they go immediately to the many shelves and bins of books to select one for silent reading time. The bins of books are alphabetized and there is an entire bin of books for almost every letter in the alphabet. As I watch the children begin, I observe that most of them are reading from simple books with large print, such as books by Ezra Jack Keats, and *Monday, Monday, I Like Monday, Letter to Amy, More Tales of Oliver Pig,* and more. When I sit down near a table of readers, I am asked repeatedly to "listen to me read." I abandon my note taking and listen. I find that most of the children are easily reading the books they choose. They appear very pleased and proud, and they use delightful and appropriate expression when reading aloud.

During this time, I notice that Bob and the parent volunteer are also listening to children read, recording the book choices as they do so. Again, this reading activity accommodates the diversity of reading ability among the children and at the same time provides a chance for them to pursue their own interests.

After about 10 minutes, a pleasantly fragrant cart of steaming food arrives at the door. Another adult is there to help serve the food. The children wash their hands, and several of them assist Bob with the distribution of napkins, utensils, straws, and milk cartons. Children pick up their trays and come to Bob and the other adult for their plate of food. Bob doesn't miss a learning opportunity and asks each child for a math fact, such as, "What's three times three?" After everyone is served, Tyrone asks his own math question, "What's infinity?" He hears a variety of responses:

"The highest number in the world."

"Infinity goes everyday."

"Infinity keeps on going and going."

"A whole bunch of zeroes."

"I think I know how to make infinity. It's sort of like a sideways 8."

The conversation ends and children focus on their food. Today's menu is chicken nuggets, rice, tossed salad, and banana halves. Children are happy with the food choices and eat heartily. Only one child has brought his own lunch.

Once the children are served, Bob leaves the room in charge of an aide and goes to the staff lounge. It is a comfortable room with round tables, couches, a small kitchen, and shelves of teacher materials. After eating and engaging in casual social conversation, Bob chats with his teammates about a special event being planned and they complete their arrangements for it.

Storytime

When Bob returns to the classroom, he immediately gets the book, *Ramona Forever,* and I remember one of this morning's journal writing alternatives—a wedding picture from the book. I hope to have my curiosity satisfied now. I wait as the children return from the bathroom and place their jackets and sweaters on the floor and use them like pillows. Most of them spread out on the floor, lying on their stomachs. Bob begins with, "I noticed that a number of you were happy to see the wedding picture from yesterday's chapter." I begin to understand as he continues, "You had so much to say about weddings that I thought you might like to write about them for today's journal-writing time—and you did." He tells them that the sheets will be available for a few more days if they are interested, then begins reading a chapter of the book by Beverly Cleary. He ends up reading several chapters, using quiet expression and obviously enjoying the book as much as the children. I see that a number of the children are rubbing each other's backs, as I have seen Bob do frequently this morning.

When Bob stops reading, I notice that three of the children are sound asleep. The other children get up and are careful not to disturb the sleepers. Bob goes to those who are asleep and gently tries to awaken them. He rubs their backs and talks softly about the next activity. Those children whose sleep is so deep that they can't awaken are left to sleep.

Math: Large Group and Individual Contracts

After a quick bathroom break, those children who are awake gather with Bob in front of a chalkboard and calendar. He begins with a direction, "Look at the clock and raise your hand if you know what time it is."

Rudy raises his hand and responds, "One o'clock."

Bob asks, "How did you know?"

Rudy answers, "The little hand is on the one and the big hand is on the twelve."

Bob agrees enthusiastically, and moves to the calendar, "Today is the 10th— read the date for us."

The class chants in unison, "Today is May 10, 1993."

Bob smiles and says, "Since it is the 10th, let's work on 10 today." As children's hands go up, he adds, "Let's start with additions."

Individual children contribute the following additions and Bob writes them on the chalkboard:

5 + 5 = 10
1 + 9 = 10
2 + 8 = 10
3 + 7 = 10

At this point, Bob stops the listing of answers with, "Can you see the pattern already?" Children nod their heads, then continue the pattern until all the possibilities are listed on the board. Bob asks, "Any other additions?"

Rudy suggests, "2 + 2 + 2 + 2 + 2 = 10," and gets a cheer for his idea.

Bob then suggests that the children begin to think of subtractions. Soon, he has a list on the chalkboard that includes:

11 − 1 = 10
12 − 2 = 10
13 − 3 = 10

After someone suggests 20 − 10 = 10, Mitchell raises his hand and suggests, "21 − 11 = 10." Bob asks, "How did you figure out that subtraction?"

Mitchell responds, "I heard Solomon do 20 − 10, so I put one more and subtracted one more." Bob congratulates him on his thinking. He then turns to the group with the directions, "If you know another way to make 10, tell the person next to you." After this math sharing quiets, Bob encourages the children to get their math folders and use the time to work on their math contracts.

Three children go to the chalkboard and continue listing additions and subtractions for 10, while the rest of the class begins working on their math contracts. I see that some of them are playing cards, some are working with unifix cubes, some are working with dice and dried beans, and some are using an abacus. Their contracts are hand drawn and appear to be different for each child. To help you visualize them, a sample of one of the contracts is shown in Figure 8–1. When I ask about this individualized activity, Bob replies, "Yes, the contracts are different for each child. Children help design their own contract sheets, and I suggest some of the content. One of the things the contract teaches is how a grid works. Children work at their own pace, and they have the option of changing an activity if they choose to. They get a round of applause and another contract when they finish."

I wonder about competition as I watch some of the children hurrying to complete a task or game so that they can color in a square. Bob comments, "In the beginning there was some talk of 'I'm on my fourth contract,' that kind of thing, but it diminished. I didn't hear any of that talk after a few months."

I watch the children very intensely involved with their varied math activities. There is a good productive hum in the room as everyone works, some in pairs, some

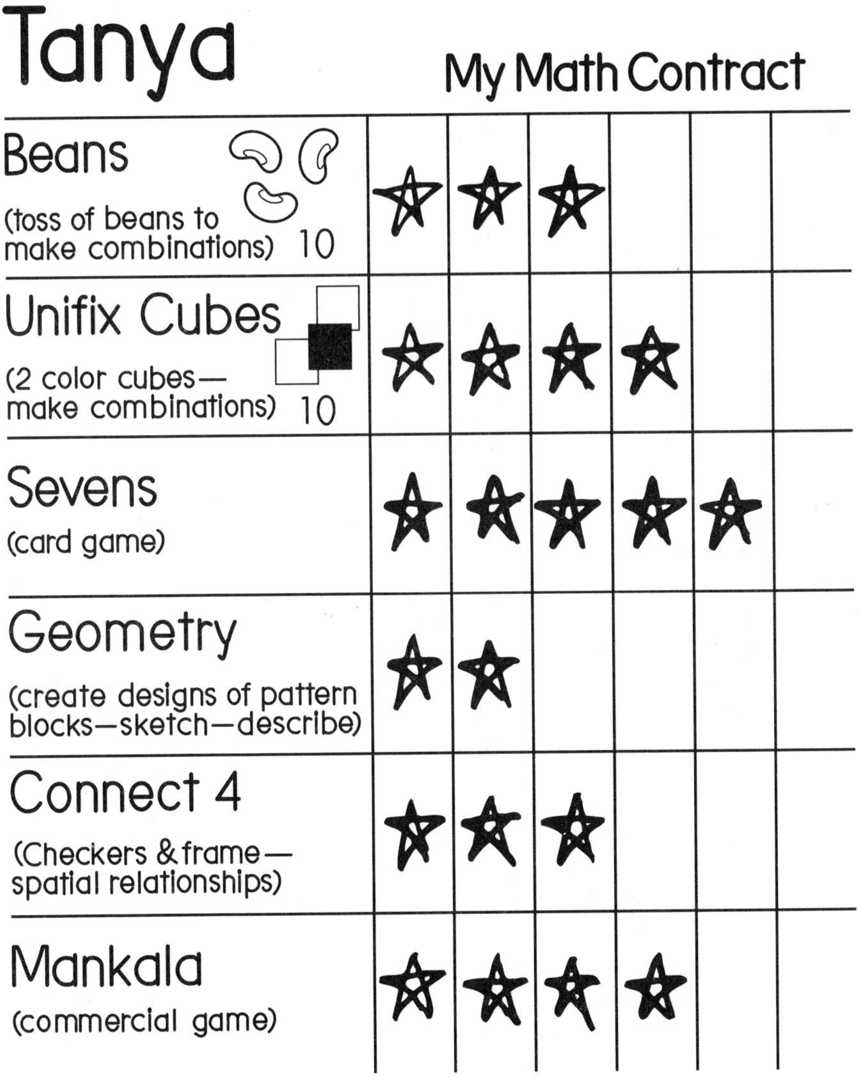

Tanya

My Math Contract

Beans ✎✎✎ (toss of beans to make combinations) 10	☆	☆	☆		
Unifix Cubes ☐■ (2 color cubes— make combinations) 10	☆	☆	☆	☆	
Sevens (card game)	☆	☆	☆	☆	☆
Geometry (create designs of pattern blocks—sketch—describe)	☆	☆			
Connect 4 (Checkers & frame— spatial relationships)	☆	☆	☆		
Mankala (commercial game)	☆	☆	☆	☆	

FIGURE 8–1

Source: Bob Tourtillott, Sabin Elementary School. Reprinted by permission.

in groups or three or four, and some alone. The classroom aide who came in to help with lunch has returned and I see that she is working with some of the children. I watch as Tanya shows Bob that she has finished her contract. He tells her that he will make a copy of it and then she can take it home. He lets her know that they will give her a round of applause at the end of the day. She goes to the chalkboard and begins to add more equations to those listed:

$$50 - 40 = 10$$
$$60 - 50 = 10$$
$$70 - 60 = 10$$

She continues to 100, then stands back and reads them to herself.

The tune from "Jeopardy" is heard again and the children listen as Bob lets them know that they can begin another choice time whenever they are ready to stop working on their math. I see that most children continue until they are able to color a square or fill it with a star, indicating completion of another practice or task. Then they disperse to a variety of activities: computer work, book making, art, and other math activities. Meanwhile, Bob and his classroom aide continue to work with individuals, tutoring them in math.

Classroom Tensions

During the free-choice time this afternoon, a situation arises with some intriguing dynamics. It began when Jasmine, an African American, went over to the window shelf to work on a design she began making this morning. Earlier today, she left the partially completed design of pattern blocks and placed a "Do Not Disturb" sign on her work. Now, several hours later, the sign is gone and her pattern pieces have been put away. As she begins to get upset, Sylvia, who is sitting nearby, tells her, "Nita did it."

Jasmine is crying but angry when she goes to Nita and begins to scold her. Within a minute, another Hispanic girl, Rose, joins Nita and stands next to her. Jasmine is then joined by three African American girls who join her in scolding Nita. Nita looks frightened and her head is down. Jasmine demands, "Why did you broke my design apart?"

It is quiet for a minute, then Nita walks to the shelf where the design was left, points to it, and says, "I cleaning up." She repeats, "I cleaning up." Jasmine continues to be upset and gets louder with, "She messed up my design and I put a sign to say 'Do Not Disturb.' " The two groups of girls are now standing facing each other and the tension is high.

Rose steps forward and says to Jasmine and her friends, "She can't read—she can't read!" Jasmine breathes a sigh and walks away, followed by her friends. Nita and Rose return to their activities and the incident seems to have ended. Rose's explanation appears to be acceptable. I watch for a while as everyone resumes former activities and Jasmine begins to make a new design. I am struck by these children's acceptance of the diversity of abilities that is so much a part of this class.

The rest of the afternoon is relatively quiet and the children play outside briefly before dismissal. Just before dismissal, they gather in a circle for "Appreciation and Regrets." It is a quick sharing and I hear sentiments expressed in fairly neutral tones:

"I appreciate all my friends who played with me on the jungle gym."

"I regret that when we were outside Tiranna and I saw two baby birds that fell out of the nest."

"I appreciate that I have only two more spaces left on my math contract."

"I appreciate that my cousin was in the newspaper."

"I regret that Nita and Rose were saying bad stuff to me."

This last sentiment is expressed by Jasmine with a mean look on her face, and it tells me that perhaps the earlier incident wasn't forgotten as quickly as it appeared to be.

When each child who wishes to do so has expressed an appreciation or a regret, Bob begins to sing a song in which he creates a rhyme with each child's name. He strums his guitar to the tune and I hear "Willabee Wallabee Wanya, an elephant sat on Tanya" and "Willabee Wallabee Wonald, an elephant sat on Ronald." When children hear their names, they leave the circle and get their possessions from their cubbies. I notice that Pauletta has stuffed her cubby with a huge mass of computer paper and a life-size watercolor painting of a person, so she's struggling to get it all together to take home. She succeeds and soon the entire class is ready to leave. There are a lot of hugs and "Bye"s.

As the children leave, I realize that I already have some helpful ideas and answers to my questions about mixed-age grouping. I hope there will be some time to ask Bob more questions and probe his thinking about what I have observed. I want to check my interpretations and expand on the ideas for working with children in mixed-age classrooms. When he returns from taking children to their buses, Bob agrees to satisfy my curiosity.

Answers to My Questions

Bob begins with a little background on the program at Sabin. The decision to experiment with mixed-age classes was teacher initiated. However, when it appeared that three classes would result from "mixing" the current kindergarten, first-, and second-grades, only two teachers were willing. Bob explains, "No one was willing to take the risk because a cornerstone to the commitment of starting a mixed-age group was taking many of the same children for three years." Bob was willing. He was recruited from another district because of his successes with integration—meeting the needs of children who are disabled and gifted in the regular classroom.

The mixed-age classes were set up by the team of three teachers after informing parents and gaining their approval. I now feel that this important step is one that must be considered when making change. I remember the way Rogers School worked with parents and the community before revamping the entire assessment process. Bob describes a summer of work, forming schedules, developing assessment procedures, and selecting individual children for the three classes. The selection of children was directed toward achieving a balance of gender, ethnicity, and ability in each of the three classes. "The classes needed to reflect the racial mix of the school—70 percent African American, 4 percent Hispanic, and the remainder Caucasian," he informs me.

Bob and his teachermates wrote a grant proposal and were funded to spend some of their summer studying and attending workshops with educators such as Lilian Katz, Constance Kamii, and John Goodlad. From there, they spent long sessions in planning strategies for the coming school year. Bob says that many of these sessions were truly philosophical discussions and opportunities to inform each other of his or her beliefs. "Basically," he says, "we couldn't get to the 'how to do' without talking about how children learn—with everything!" Bob is candid in describing many of these sessions as difficult. He attributes this to the possibility of change and admits, "The difficulty with change is that it involves looking back and the possibility that something wasn't right or perfect." In the end, the three teachers used three approaches to the same goals. "Our classrooms look different, our time is spent differently, and our management systems are different," Bob explains.

I ask my question about accountability to school district goals or curriculum within a mixed-age classroom. Bob talks about his math program and says that he used the Portland Public Schools curriculum guide as a starting point. From the district goals, he began planning "how to get there." His plans were inspired by the Math Their Way approach, and the work of Constance Kamii with math games. His decisions about activities reflected a concern that they move from concrete to symbolic thinking. My observation during the last month of school didn't give me a chance to see much of the concrete beginnings, although the contract activities did involve both kinds of thinking.

Bob wants to make sure that I realize that two very important goals are being addressed in this class—the goals of independence and social abilities. I've noted the opportunities for children to be "in charge" and in decision-making roles throughout the day of observations, but I had not highlighted the social opportunities related to many of these instances. "A mixed-age class holds more opportunities for interacting with a diverse group of peers and I think these children are becoming quite sophisticated in their social abilities." Bob reports that he gets frequent feedback about the social skills of his children from other teachers in the building and from the community when they are out on field trips. It is obvious that he takes a lot of pride in this growth. "This class is a study of agreements between people" is his way of describing it. As I think back on the situations of the day, I agree.

It is time for both of us to go home, so we end this conversation about mixed-age classrooms, specifically Bob Tourtillott's class. I express my thanks and bid farewell, aware that I don't have all the answers to my questions. As I drive home, I reflect on my visit and my conversation with Bob. Although I place his ideas in the context of his acknowledged "beginning" with the mixed-age approach, I find myself very inspired by his thinking. It starts with children in almost every instance, and from there, *he's* learning along with the children. I remember him describing himself as a "learning partner," and that is probably the best answer to my first question, How does one start teaching in a mixed-age classroom?

Questions and Issues

1. Bob used a management and discipline approach on two occasions that consisted of "removing privileges." Children were not able to use the computers for a day, and they were not able to use the entire playground for a period of time. Discuss this approach and include the following topics:

   - Possible reasons for using the approach in these situations
   - The message communicated to children
   - Alternatives to the approach
   - Consistency with the total management system of the classroom

2. Visualize a situation in which Jasmine's confrontation with Nita was not handled by the children, and the tension and fighting increased. Other children became involved, and

Nita began crying. As the teacher, how would you handle the situation? Predict how Bob Tourtillott would handle it.

3. A major goal for these children is independence. Many of Bob's routine work is focused on that goal, and he frequently reminds the children how independent they are. Review the day again and find other opportunities for children to become even more independent.

4. Imagine that the parents of the more academically advanced children are concerned that their children are not being challenged in this mixed-age classroom. There is also some concern that those children are helping other children so much that their own learning is being limited. Respond to both of these concerns.

References

Anderson, R. H. (1992). *The nongraded elementary school: Lessons from history.* Paper presented at the annual meeting of the American Educational Research Association, San Francisco.

Connell, D. R. (1987). The first 30 years were the fairest: Notes from the kindergarten and ungraded primary (K–1–2). *Young Children, 42* (5), 30–39.

Gaustad, J. (1992). Nongraded primary education. *ERIC Digest No. 74.* Eugene, OR: Clearinghouse on Educational Management.

Greenberg, P. (1993). How and why to teach all aspects of preschool and kindergarten math naturally, democratically, and effectively. *Young Children, 48* (4), 75–84.

Halliwell, G. (1989). *Teachers initiating change towards more flexible curriculum practices.* Paper presented at the International Conference on Early Education and Development, Queensland, Australia.

Hilliard, III, A. G. (1992). Why we must pluralize the curriculum. *Educational Leadership, 49* (4), 12–14.

Katz, L. G., Evangelou, D., & Hartman, J. A. (1991). *The case for mixed-age grouping in early education.* Washington, DC: National Association for the Education of Young Children.

Pratt, D. (1986). On the merits of multiage classrooms. *Research in Rural Education, 3* 111–115.

Webb, T. B. (1992). Multi-age grouping in the early years: Building upon children's developmental strengths. *Kappa Delta Pi Record, 28* (3), 90–92.

9

Garderie Papillon: Quebec Society for Disabled Children

Building Self-Confidence and Embracing Diversity: How Many Resources? How Much Commitment?

Prior to my decision to visit Garderie Papillon, I spoke with a number of early childhood educators in the province of Quebec. Each time, they recommended Garderie Papillon (Papillon Day Care) as a "special" place to visit. The program, which opened in 1976, is the only child-care facility in Quebec that reserves as much as 40 percent of its enrollment for children with disabilities.

The Papillon goal is impressive: to offer "real integration opportunities" for children at an early age in a child-care setting. Approximately 60 children are served at Papillon, ranging in age from 18 months to 5 years. The staff have credentials in either early childhood education or special education, and each classroom has a pair of "educators" (their name for teachers) representing the two specializations. There is a ratio of one adult for every six children aged 3 to 5 and one adult for every five children under age 3. The center is open from 7:30 A.M. to 5:30 P.M. to accommodate the many working parents who need child-care facilities. This basic information, especially the staff credentials, drew my respect and prompted me further to investigate the Papillon program. Before learning more about Papillon, I was already concerned about resources. What does it take to offer such a program?

Context and Community

My reading and conversations about Papillon provided enticing details for the upcoming visit. The center is located centrally in downtown Montreal, close to businesses and shopping, which is where many parents work. This very metropolitan location, coupled with Papillon's reputation, attracts a diverse population of families, thus children of many ethnic backgrounds attend the center. There are two official languages spoken by children and teachers: French and English. However, there are many other languages spoken informally by children and families and staff.

Garderie Papillon is actually one of a comprehensive set of services offered by the Quebec Society for Disabled Children. The society is a private nonprofit organization founded in 1930 and its services include transportation, residential care, family support, and educational programs. This breadth of services offered by the Quebec Society for Disabled Children communicates the society's sensitivity to the comprehensive needs of children and families, especially those with disabilities.

My investigation tells me that Garderie Papillon is a major component of the Quebec Society's services to children and families. So, my expectations are high, not only for unique child-care services but also for child care that is integrated with the broad scope of the society's work. Integration of services may be one answer to my initial concern about how many resources the child-care program requires.

Approaching Garderie Papillon

It is only six blocks to Papillon, but I must bundle up to walk in the severe winter temperatures of 10 to 17 degrees *below* zero. There is so much snow that people are walking single file in a path through knee-high drifts.

Garderie Papillon is located on Rene-Levesque Boulevard, adjacent to the busy Atwater Metro station and within blocks of the major thoroughfares of the downtown area. Most of the buildings in view are department stores and businesses, with one exception—an old and historic Franciscan church. Many of the side streets are packed with blocks of old row houses, a number of them under reconstruction or being refurbished. The Metro station and the business activity of the area confirms my hunch that Papillon is accessible for working adults.

Rene-Levesque Boulevard is well plowed and heavy with traffic in spite of the weather. Across from the Papillon facilities is an old red brick building that houses the Hopital de Montreal pour Enfants (Montreal's Children's Hospital) that spreads over several blocks and three stories. The proximity of this facility surely is an advantage for the families at Papillon.

I reach my destination—a contemporary brown brick structure with starkly sloped roof lines. On either side of the doorway are two flags snapping in the wind. They are bright blue, imprinted with white butterflies, the emblem of Papillon services, and they announce the Société pour les Enfants Handicapés du Québec. Also on the front of the building is a large bright blue butterfly. By the way, if you haven't figured it out, *papillon* means butterfly.

Arrival at Papillon: Winter Hassles

Double glass doors open automatically as I approach, followed by a second set of glass doors that do the same. Just beyond the doors is a reception area for the entire facility and a friendly staff member greeting and helping those who enter. To the side of this entry is a "boot room." You are expected, immediately upon entering, to remove your boots and to walk around the center in dry shoes. I notice that part of the boot room is filled with various types of wheelchairs, crutches, strollers, and other equipment.

Now I enter a wide hallway bordered on each side by larger than usual cubbies for children's belongings. The floor is full of children struggling with boots and snowsuits. Several parents are helping their children and providing the usual encouragement, "Don't forget to bring your mittens home." I hear French, English, Spanish, and Vietnamese being spoken. I notice a smiling 5-year-old, Teresa, arriving in a wheelchair. She's greeted by several teachers with, "Bonjour," and she looks at me

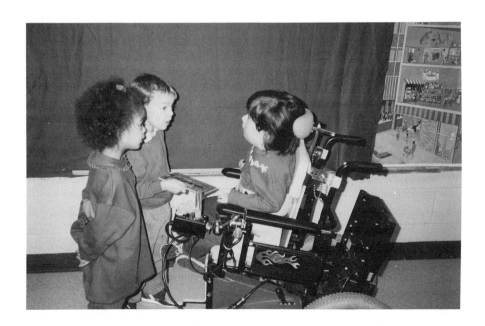

with an inquiring expression. "Bonjour. Comment ca va?" she asks. I respond with my best French, telling her that I am fine, and she smiles. Her friend, Natalie, begins to remove Teresa's jacket, talking softly to her in French. When she finishes, she places Teresa's belongings in her cubby, and puts soft slipper-like shoes on her friend. Natalie wheels Teresa into the classroom and pushes her chair up to one of the amoeba-shaped tables. She then gathers paper and crayons, and seats herself at the table next to her friend. She places several colored markers and a paper on a raised stand in front of Teresa on the table. As I watch the two friends, I am touched by the opportunity that both of these children have for learning about differences. Later, I realize that this is the first of many advantages of inclusion, the integration of children with varying needs and abilities.

Back in the hall, I hear "Ooh la la" from adults in response to childen's efforts and successes in removing their difficult, bulky, winter clothing. It is a pleasant change from the usual "Great job." I also hear Gaby, one of the educators, greeting Robert, who is sitting on the floor fully clothed in his winter wear, and asking, "Is anyone undressing you?" He shakes his head to indicate that no one is assisting. Gaby follows with, "OK, which leg is your prosthesis?" He points to his right leg, and she carefully removes a boot from his right foot. She insists that he help by indicating where his clothes go: "Show me where your hook and your cubby is." Once Robert is ready for the day, Gaby encourages him to use the side rail and he scoots down the hall to his classroom. As I reflect on this brief episode, I recall Papillon's goal of building self-confidence. I am aware that Gaby provided Robert a chance to "be in charge" even while helping him.

What to Observe at Papillon

Even before I arrived at Papillon, I felt that I could not limit my observations to one classroom, especially if I wanted to see the comprehensive quality of program resources and services. If I am going to answer my question of how to offer such a program, I will have to go beyond one class. Since the children are placed in classrooms according to age, I decide to observe children ages 3 to 5 years old, rather than focus on just one age group or one classroom.

My decision to observe in more than one room is supported by the easy flow of one room into another, and by the staff's commitment to all the children. This commitment is evidenced to such extent that I find it difficult to determine which teacher works with which age group. I also see children moving easily from one room to another, to visit friends or to watch or join an activity. One more factor supports my decision to observe more generally. A special activity is scheduled during my visit today—one that brings together children of several age groups. Children, ages 3 to 5, are going ice skating. It is their fourth week to skate, and the activity is a regularly scheduled component of the winter program for three months.

When I hear of the activity and try to picture the 3-year-olds, I am puzzled. "Ice skating?" Kathleen Hobbs, the coordinator, responds with, "But, of course. This is Quebec." She reminisces that she began skating at age 2. The rationale satisfies me, but now I really have questions about the resources needed for such an activity with children of such diverse abilities.

Full of Choice

I look forward to the ice-skating experience as I enter the classrooms this morning. Natalie and Teresa, still in her wheelchair, are at the table drawing, and near them is Marian, who has been quite productive since her arrival. Using colored paper and pipe cleaners, she has made about 20 flowers with stems. She leaves them in a pile at her place at the table and goes to the shelf of art materials. I see her poke through the various bins of material and return with about eight empty toilet tissue rolls. She glues several flower "stems" in each roll, producing a kind of vase full of flowers. Gaby, the educator, comes by and comments, "Ah, I see that you have been running a production line." Marian responds, "These are for all the mommies." She continues to work on her creations for 10 more minutes, then gathers them into a bag and places it in her cubby.

Four other children have followed Marian's example and are now concentrating on making their own flower-filled vases from the same materials. Alexandria, who appears to have difficulty with fine motor control, asks for help. Lois, another educator in this room, responds by asking her where she wants the stem placed, "Ici?" (Here?) Alexandria nods and Lois holds the stem for her, "Les fleurs—ici. Bon!" (The flowers—here. Good!)

Teresa wheels her chair over and watches the vase making for a few minutes. She tells the other children that their flowers are pretty, then approaches a student teacher sitting at a nearby table. What happened next was inspiring to watch, and another example of how to respond to diverse needs. The student teacher and children with her are threading large wooden beads. Teresa expresses an interest and pulls up to the table. She is given some beads and a string but is unable to manipulate them. Gaby comes by and asks, "Let's see—how can we set these up so that Teresa can use them?" Children make suggestions and even try to put things in Teresa's hands, but without success. Gaby gets a lump of playdough from the nearby table, secures it to the table top, then places a wooden stick in the dough. The height of the stick allows Teresa to thread the beads on it. She grins as she places the first two beads successfully. "After you fill up the stick, we'll slip the beads onto a string," assures Gaby.

Other children in this classroom are busy at a nearby large rectangular table, playing with playdough or puzzles. I hear Harold announce, "At home I have deux (two) puzzles—Aladdin and Little Mermaid. I had already noticed that both adults and children mix their French and English in the same sentence.

At this same table, I also observe Amie flattening her modeling dough with different body parts: hand, elbow, wrist, chin, and cheek. She slowly experiments and checks the impression she has made. Lois approaches the table with a pair of shoes and asks Harold, "Do these belong to you, monsieur?" Harold smiles and takes the shoes. Lois notices Amie's activity and sits down next to her and asks about her playdough prints.

Assessing the Environment

There is a quiet hum of activity around this room, but not much conversation, so I take this opportunity to observe the environment. On one side of the room is a low-shelf supply cabinet topped with a counter and two sinks. One of the sinks is at the right height for Teresa. In front of the other sink is a sturdy set of stairs for children. On the counter is a rack of toothbrushes, a soap dispenser, and paper towels, all within children's reach. Nearby are two large easels and shelves of miscellaneous art supplies. On another wall are low shelves of manipulative toys— beads and cords, wooden train and tracks, several sets of interlocking pieces, and puzzles. Adjacent are several flannel boards and displays of books, many hung on heavy colored cord for easy access to children. There is a large area for blocks with shelves of blocks, several large toys, and lots of wooden people figures. My impression is that there is very little that is not easily accessible to children.

Above all of the low shelves is an abundance of children's artwork hung by the artists themselves. Just above the children's work are teacher-made materials displayed: vocabulary cards in French and English (such as *poisson—fish, fleur— flower, bateau—boat*), posters about safety and manners, a calender, a birthday list, and so on.

Other than the French language displayed, the environment and materials appear to be quite standard for an early childhood setting, not more extensive or unique from what I would find in many places. However, I do notice that there are very wide spaces between furniture in this room and in adjoining classrooms, most likely to accommodate Teresa's wheelchair and to support those children who walk with crutches.

As I gather details, bowls of applesauce have been brought into the room, and children are putting away their play materials. It is a casual routine; children appear to be moving at their own pace. I decide to move next door to watch a younger group.

Looking for Differences

Among the 3-year-olds next door, three different activities are taking place. Four children are finishing their applesauce, while other children are busy in the dramatic play center (a store and a housekeeping area) or in the block center. As I stop to observe, I can't help but notice that, for several children, eating is a laborious process. One particular child, Amanda, has more applesauce on her face than the amount she is able to get in her mouth. Nevertheless, she continues her eating until her bowl is empty, and she appears in no way bothered by "the mess." Her teacher, Maria, is nearby. She has been encouraging Amanda, and now wipes her face.

Amanda heads for the blocks and dumps out a box of small wooden accessories. I notice that she, like so many children in this room, prefers the floor for her play. Amanda begins to place the wooden pieces in her mouth and watches other children at play. I notice that she moves her body to the rhythm of the song playing on the phonograph. After a few minutes, Maria comes over and sits down next to her. She holds Amanda's hand, places one wooden item in it, and helps her clutch it while guiding her hand to the box. She continues to assist Amanda to pick up the wooden accessories and place them in their box. With each item, Maria encourages Amanda with, "Bon." (Good.)

I am distracted from watching this interaction by a child who is moving the furniture around the room. At the moment, he is pushing the stove from the dramatic play center through the open spaces to other parts of the classroom. Maria acknowledges his movement with, "Oops. It's Louis's Moving Company at work again." I watch Louis for a while and realize that walking on his own—that is, without something to push or to hold onto—is very difficult. The furniture provides support by enabling him to balance himself. I can't help but wonder about Louis on ice skates.

The dramatic play area with a large space devoted to grocery store accessories is quite popular with this age group. There is a box of paper grocery bags and a shelf of baskets, and four of the children fill a bag or basket with grocery items (empty cereal boxes, empty plastic juice containers, etc.) and go around the room "selling" their merchandise. The adults use this opportunity to interact and promote language growth:

"What are you selling today?"
"Do you have any juice?"
"What kind of juice? What kind of cereal? What kind of soup?"
"How do I cook with this?"
"How much is it?"

A great deal of buying and selling of grocery items takes place. Fortunately, there is a very large supply of these items, so children can continue their selling for a full 30 minutes and not run out of supplies. There are also plenty of adults to support the children's use of language—two educators and two student teachers. I realize that student teachers are likely an important resource for Papillon and that Papillon is probably an important resource for educational programs at nearby universities.

Time to Get Ready for Ice Skating

Before I realize it, an hour has passed, and children and adults begin preparations for the outing to the skating rink. I watch and then become involved in the dressing of children—snowsuits, scarves, hats, mittens, and boots—quite a task for even the most independent of the children. Many of them need a great deal of assistance, so adults are kept busy with this preparation. It seems like these children just barely got out of all this clothing and here we are putting it all back on. I think to myself, The staff must have discovered that the skating activity is worth it.

The vans arrive (the same transportation vehicles and personnel that bring children to Papillon) and children and adults fill up every space in the buses. When I look into the vans, children look like they are stuffed into their seats. The bulky clothing gives the impression that they cannot move. I notice there are now many more adults than I observed in the classrooms, and I wonder who they are.

On the way to the rink, I ask Kathleen Hobbs my questions. I learn that, when the children go skating, many of the administrative staff of the Quebec Society for Disabled Children and some parent volunteers accompany the Papillon teachers. I later meet two additional helpers—young Mormon women who volunteer at Papillon once a week. They appear to know the children very well. So, the ratio of adults to children has at least doubled for the ice-skating activity.

It is probably premature but I find myself questioning the value of the skating experience in view of the obvious and enormous effort, time, and expense. I subtley suggest this issue to Kathleen as we talk, and she agrees with my concerns. She explains, "This is an issue for all of the staff and the parents, and we have addressed it many times in our meetings. We felt all along that skating helped many of the children develop confidence, but we still found ourselves questioning. Recently, one of the teachers decided to develop a list of aspects of motor development related to ice skating. After several revisions, it was developed into a checklist [see Figure 9–1], and now we use it to document another area of growth besides self-confidence. I think that we all feel more secure about the value of the experience since we began to observe some other outcomes using the checklist."

I feel a little less guilty about my concerns, knowing that they were shared by the staff and parents. I am also impressed by the thoughtful approach to accountability that emerged from the staff. In less than half a day, I am already aware of the creativity and reflective decisions that support the services offered to children and families at Papillon.

Once we arrive at the rink, I put my questions and concerns aside, because there is more work to be done before the skating can begin. All the children wear helmets as well as skates. Fortunately, they keep most of their winter clothing on because the rink is cold, but they need help with skates and helmets. I learn that some of the children own their own skates and helmets, others rent the equipment or use what is provided by the Quebec Society. One way or another, everyone has the opportunity to skate.

This particular rink was chosen by the Papillon staff because it provides walkers for all the children. This time of the week is also a time when the Papillon group has the entire rink to themselves. I am intrigued by the walkers—they are made of wood, are child height, and are painted in bright primary colors. As the skating begins, almost every child takes a walker out on the ice, using it for balance and for getting started on skates.

SOCIÉTÉ
POUR LES
ENFANTS
HANDICAPÉS
DU QUÉBEC

QUEBEC
SOCIETY
FOR
DISABLED
CHILDREN

GARDERIE PAPILLON

SKATING PROGRAM
EVALUATION

STUDENT'S NAME: _____

DATE OF 1st TEST: _____

DATE OF 2nd TEST: _____

DATE OF 3rd TEST: _____

DATE OF BIRTH: _____

BALANCE

1.
Stands on one
foot

	wk 1	wk 5	wk 10	
Y				
N				

2.
Falls and gets up
(without help)

	wk 1	wk 5	wk 10	
Y				
N				

3.
Walks on skates

	wk 1	wk 5	wk 10	
Y				
N				

FIGURE 9–1 Skating Program Evaluation

Source: Garderie Papillon, Quebec Society for Disabled Children. Devised and used exclusively by Papillon Daycare. Reprinted by permission.

4.
Picks up object

	wk 1	wk 5	wk 10	
Y				
N				

WALKERS

5.
Weight on forward
leg

	wk 1	wk 5	wk 10	
Y				
N				

WALKERS (suite)

6.
Uses walker for
balance (not
support)

	wk 1	wk 5	wk 10	
Y				
N				

7.
Keeps arms
straight

	wk 1	wk 5	wk 10	
Y				
N				

8.
Pushes with
alternate leg

	wk 1	wk 5	wk 10	
Y				
N				

GLIDING

9.
Standing feet
together

	wk 1	wk 5	wk 10	
Y				
N				

10.
Knees bent, feet
together

	wk 1	wk 5	wk 10	
Y				
N				

FIGURE 9–1 Continued

GLIDING (suite)

11.
Pushing off the
boards

	wk 1	wk 5	wk 10	
Y				
N				

12.
Feet parallel;
knees bent; push
one foot out to
side

	wk 1	wk 5	wk 10	
Y				
N				

COMMENTS:

_____

_____

_____

_____

_____

FIGURE 9–1   Continued

On the Ice: Confidence and Performance

Within 10 minutes, I notice that about eight of the children have abandoned their walkers and are skating with ease. Within a half hour, I notice that more than *half* of the children have abandoned their walkers. I have to remind myself that this is only the fourth time ice skating for many of these children.

As I watch the children and adults on the ice, I see delight and pride on most children's faces. There are frequent spills, but no one seems bothered. In fact, the children generally laugh when it happens. I look for Louis, of Louis's Moving Company, and am amazed by his balance and agility. He certainly fares better on ice than on floors. I see Teresa and another girl, who also uses a wheelchair, go by. They are both strapped into chair-like contraptions designed to allow them on the ice— like a wheelchair without wheels. I notice that children take turns pushing both girls around the rink, and that the chairs provide support for the skaters. Teresa looks pleased and so do those who are pushing her.

As I watch the scene at the rink, I think to myself, These children don't look like 3- to 5-year-olds. Many of them skate beautifully, even rhythmically, to the music, and with expressions of care-free confidence. There are frequent requests for "Look at me" or "Look at what I can do," and there are many adults on the ice who are willing to look and respond.

Those children who continue to use the walkers do so in varied and creative ways. Sometimes, two children use one walker, with one child skating forward and one child skating backward. After about 30 minutes, children occasionally leave the ice, come to the bench for a few minutes, then return to the ice. After an hour and 15 minutes, most children are leaving the ice and are ready to quit. They look and act quite weary. Again, the process of removing skates and helmets is undertaken by children and adults.

Seven children choose to remain on the ice for another 15 minutes, and they happily continue their recreation. They are all from the 4- and 5-year-old class and they look like they've been skating longer than a few weeks. They also look tickled to have the rink to themselves.

On the way back to Papillon, adults lead children in singing a variety of songs: "Frere Jacques," "My Little Red Wagon," "Itsy Bitsy Spider," "Bon Matin Mes Petit Amis" (Good Morning My Little Friends), and other familiar songs. Many children are fighting the urge to sleep, and the singing helps. "It really messes up their schedule if they fall asleep now," Gaby informs me. She and other adults keep the children involved all the way back to the center.

Back at Papillon: Satisfying Hunger and Fatigue

During the undressing process once back at Papillon, I see children helping each other and talking excitedly about their skating experience. I listen:

"I went really fast today."

"I didn't fall down even one time, did you?"

"I'm going to go skating again with my mom and dad."

"I skated with Kathleen and she said I'm doing good."

While children wait for others to finish undressing, they browse through books. When it looks like everyone is back in the classroom, Lois sends Aaron to the kitchen with, "Tell the cook that we're ready for lunch." He returns, followed by an elderly Vietnamese woman with a cart of food. Lunch is served family-style and the menu is chicken, rice, and green beans. As children seat themselves, there is a brief commotion. Alphonse objects to Teresa sitting next to him. He wants her wheelchair moved, and Lois first informs him that Teresa's chair fits only in that particular place. Lois next informs him that if anyone moves, it will be him. He sulks and sits down at the table, obviously not looking Teresa's way. There's no more comment about his objection. I wonder how Teresa feels.

As the serving begins, I hear, "Bon appetit!" Gaby says to those children at the table with her, "Remember how we hold our knives." Children are seen cutting chicken off the bone and struggling with the process. Some ask for help, while others persist in doing it themselves. Finally, most pick up the entire piece of chicken and nibble off of the bone. There is some conversation about chicken bones, and another about eating with chop sticks. I hear "Passez la sauce" whenever someone wants the gravy.

During the meal, a student teacher has been feeding Teresa some of her lunch and placing "finger foods" within her reach. Teresa eats with a good appetite and shows no visible reaction to Alphonse's rejection. When her meal is finished, pieces of cookie are placed near her hand so she can feed herself. Teresa pauses before finishing her dessert, looks at me and asks, "Why do you not speak such good

French?" She certainly had made an accurate assessment and she catches me off guard. I try to explain that I don't have much chance to speak French, and she asks, "Why?" I tell her that I come from a place where no one speaks French, and that it is in the United States. She accepts my reasons and tells me that I can practice with her. "Merci beaucoup," I respond, and she grins.

Dominic asks for more milk by pointing to his empty milk carton. I haven't heard him say any words all morning. Gaby urges him to go to the kitchen to get some more milk. He looks worried and hesitates. Gaby encourages him, and eventually asks if he would like some help. He smiles, and she asks Nadine to go to help hold the door. Dominic soon returns. He has *three* cartons of milk and a very large grin. It looks like a grin of confidence to me.

A few minutes later, Alphonse drops his fork and gets Gaby's attention. She tells him that he can go to the kitchen and say, "I need a new fork." She is firm with him when he whines, and says again, "You have to ask for it." He reluctantly leaves and returns quickly with both a new fork *and* a new plate of food. His grin is huge as he takes them to his place at the table—another one of those looks of confidence!

Kim and Latoya have been playing with their food while they talk silly and laugh. When they are encouraged to finish their lunch without some of the silliness, Kim looks intent as he begins to eat. Latoya continues playing and tries to entice Kim back into the silliness. Lois urges Kim to say, "I don't want to fool around anymore." She adds, "Tell her you want to eat." Kim communicates to Latoya using Lois's words with a very serious expression, and even repeats the message when Latoya teases a little. She stops and both children finish their lunch.

Andrea's mom appears at the door at this point and speaks to her in French, reminding her of her doctor's appointment. Andrea resists and responds in English, "No, no. You came too early." Andrea becomes upset, and is quieted only by her mother's promise to bring her back to Papillon after their appointment.

Lunch is finished and several activities occur simultaneously: brushing teeth, using the bathroom, sweeping the floor, and cleaning the tables. Children are very involved with the cleaning tasks, and conduct their own tooth brushing with complete independence. During this time, Dominic becomes intrigued with the belt I am wearing. He works to unbuckle the unusual clasp with great patience. When he is successful, he takes it off and tries it on himself. It slips to his feet. He tries several times, then abandons it. He leaves me, and in a few minutes, appears with a belt from the dress-up clothes. He takes a little time to put it on, and then points to mine and to his while producing a facsimile of the word *belt*. This is the first word I have heard from Dominic. He is quite thrilled and wears the belt the rest of the day.

Children are listening to a story as the cleaning is completed, and mats and blankets are arranged on the floor. Before very long, the room is full of the heavy breathing of children's sleep. Several adults look like they could easily settle onto a mat and do the same. It has been a busy and tiring morning.

Papillon's Services

During the quiet of children's naps, I have a chance to browse through the many materials that the coordinator, Kathleen Hobbs, has provided me. There is extensive documentation kept on each child. Kathleen explains that it is extremely important to conduct such observations and recordings, especially for many of the children who need additional services and will need appropriate placements after leaving Papillon. I ask about the disabilities that I have been observing in the classrooms today. She names six children who have severe language delays, four with delays in motor development, and several with developmental delays. There are also a few children with severe behavior problems. Other specific conditions include spastic diplegia, arthrogryposis, and mucolipidosis.

For some of the children, there is also emotional trauma in being separated from parents or family members for the first time. Kathleen continues, "Many families here are from a culture where you don't give up your child to anyone, so it's also hard on many of the parents." She continues with a striking example: "One set of parents had so much difficulty with the separation that we needed to do something special to ease their fears and anxiety. Instead of them telephoning us several times a day, we agreed to write a letter or a kind of journal entry for them each day about their child's experiences. Well, the father often writes back in journal form about the remainder of the child's day—that is, after he leaves Papillon. We have learned so much from this interaction, and the parents are much more relaxed."

I am impressed by the sensitivity of the staff and by the commitment to families. I am also aware of the time demands of such sensitivity, and begin to wonder about the energy level of the staff. I question Kathleen further. I learn that the teachers do have several short breaks each day and six hours of paid "prep time" per week for planning. There are sick days, personal days, and 13 paid holidays.

There are two staff meetings per month, mostly for discussion of concerns, group problem solving, or special event planning. I am pleased to learn that there are government supplements for child care. "One in eight children are subsidized in day care," Kathleen tells me. She adds, "There is also money for teacher training, conference attendance, and paid substitutes during those times." This information helps me understand how many of the parents can afford the kind of care I am witnessing.

An Afternoon of Exciting Moments

The 4- and 5-year-olds begin to stir, and as they awaken, they may go to the indoor playground with Lois. Gaby stays in the classroom with those who continue to sleep. The indoor playground is in a large room at the end of the hall of classrooms. It is well equipped for active play and large muscle activity. One massive structure fills a third of the room. It is built of giant interlocking pieces with several tunnels, two slides, climbing spaces, and hollow squares and rectangles with child-sized openings. There are also mats for tumbling, large balls, and several benches on the edge of the room. I see Teresa wheeling around the room with one of her friends riding on the back of her chair. Both are laughing and talking happily. This looks like "embracing differences" to me.

Just outside of this room, through a set of double doors, is an outside playground, bright and colorful and surrounded by a royal-blue fence. There is a red and yellow slide, a wooden bridge, several climbing structures, and varied wheel toys. It looks inviting except for the snow and ice. As I survey both the interior and exterior play spaces, I surmise that the equipment and environment truly support children's development. However, they are *not* "out of the ordinary" resources. What is different is the way that they are arranged to accommodate the varied needs of the children: large open spaces for wheelchairs, mats for those children without mobility, climbing structures requiring different levels of skill, and so on.

About this time, a parent arrives, carrying her child who looks about 3½ years old. Cheryl, the mother, is quite ecstatic, and several staff members gather around her to hear her news. It seems that she and Dannelle, her daughter, have just been to their regularly scheduled series of appointments with therapists, and several advances have been made. One major development for Dannelle has been toilet training, and there's much success to report.

A second bit of news, and one that is accompanied by much more excitement, is about Dannelle's use of a contraption rigged up by the therapy team to enable her to call her mother. On the contraption is a large red button that, when pushed, prompts a tape recorder to play a message that says, "Mommy, I want you." This morning, Dannelle learned to use the invention to call her mother, and each time she used it, Cheryl kissed and hugged her to reinforce this new learning. This is a major breakthrough and everyone shares the excitement with Dannelle and her mom. I watch as staff members hug Cheryl and I also see a few happy tears over the success. When it quiets a bit, Cheryl describes plans for other buttons to be added, so that Dannelle can play her favorite music or communicate other messages. She will eventually be able to use it at Papillon.

During this joyful interaction, I observe that Dannelle has almost no movement ability. A student teacher takes her out of her mother's arms, lays her on the floor, and removes her winter clothing. Then she carries her into the classroom where a few 3-year-olds have awakened. They are seated at one of the tables and began to play with playdough and puzzles. The student teacher joins them with Dannelle in her lap, enabling her to watch the other children.

Dannelle's parent learns of my visit to Papillon and stops to tell me about her experiences with the center. She describes the cooperation between the therapy team and the Papillon staff, and the resulting progress. There are frequent observations at Papillon, and consultation with the educators. She also states clearly that her life would be impossible if not for the child-care services. Dannelle's days at Papillon enable her mother to have time for a younger sibling, to take care of household tasks, and to have a little time for herself. She describes her current search for a placement for her daughter when she reaches age 6, and admits that she's "starting early." Apparently, there are so few places and so many waiting lists, that she must begin at least two years ahead of need.

In a later conversation with Kathleen Hobbs, I find that Dannelle's mother, Cheryl, is probably one of the most frequent volunteers at the center, and that she's very involved with the parent board. The parent board reviews and reforms policy, oversees fund-raising activities, and sponsors parent education events. As I listen, my list of resources continues to grow. I notice that Cheryl has stayed this afternoon and is helping in the indoor playground. I follow her lead and return to watch the children's activity.

Afternoon Play and a Unique Water Activity

Children begin to play here in the indoor playground rather quietly. Their play is subdued as they continue waking up. As time goes by, and more children join them, the room is filled with activity and noise. They are able to stay here for 45 minutes, and most children seem to be very involved and happy. When they begin looking and acting tired, bored, or both, Lois and Gaby take them back to the room in "a train."

Their snack, cantaloupe slices, is waiting, and they appear hungry again. It is a quick snack—everyone seems anxious to get to other activities. I chuckle when I hear Erica say to Albert, "You have to sit right to have a snack." She uses an adult voice of authority. There are lots of "more please"s as the bowl of cantaloupe is passed around the table several times.

I look across the table and see Alphonse reaching across the table and timidly placing a piece of cantaloupe in Teresa's hand. He is quite hesitant, but smiles a little when she eats it. She thanks him. Gaby comments, "Wow, Teresa, you got another bite." A few minutes later, she comments to Alphonse, "Alphonse, you have such nice table manners—so polite." I remember Alphonse's discomfort at lunch when Teresa sat next to him. His voluntary help for her now looks like a change of attitude. Like many of us, he may just need more experience with differences.

I look next door and see that the 3-year-olds are finishing the same snack. I decide to visit them when I hear what is planned for the afternoon. Maria has gathered the children in a circle and describes the afternoon activities: "We have two things to do—you can be a hairdresser or you can go to the 'salle de collage' (art room) and work with hammers." She calls children by name and offers again, "Coiffeurs" or "Collage."

The other educator takes a group across the hall to the "salle de collage" where they have small hammers, pieces of wood, and nails with large heads. They all wear safety glasses, and become immediately involved in their hammering. The student teacher and educator help them get their nails started, then back off so that children can pound on their own. I observe that Dannelle is on the floor off to the side, watching the activity.

Back in the classroom, Maria has donned a large plastic garbage bag with holes for her head and arms. The four children who chose coiffeurs have donned plastic painting smocks. The water table is full of warm water, and there are containers floating in it. Maria sits in front of the water table and asks the children what hairdressers do. There is silence until Simone shouts, "Haircut." "Yes," agrees Maria, "and shampoos." She puts her head down over the table, and encourages the children to get her hair wet for a shampoo. They begin rather hesitantly, but soon get very involved pouring water over her hair. There is no conversation—just concentration.

After her hair is completely soaked, she squeezes a little shampoo in the hands of each child, and encourages them to wash her hair. While they do so, Maria asks each child by name, "Monique, lavez mes cheveux?" (Monique, are you washing my hair?) The children barely answer—they are so completely involved in their work. After a time of shampooing, Maria puts her head closer to the water, and once again encourages the children to pour water over her head to rinse her hair. This time they do not need much encouragement, and they become quite active in the rinsing. Maria checks her hair to be sure that the soap is out, then wraps a towel around her head. She suggests that the children dry their hands on some nearby towels, while she pushes the water table out of sight.

Now, Maria gives hair dryers to two of the children and gives hair brushes to two others. Again, they need little encouragement. They each go about their task with great seriousness. Maria must say repeatedly to those with the brushes, "Doucement, doucement" (Gently). Ara tells her, "It's dry" and moves to another part of her hair with the dryer. After a few minutes, the children exchange brushes and dryers, so they have a turn with each. They do this easily. I find myself so intrigued with this activity and completely enchanted with the pleasure I see on the children's faces. When I reflect on this scene, I interpret the facial expressions as more than enjoyment. They are those looks of confidence again!

During the activity, children from other rooms have come in to watch, and stare longingly as the 3-year-olds go about their work on Maria's hair. Maria asks them, "Est-ce que mes cheveux sont beau?" (Is my hair beautiful?) and they tell her that indeed it is beautiful. She responds, "Ooh la la." The children continue to work on her hair, and obviously think of this as very important business. Maria patiently sits for as long as they are interested in their work.

I can barely tear myself away from this scene, but I'm curious about the hammering activity. In the salle de collage (art room), children are equally absorbed in their work. Some are hammering their third and fourth nails into the same piece of wood, while others are painting their creations. Again, children from other classes are observing and sometimes offering advice. Andre has just finished hammering in his second nail, and he's thrilled. He shows it to several

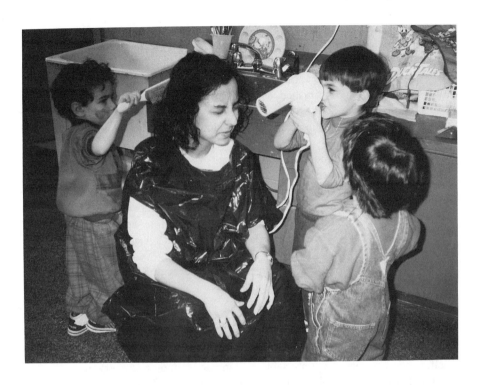

children and adults, then takes the piece of wood to his cubby. When he puts it on his shelf, he exclaims, "It fits" and grins with that look of assurance that is becoming so familiar.

Slowing Down

The woodworking activity seems to be finishing. Children are removing their safety glasses and heading down the hall to the indoor playground. I decide to return to the older children and see what is happening. They appear to have been reading stories individually, but Lois is calling them together to look at a book as a group. She begins, "We've finished the surprise we were working on." She then asks, "Do you remember the name of the book we were making?"

Several children respond, *"The Very Hungry Caterpillar."*

"Yes," Lois agrees, "And Erica did the illustrations for this." She begins to show the book and the children read along with her. Halfway through the reading, Kim is playing with a truck and is disturbing the group with movement and noises. Lois attempts to change his behavior with, "Please play with it quietly at your feet."

Aaron has a suggestion: "He could play with it on the rug in the quiet room." Lois agrees, and tells Kim that he can choose between the two choices. Kim stays in his place and is quiet.

The reading of *The Very Hungry Caterpillar* continues without further interruptions. When the book is finished, several children talk about making more books. Lois suggests, "If we keep working as a team, we can make lots of books." After this, Gaby joins the group and asks the children to form a circle. I hear her encouragement:

"We have to make room for all our friends in the circle, Kim."

"Can you find a place on the floor in the circle, Latoya?"

When everyone is seated, Aaron observes, "This isn't a circle—it's a hot dog." Gaby agrees, and asks if the children want to move. There's not much response, so she proceeds, "Let's talk about our day before we go to our journals." She continues, "It was a very busy day and you did a lot of activities." Children burst in with:

"I was a fast skater today, and I got to stay later with Kathleen."

"I passed the snack to everyone today."

"I didn't like what Kim did to me today."

"I saw them wash Maria's hair. Can we do that?"

When the children's responses slowed down, Gaby suggests that they get their journals and write and draw something about their day. All the journals are on one shelf, so there is some uncomfortable pushing and bumping as everyone tries to get a journal at once. Fortunately, the confusion is resolved quickly, and partly due to children helping each other: "Here, Kim, I got your journal for you." I notice that the journals are regular composition books, with the covers decorated by the authors. Some of the 4- and 5-year-olds begin drawing, and some write individual letters or strings of letters in their journals. Aaron writes an interesting paragraph using invented spelling:

I skatd fast toda. It waz funn. I want to go agan.

Kathleen Hobbs, the director, joins the class during the journal writing, and assists by taking dictation from the children about their pictures and the events of their days.

Ending the Day

The afternoon gets quieter as children begin to leave for home. When only a few children are left, they are placed together in one room with manipulative toys and books and two educators. The remainder of the staff is in the staff room discussing problems and plans for the next day. The conversation is full of sharing—the sharing of stories and the sharing of ideas. They look tired but the climate is positive and friendly. There are extensive files in this room, and I learn that most are for children's background information and progress reports. I observe several educators completing observational records on children and placing them in the files.

Outside the staff room in the hallway, the bus drivers are coming to take children home. I see the same individuals I observed in the morning bringing children into Papillon. I notice that each child is called by name by the drivers and taken to the bus either individually or in pairs. Those children who cannot walk are carried by the drivers, who demonstrate real affection for them and for all the children. I hear them conversing with the children about ice skating, favorite books, and washing Maria's hair.

What Makes Papillon Work?

The day is ending at Papillon, and I feel the weariness of those who have been working all day. On my way out, I see that two of the classrooms are being painted by several young men, again from the Mormon church. I am struck with the amount of physical and emotional energy that is expended in this environment—by staff, by parents, and by volunteers.

As I continue reflecting on the day, my conversation with Dannelle's mother is still vivid. Her descriptions of the collaboration between her child's therapy team and the staff of Papillon are easily recalled. Many scenes from the ice-skating rink still fill my head, and I remain in awe of the weekly preparations for that activity. I am convinced that the staff is achieving their major goal of building self-confidence. It is also clear that the adults are embracing diversity and that the children are learning to do the same.

I return to my concerns about what it takes to provide this kind of integrated care and education for young children. I mentally list the human resources and the environmental ones. However, as I continue my list making, I realize that I have left off the more abstract characteristics such as commitment, "esprit de corps," and beliefs. I can't imagine this program without these qualities. Kathleen Hobbs's very long days and multiple roles are observed because she is committed to the integration concept.

At Papillon, the beliefs about children are strong and each child is seen as an individual. Aaron, a bright, active 5-year-old, was challenged and able to extend his understandings in the activities I observed. At the same time, Dominic, who was developmentally delayed, participated at his own pace, adding vocabulary and concepts through his activity and interactions.

The same abstract qualities of commitment and beliefs result in the obvious attention to parent relationships, the successful teaming with various medical and therapeutic teams to meet individual children's needs, and the shared resources of the Quebec Society for Disabled Children. These also demonstrate an approach characterized by communication, collaboration, and respect.

One of the strategies recommended to address attitude barriers to preschool mainstreaming is to "visit programs that are already integrating children with disabilities" (Rose & Smith, 1993, p. 61). As the day ends at Garderie Papillon, I hope that our visit to this child care center in downtown Montreal has been a productive one that responds to the concerns and issues that all of us may have. I hope that you and I have begun to answer the questions of How many resources? and What does it take?

Postscript

In a telephone conversation with Kathleen Hobbs, the director, eight months after my visit, I learn that Dannelle is now creeping across the floor at Papillon, much to everyone's delight. Kathleen also tells me with excitement that all but one of the children in Lois and Gaby's classroom have been accepted to begin public kindergarten. The pride in her voice is one more answer to the question, What does it take?

Questions and Issues

1. If you were contemplating integrated child care for your community, how would you answer the questions How many resources? and How much commitment? Identify some sources of resources and commitment.
2. Analyze the ice-skating experience for parents who may object to the activity for reasons of cost, danger, or schedule (a whole morning).
3. Make a list of the "ordinary" and the "out of the ordinary" resources you noticed at Papillon. Comment on the essentialness of your items.
4. Analyze the commitment we witnessed at Papillon. Suggest reasons why staff and parents display an almost unlimited quantity of this force.
5. Consider the potential for attitudinal barriers in your community regarding an integrated child-care facility. What are those attitudes and how could they be addressed?
6. The motto for Papillon's services is "Donnez les ailes." (Give them wings.) Many of the opportunities offered to children at Papillon do "give them wings." In addition to building self-confidence, what other potential areas of growth did you observe in the program?

References

Anderson, M., Nelson, L. R., Fox, R. G., & Gruber, S. E. (1988). Integrating cooperative learning and structured learning: Effective approaches to teaching social skills. *Focus on Exceptional Children, 20* (9), 1–8.

Ayres, B., & Meyer, L. H. (1992). Helping teachers manage the inclusive classroom: Staff development and teaming star among management strategies. *The School Administrator, 49* (2), 30–37.

Bailey, D. B., & Winton, P. J. (1989). Friendship and acquaintance among families in a mainstreamed day care center. *Education and Training in Mental Retardation, 24* (2), 107–113.

Child Care Information Exchange. (1993). *Issue Number 93.* Redmond, WA: Child Care Information Exchange.

Cook, R. E., & Armbruster, V. B. (1982). *Adapting early childhood curricula: Suggestions for meeting special needs.* St. Louis: Mosby-Year.

Eggers, N. (1983). Influencing preschoolers' awareness and feelings regarding depicted physical disability. *Early Childhood Development and Care, 12* (2), 199–206.

Green, M., & Widoff, E. (1990). Special needs child care: Training is a key issue. *Young Children, 45* (3), 60–61.

Heitz, T. (1990). How do I help Jacob? *Young Children, 45* (1), 11–15.

Holder-Brown, L., & Parette, H. P., Jr. (1992). Children with disabilities who use assistive technology: Ethical considerations. *Young Children, 47* (6), 73–77.

Hundert, J., & Houghton, A. (1992). Promoting social interaction of children with disabilities in integrated preschools: A failure to generalize. *Exceptional Children, 52* (3), 311–320.

Jenkins, J. R., Speltz, M. L., & Odom, S. L. (1985). Integrating handicapped preschoolers: Effects on child development and social interaction. *Exceptional Children, 58* (1), 7–1.

Peck, C. A., Carlson, P., & Helmstetter, E. (1992). Parent and teacher perceptions of outcomes for typically developing children enrolled in integrated early childhood programs: A statewide survey. *Journal of Early Intervention, 16* (1), 53–63.

Rogow, S. (1991). Teachers at play: Observed strategies to promote social play between children with special needs and their non-handicapped peers. *Journal of Special Education, 15* (3), 201–208.

Rose, D. F., & Smith, B. J. (1993). Preschool mainstreaming: Attitude barriers and strategies for addressing them. *Young Children, 48* (4), 59–62.

Ross, H. W. (1992). Integrating infants with disabilities: Can "ordinary" caregivers do it? *Young Children, 47* (3), 65–71.

Sanford, P. (1989). *Integrated teaching in early education: Starting in the mainstream.* New York: Longman.

Sasso, G., & Rude, H. A. (1988). The social effects of integration on nonhandicapped children. *Education and Training in Mental Retardation, 23* (1), 18–23.

Souweine, J., Crimmins, S., & Mazel, C. (1981). *Mainstreaming: Ideas for teaching young children.* Washington, DC: NAEYC.

10

The Traveling Preschools: The Kamehameha Prekindergarten Educational Program

A Barrier-Free, Literacy-Rich Opportunity for Families

When I first heard of them, Kamehameha's Traveling Preschools sounded like a unique idea and one that could be replicated in many communities. The Traveling Preschools were briefly described as a "mobile educational program transporting learning to young children and their families wherever they might be." I immediately thought of the potential for cost-effective and easily accessible early childhood education experiences for large numbers of children. As I explored the background of the Traveling Preschools (TPS) and interviewed the individuals responsible for their curriculum development and administration, I began to comprehend the complexity of the program and to see the potential for many more

177

effects. In writing about the Traveling Preschools, Ginger Fink (1990b) described this potential:

> *In 1987 Kamehameha's PreKindergarten Educational Program undertook an innovative project, one that has expanded not only the availability of educational services to Hawaiian families, but the concept of "school" among local educators. With the piloting of the Traveling Preschool, an adventure in true community-based learning programs began, one that has changed the complexion of early education in Hawaii. (p. 17)*

Her description convinced me that I would be seeing much more than "mobile early childhood education." I also learned that the Traveling Preschools are one of a continuum of services offered to Hawaiian families by the Kamehameha Pre-Kindergarten Educational Program. The continuum begins when a baby is expected and continues until the child is ready to enter kindergarten. The first service, the Home Visiting Program, provides support and information to the family during pregnancy and until the baby is 2 to 3 years old. From that time, the family is encouraged to attend a Traveling Preschool. When the child is 4 years old, he or she can go to a center-based preschool.

The potential of the Traveling Preschool and its role in a continuum of services from birth to kindergarten enhance its uniqueness for inclusion in this book. Before traveling to the 1 of the 32 sites visited by the Traveling Preschools, some additional program description will be helpful for interpreting what we see. The preview will begin to reveal why this chapter is subtitled "A Barrier-Free, Literacy-Rich Opportunity for Families."

A Preview of the Traveling Preschool

I read in the program description that the target age for the Traveling Preschools is the 2- and 3-year-old child, but younger and older siblings are welcome. I think to my self, So, one could bring an infant along with one's toddler. How does that work? I am further intrigued when I read that "a parent or other caregiver of legal age must accompany and remain with the child during the preschool program." This preview suggests that there might be parent education opportunities and extensive adult/child interactions to be observed. I try to anticipate the role of parents and the role of teachers. What will a preschool be like when all children have a parent or family member with them?

The program description also says that the Traveling Preschools are designed to be as "barrier free" as possible. This causes me to wonder what other accommodations will make it easy for families to attend the program. Additional program information states that the intent is to help parents and other care-giving adults feel secure and valued in the program. To achieve this, one of the program's priorities is the inclusion of children's and families' culture in many aspects of the program. Will this program, I wonder, go beyond the usual cultural materials and activities? Another major intent of the Traveling Preschool is to promote language and literacy development. This program emphasis is connected to the belief that children learn language naturally when they are communicating with adults about the things they are doing and feeling. Those who have studied Hawaiian children (Speidel, Farran, & Jordan, 1989; Berman, Izu, McClelland, & Stone, 1988) have found that they tend to have well-developed visual thinking, but may have difficulty with the kind of language required later in school. I begin to anticipate the opportunities for oral expression and literacy that are possible in the program I am about to see.

More questions are forming as I speak with staff members to schedule my visit. I hear a contagious enthusiasm and a clear commitment in these conversations, so I am anxious to get to one of the TPS programs. Fortunately, there is a site near my temporary home, and it's in an old Hawaiian community. Come with me as I drive to Waimanalo on the island of Oahu.

Approaching Waimanalo and the Traveling Preschool

The Waimanalo site is well outside of the Honolulu downtown congestion and the glamour of Waikiki, and just past the suburb of Hawaii Kai and the famed Hanauma Bay. I am following the Kalanianaole Highway (yes—pronounce every single vowel). It is difficult to keep my eyes on the road as I pass the island's most stunning stretches of coastline—steep, rocky cliffs edged by silvery sand and sparkling emerald water. The scenery is further enhanced by spectacular vignettes of human activity—surfing experts riding giant waves, novices of the sport tossed about within those same waves, windsurfers skimming the water on boards with brilliant sails, groups of divers suited up to explore the underwater depths, and anglers lazily perched on the dark volcanic rocks along the shore waiting for a nibble.

The community of Waimanalo appears before me with flat stretches of beach on one side and rugged foothills and mountains on the other. Most of the homes I see are quite simple. Many have the look of coastal dwellings I have seen on the Oregon shores: a bit weather beaten by wind, salt, and water; faded trim and siding; and temporary roofs. To my right is a grassy recreation area next to the beach, and I see a gathering of tents and temporary shelters. Many of the shelters are simply large, blue plastic sheets stretched as covers over collections of belongings. There is an abundance of folding chairs, cots, barbecues, clotheslines, and cooking equipment and tools. The gathering has a crowded look. The shelters are quite close together, although there are large open spaces around them. I see a horseshoe game off to the side and a card game at a nearby picnic table.

Most of the people appear to be of Hawaiian descent, and they look relaxed and happy. There is a group of children on the adjacent beach, and several older teenagers who appear to be supervising them. It's a very peaceful scene, but it leaves me with questions. Is this a vacation? Are these people homeless? Where do they come from? I add these to my list of questions as I approach the Traveling Preschool site.

As I drive through Waimanalo, I notice several convenience stores, a tiny dark Mexican restaurant and an outdoor Hawaiian barbecue shop, a polo field, MacDonald's, and a colorful souvenier shop with an array of mu'umu'us, windchimes made of shells, painted velour beach towels, and kites dancing in the breeze. It appears that, without transportation, families here do not have access to many services. Before I can consider this possibility further, I see the Waimanalo Elementary School at the edge of those small businesses.

Where and When Are the Traveling Preschools?

The Waimanalo Elementary School grounds are one of the sites for the Traveling Preschools, and Pope Elementary School is the other Waimanalo site. Each site is scheduled for two days a week (Monday and Wednesday, or Tuesday and Thursday), but families can go to one or both sites, depending on their interest, their proximity to the site, and their own schedule of activities. So, a family may attend as often as four mornings per week.

The Traveling Preschools are open year-round with a break in August for staff vacations and in-service. The sites include elementary school buildings and grounds as in Waimanalo, but they also include recreation centers, parks, churches, and other community facilities. The Hawaiian weather makes it possible to use varied outdoor locations; however, there is always a need for some shelter in case of inclement weather. In my conversations during the day, I will learn that the site selection is primarily based on proximity to families. Other considerations include location of community resources and availability of bus transportation. The schedule and location information begins to satisfy my curiosity about how the programs are made "barrier free," but I wonder if there are even more provisions for families, more ways to encourage their attendance.

As I pull into the parking lot, I notice that the public library is located on the school grounds, and think of all the advantages that this brings to the school and the preschool program. I also see that the Traveling Preschool van is parked in the back of the buildings, so I know I am in the right place.

Creating a Preschool in 30 Minutes

Cathy Javor and Lorna Hines are opening the back doors of the blue van with a Kamehameha Traveling Preschool sign on its side. Cathy is the preschool teacher and Lorna is the paraprofessional aide at the Waimanalo site. On this particular morning, they are debating the possibility of rain as they begin to unload the van and set up the "preschool classroom." Since the families prefer to be outside, they decide to take a chance with the weather and set up on the lawn near the school.

I watch as Cathy and Lorna arrange large (6′ × 9′, 9′ × 9′, and 9′ × 12′) grass mats under an enormous Jacaranda fern tree. The mats are placed close together and there is not much room to walk between many of them. On half of the mats are folding tables (2′ × 3′) that are only a foot and a half high. I am curious about these tables, but Cathy and Lorna are very involved making decisions about selection and placement of materials, so I wait to ask my questions. As the van is unloaded, learning centers appear before my eyes. On one mat I see colorful Tahitian print pillows, large baskets of books, and a collection of "take home" book bags. On another mat is a hamper of dress-up clothes, including a grass skirt, a lei, sandals, a Hawaiian shirt, and a box of musical instruments containing a ukulele, gourds, rain sticks, and drums. I also see a mat with blocks and accessories (cars, signs, people, etc.). On the tubs and boxes holding these materials are signs:

BLOCKS   Have your child stack them.
                Have your child build with them.
                Have your child pretend with them.
BLOCKS   Build small muscles.
                Build imagination.
                Build thinking skills.

There's also a table with tubs of playdough, colorful Tahitian print placemats, and kitchen utensils. The largest center consists of three straw mats placed side by side and three tables with art materials (scissors, glue, paint, markers, paper, staplers, and brushes). There is also a small table with a sign identifying it as the He-Makana-ia-oe, or the Giving Center. I look closely and find that it is a center in which to make something for someone else. There is also a mat with infant toys and a table with "More for Fours" folders. I remember that families can bring younger and older siblings.

Cathy stops her setup to tell me that this arrangement of mats is unique for Waimanalo. "If we were in another community, this would look different. For one thing, the mats would be spread out with lots of space between them. The families here like to be very close together. They like to visit and to see each others' children." As I listen to her explanation, I remember the staff commitment to making families feel comfortable. This seems like such a minor detail in the setup, but I expect that it really supports the comfort and feeling of community intended by the program.

Just when I think that Cathy and Lorna are finished, I see them add one more center next to their van—a "Fish and Ocean Life Center." A beautiful underwater scene is propped against the van as a backdrop. On it are labels for the fish in the scene, and their names are printed in English and Hawaiian: *whale—kohola, squid—he'e, sting ray—hihi manu, flying fish—malolo*. On the mat is a basket of shells, a plastic box of fish lures and a pair of tiny tongs, and a spectacular collection of books about fish and sea life.

"We went to Makapu'u Beach yesterday and looked at the tide pools," Lorna informs me as she and Cathy fill two plastic tubs with water. They add six very small nets and float colorful fish lures in the tubs. I can just picture the toddlers' faces when they see these tubs of "fish."

Meeting the Families

It is arrival time, and I watch as each child and adult is greeted individually by Cathy and Lorna. The greetings are not just "hello" but hugs and kisses and warm conversation. I hear the two educators being referred to as "Auntie Cathy" and "Auntie Lorna," and remember that one of the goals of the preschools is to create *'ohana,* or a sense of family. It occurs to me that something as simple as how families address the teachers begins to communicate the *'ohana* so well.

I think that there are other, more subtle messages within the title "Auntie." One of them is related to the philosophy of the TPS about the role of parents as the most influential teachers of young children. Parents are encouraged to take on a teaching role in the program. Thus, Cathy and Lorna's roles and titles are quite different from those of most preschool teachers. They are facilitators who encourage parents, provide resources, model approaches and strategies, and assist when needed. Rather than focus on interactions with children themselves, they guide and promote family interactions. They are "aunties," or family members, who help other family members.

It doesn't feel comfortable to stand there simply observing them, so I introduce myself to the adults and children. I am immediately "Auntie Amy" and my discomfort disappears as I make connections with the families. Some of the children are with mothers, some are with fathers, and some are with grandparents or combinations of adults. There are also two nannies with children. Within the group of 26 children, there are 3 infants and 2 older children. A number of the mothers are quite young and I notice that they stay especially close together.

Those adults and children who are "regulars" are easily recognized. They go immediately to the sign-up table, complete the routines (posting the child's name tag, checking information sheets), and begin to play. When I look at the previous month's check-in sheet, it appears that families come according to their own schedule. This "drop-in" feature definitely makes it easier for families to attend. I inquire of several parents and learn that there is no charge. Another barrier eliminated!

Those who have come for the first time are escorted by Cathy or Lorna or one of the "regular" parents or grandparents. I listen to Cathy's tour: "We always have blocks and we always have playdough. Many of the other centers change. All of this science area is a follow-up to our field trip to Makapu'u Beach yesterday and to Sea Life Park last week. We provide materials that will prompt children to talk about their observations and to continue their experiences."

Cathy escorts a young mother to the sign-up sheet, shows her the monthly calendar, and extends her warm welcome to the Traveling Preschool. Of the 20 adults, only 2 appear to be new to the program. They stand on the edge watching, but their children soon spot the materials and lead their parents to the mats. It is a wonderful scene in front of me—2- and 3-year-olds leading adults by the hand to centers.

An Overview of the Preschool Scene

As play begins, I see a reason for the low tables. Adults and children can sit on the mats and participate side by side. For the youngest of children, the tables are just the right height when they stand. I think to myself, Here is another program feature that contributes to comfort and truly encourages adult/child interaction and play.

I watch a variety of activities: children and adults squeezing playdough through a garlic press or pasta maker; a parent reading Janet Craig's *Now I Know What's Under the Ocean* (Troll, 1982); a mom and her twin sons creating a block structure; and two toddlers fishing in the "tide pools." In each activity, I hear an easy flow of conversation. I hear talk among the adults themselves and I hear conversations with their children. There are enthusiastic comments about the previous day's field trip to the beach and tide pools. The materials seem to prompt those comments. I see Keaka's mom pointing to the malalo and the hihi mano, saying, "Look, these are like the fish we saw yesterday at Makapu'u."

In the background, a tape plays children's songs in Hawaiian. I notice that Cathy and Lorna are setting up one more center: a small blue and grey tent. They place a hibachi off to the side of the entrance and provide cooking tools. There is also a cardboard boat, dolls, overnight bags, flippers and a snorkeling mask, camping equipment, and more dramatic play materials. Lorna sees me watching and explains, "Camping by the beach is the favorite activity of the Hawaiian families. The families here in Waimanala love to be all together by the ocean with tents and lots of cooking equipment. It doesn't matter if they live just a block away from the beach—they like to live outside, especially during the summer."

Her description recalls for me the camping community I saw as I entered Waimanalo. I ask Lorna about the scene and she confirms that the "campers" are mostly residents of the surrounding community. I realize that the camping center I am seeing at the preschool is a way of re-creating the community. I turn back to the camping center set up on the lawn amongst colorful Kamani trees, and watch Jess and his brother take cooking gear in the tent to play.

Circle Time: Aloha and Morning Activities

About 10 minutes after most of the families have arrived, Cathy calls everyone over to one of the large mats for "circle time." It's a lively circle with all the adults and children, and again, it feels like 'ohana, with friendly conversation and parents greeting and checking on each others' children. Cathy begins "circle time" with a

song that wishes each child "aloha" by name. There are lots of smiles with this one. The next song is an adaptation of "Did You Ever See a Lassie?" substituting, "Did you ever see a palm tree sway this way and that way?" The song continues with verses like, "Did you ever see an aki swim this way and that way?" After the song, Lorna introduces the art activities for the day. First, she displays a basket of plumeria (a native flower) that she and a parent just picked from nearby trees. She demonstrates the simple printing process of dipping the blossoms in paint and pressing them on paper. Next, Lorna introduces a painting activity, one in which children will roll kukui nuts through paint and on paper set in boxes. The last activity involves stuffing precut paper fish with newspaper ripped and crumbled into small pieces. She shows all of the activities with very little detail about how to do them. She does, however, remind the parents to use the names of all the materials, to do as little as possible for the children, and to enjoy the activity together. After her directions, Lorna leads the adults and children in the dancing the Hokie Pokie, with body parts sung in Hawaiian.

After their lively participation, everyone sits down and Cathy introduces the cooking activity for the day—pancakes with coconut syrup. She also encourages parents to allow children to do as much as possible. She suggests that children can stir, pour, and help flip the pancakes. She also encourages the adults to comment on the changes that occur when the pancakes are cooking and on the taste of the coconut syrup. She notes for parents that the cooking is a one-on-one activity. She shows the children the coconut syrup and holds up coconuts. One is in the shell and one is not. She reminds everyone that there are coconuts near the camping center, and that there are hammers and nails to use with them.

"Circle time" comes to a close with reminders of coffee and cold water available and the location of bathrooms. Another "aloha" song signals the end of "circle time." Amazingly, most of the 2- and 3-year-olds are still on the mat with the adults. It is obvious that Cathy and Lorna keep "circle time" very brief to accommodate the short attention spans. They also mix parent information with activities, such as songs and fingerplays. Some of the adults continue to sing as they leave the mat to go off to a center.

Observing Family Interactions

For the next hour and a half, I observe many family interactions on the mats before me. As I watch, I am frequently reminded of how unique this program is. There is no teacher in a traditional sense, there is no schedule, there is no insistence on interaction among the children (that is, no one is insisting that "Malea play with Jerri"). To capture this Traveling Preschool experience for you, I have decided to take you walking with me from mat to mat.

As you watch what is happening in the centers, remember the staff's intent to make the preschool reflect the community and to respect the parents as teachers of their children. Another priority to remember is the emphasis on language and literacy development. It is intended that the materials and activities will stimulate children's talk, and that parents will talk with their child about what he or she is doing. Be sure to notice the role that Cathy and Lorna play as facilitators of those family interactions.

Alicia and her mother are sitting at a table with puzzles. Lorna stops by and sits across the table from them. This is their second visit to the preschool, and on the previous day, Alicia had become very fatigued and miserable at the end of the field trip. Her mom expresses worry about Alicia coming to preschool. Lorna encourages Alicia's mother to "feel free to take her home when she begins to get tired so she won't get too worn out today." Alicia's mom agrees, saying that she doesn't want to repeat the unhappy ending. "She really wanted to come today, so I want it to end on a good note."

As they talk, Alicia is very involved with puzzles, the kind with only three pieces. Her mom asks, "Where can I get simple puzzles with knobs like this?" She continues, "Alicia can't get the pieces out of her puzzles as home, so she gives up and doesn't use them." The parent and Lorna watch Alicia for a minute and they agree that she really enjoys the puzzles and can assemble a simple one.

Lorna says to the child, "Alicia, you are putting all the pieces in the puzzle." Then she promises Alicia's mother that she will look for some catalogs with information about appropriate puzzles. As she begins to move on, Lorna watches as

Alicia's mother talks with her daughter about the puzzles. She hears, "You put all the pieces in—can you do it again?"

At the "Fish and Ocean Life Center," a toddler, Jerri, and his dad are looking at the shells. Matt, the father, lifts a large conch shell to his ear to demonstrate listening to the sounds of the ocean. "If you listen, you can hear the waves." Jerri gets the basic idea of holding the shell to his ear, but soon uses the shell as a telephone. Matt acknowledges his idea, and begins to respond to his telephone conversation.

The pancake batter is ready and adults and children begin taking turns making and eating pancakes. Cathy is nearby, coaching the adults:

"Talk about the bubbles on the top of the pancake."

"Help your child notice that the pancake gets brown as it cooks."

"We're tasting coconut syrup because we've been talking about coconuts and experiencing the different ways we use them."

As the first batches are being eaten, I hear a grandmother say, "He doesn't eat this well at home." Another adult comments, "Yum, I like this coconut syrup." She looks at her two sons, and asks them if they like it too. They're both very involved in cutting their pancakes into pieces with small plastic forks, and they don't respond to her question. She waits and then comments on their cutting, "You are cutting your pancake into lots of pieces." She continues, "Now you will have lots of bites to eat."

The art center appears to be the most popular area, and I have trouble deciding who enjoys the activities most—children or adults. I hear much encouragement at this center. "Come on, you can do it, you can do it," urges a mom to a young toddler who is tearing paper to stuff a fish. Another asks her youngster, "Do you want it like this or like this?" Several children are very involved in the activity of rolling kukui nuts through paint in a box cover, watching each new path of paint. I hear a parent comment to herself, "I never thought of doing this." She turns to her daughter and watches before asking, "What is the kukui nut doing?" She hears, "It's making the paint go this way and this way and this way" as her daughter points to each paint stream.

While observing at this art center, I also hear adult conversation focused on family concerns. One parent is describing problems with her older children fighting. Others commiserate with her and describe similar problems. Another parent adds, "You know, it doesn't get any better." She continues, "My brothers and sisters and I were like that, and now we're grown and have gone our separate ways, and now it's better." The parent who initiated the conversation responds, "I need help with it now—I can't wait till they grow up." Another parent suggests that she talk to Auntie Cathy and see if she has any ideas to help. The conversation ends, and the adults once again focus their attention on the play of their children.

I notice that Stephen has been cutting strips of paper the entire time. I comment on his cutting skills and learn that he is $2\frac{1}{2}$ years old and that he has been coming to Traveling Preschools since he was an infant. Stephen beams when he hears the compliments on his ability to cut well, and so does his grandmother.

As Lorna approaches the art center, Alika's mom stops her with, "Auntie Lorna, I have an idea for an easy art project for the children." Lorna listens. "We could gather lots of little shells to string for necklaces." They discuss the size of the shells and the need for cord or string that the young children could handle. They set a time to talk further and make plans. As I listen, I am reminded that parents are encouraged to plan activities and be involved in curriculum development at the Traveling Preschools.

Scenes of Inspiration

I continue my walk from center to center, and I am touched by the scene on a nearby mat. Three-year-old Malea is wearing a grass skirt and a yellow plastic lei. She's dancing to the taped music while her mother taps a beat on the gourds. There is a comfortable rhythm to the music and to the parent/child interactions. Malea dances for a minute or so, then hands her mom a different instrument to play. The gourds are followed by a ukelele, then a drum, then rhythm sticks. With each new instrument, her mother says the name and Malea repeats it.

I hear Paulo's grandmother instructing him to sort the fish lures by color into sections of a box, "You must put the yellow ones in here and the blue ones in here." He resists and insists on putting them where he wants them. She corrects his placements for a while, but his determination outlasts hers, and she gives up on the color sorting. Cathy walks by and comments on Paulo's use of the tongs, "His fine motor control is really developing—look at how well he's using those tongs." Grandmother looks back at her grandson's activity and soon tells Paolo, "Good boy" when he picks up a lure with the tongs.

Near the "Fish and Ocean Life Center" is a small cage of lizards. Three children and two adults have been watching them and talking about the creatures. Matt, Jerri's father, says, "See her eyes moving?" The other adult asks, "How can you tell whether they are male or female?" Matt answers that the males have horns. Lorna stops by the cage and enters into the conversation with a description of what the lizards eat. She opens the cage and places her arm near the opening. One of the lizards climbs onto her arm and the children watch intently. Matt asks, "How does he feel on your arm?" Lorna responds, "They grip—they just want to hang onto to you." She offers the lizard to him as his son Jerri watches with wide eyes. He takes the lizard on the back of his hand and begins to talk to his son about the animal. Lorna gets the other lizard out to show the other adult, Susan, and her children. One of the children is willing to hold the lizard and the conversation continues about how the lizard feels.

On the edge of one of the mats is a tray of photos and a sign that asks:

Do you remember when these photos were taken?
Can you find yourself?
Can you find your friends?

Two adults are browsing through the pictures. Their children are seated next to them but they don't appear very interested in the photos. The parents are enthused as they reminisce, "Remember this one—look at how much Roy has grown." "Oh, I forgot about Carol and her little boy. I wonder where they are living now. Here's a good shot of you and Cathy." When a photo of the children appears, the adults gather the children closer to look at it. "Remember when we went to the luau, and we ate with our kupunas (grandparents)?"

Three adults and three children are seated around a poster of numbers in English and Hawaiian. Each child has a collection of seed pods to count and place on a tray with the appropriate number. The children seem to be familar with numbers in English and in Hawaiian. Two of the adults also know the numbers in Hawaiian, but the third parent is learning Hawaiian. She shouts, "Ekolu" (three) and "Elima" (five) as enthusiastically as the children do.

Next to them is a toddler and mom playing with an egg carton and small shells. The toddler is picking up the shells with a small pair of tongs, and every time she gets one in the egg carton, her mom says, "Give me five." Throughout the process, the parent encourages the fine motor task with, "Squeeze. That's right, squeeze. You've got it—squeeze." The task is difficult for the child, but when she comes close to giving up, her mother's encouragement appears to help her persist. Her occasional success also extends her attention to the task. The mother is obviously proud of the child's efforts.

On the clothesline hooked to the side of the school building is a row of beautiful prints made by dipping plumeria blossoms into paint and pressing them on paper. I've noticed that some children are able to hang their work independently and some ask for adult help. The prints are quite beautiful, and parents are obviously thrilled with the beauty. I hear a grandmother ask, "Tell me how you made this beautiful picture." Her granddaughter points to each plumeria shape and says, "I painted the flower and then I put it on the paper." Her grandmother suggests walking to see the plumeria tree, and off they go.

At the "tide pool" (tubs of water), a mother watches her daughter fish for the colorful lures. When the child has carefully captured every single lure in her net, she dumps them into her hands and proceeds to walk away from the tubs. Her mother attempts to get her to put the lures back in the water with, "Fish have to live in the water—put them back in the pool." As her daughter hesitates, she adds, "Remember the fish we saw yesterday?" The child nods her head, and her mom continues, "They were all in the water." Her daughter reluctantly tosses the lures in the water, frowns at her mother, and walks away.

A dad and his young 2-year-old, Mandy, are sitting at the puzzle table. Mandy is playing with a simple puzzle with three fish shapes. As she places each shape in place, her dad claps enthusiastically. When all three are in place, he begins to point to each one saying, "This is the red fish, this is the yellow fish . . ." Before he can finish, Mandy gets up and walks away. Her dad follows.

I observe Cathy moving from mat to mat, informing adults and children, "Five more minutes to play before cleanup." I look around to see if there are any more scenes to capture.

In the block area, Sheena has built a wall around her mother and baby brother. She is busy using every single block, and her mother alternates between encouraging her building and cooing to the baby. I hear her mother say, "You are building this wall very high." Sheena responds, "It's higher than Joey."

A similar scene in the reading or book area catches my eye. A mother reads to three of her youngsters while her infant plays on his stomach on the mat. There are colorful homemade materials to keep the baby's interest: a fabric ball and a plastic bottle filled with clear liquid and sparkles. Occasionally, a 3-year-old comes over to play with the baby. The mother urges them to "touch her gently" or to "roll the ball easily in front of her." When she finishes the book, one of the children says, "Now *I'll* read the story." Her mom responds, "Great! We'll listen to you."

Dismantling the Preschool

As I hurry to get a few last details, I see the physical arrangement of the preschool being taken apart by children and adults. Everyone is very involved in gathering and placing materials in the van. Children and adults put materials back in bins and carry them together to the van. Cathy and Lorna respond to each child and adult:

"You've brought all the blocks to the van."

"Here's three tubs of playdough."

"This is where we put the musical instruments."

I also hear "mahalo" (thank you) frequently. Some of the mats are left in place and some are folded to put in the van. As one mother tries to fold up a mat, her daughter and a friend lay down on the mat. The mother continues her folding, laughing and saying, "Now I have a big burrito."

Circle Time: Another Aloha

The preschool is packed into the van in no time, and adults and children gather once again on the few remaining mats. After a couple of songs, Cathy begins a final "circle time." She asks, "Did everyone make a pancake today?" Lots of yeses are heard. Cathy continues, "When you poured the batter into the pan, it was all soft, but then what happened?" One child says, "It got brown." After a few other responses, and then quiet, a parent says, "The batter got hard—it cooked." Cathy follows the responses with, "These are the kind of things you can talk about when you cook at home together."

Next, Cathy introduces the book *Swimmy*. Using the cover illustration, she points to fish and reminds everyone of the fish they watched on the previous day. She explains that the story is about working together and helping each other. She adds, "It's like our family—our 'ohana here at preschool." Before beginning to read, Cathy reminds the adults, "If your child gets restless and needs to move around, just take him or her to the edge of the mat and let him walk around in a way that won't disturb anyone else."

As Cathy begins to read the story, the children move closer to her. After a few pages, one of the children stands up in front of the book and all the children. Cathy puts her arm on his shoulder and says, "You need to sit down here or sit with mommy." He goes back to sit on his mother's lap, and listens to the rest of the story.

The story ends, and several adults comment on how much they liked it. Cathy returns to the cover with its illustration of Swimmy and all the fish friends, and comments, "Look at the big family they made—a fish 'ohana." Then, Malea's mother shows a book, *Nature Pop-Up Water Life* (Hoy, 1990) that she will read at the next preschool session. Children are getting restless and tired, and Cathy acknowledges this with, "It's just about time to go. We have one last announcement." She pulls out several small plastic frames decorated with shells, beads, and colored cording, and announces, "This will be our adult project for next week. When you come to preschool next week, you can decorate one of these frames for yourself. We'll have beads, shells, cording, paint, and a glue gun for you to use. If you can think of anything else to decorate these with, please bring it with you next week."

The "circle" ends and "good-byes" are heard. "See you next week," Lorna says, and Cathy adds, "The Fish Man (a local celebrity) is coming next week too." There are hugs and kisses once again as the families depart for home. It is not a hurried farewell. Many adults continue conversations with each other and with Lorna and Cathy.

Malea's mother approaches me to ask what I think of the preschool. When my response is focused on the value of the program for young children, she interrupts with, "It's very important for the adults too." She adds, "*We* need this program—a chance to get together, to talk with adults, to support each other." As I listen, I think to myself, This is the 'ohana, the family.

Revisiting the Question: What Is a Traveling Preschool?

When our conversation ends, I look at my watch and realize that between 8:30 and 11:20 A.M., a preschool environment has been created, used by a total of 46 adults and children, and disassembled. Although the physical structure is gone, packed into the van, the preschool community remains as families continue to chat. Later in the day, I talk with Lorna and Cathy and others involved in the Traveling Preschools. I hear their stories of experiences with the program. Some are poignant and some humorous. Their tales describe well the extent of community created by the Traveling Preschools.

As we prepare to leave this innovative program in Hawaii, the stories stay with me and color my images of the preschool morning. A few examples provide documentation of how well the Traveling Preschools are meeting their primary goals.

The Story of Danny

At one of the other preschool sites, a little boy, Danny, appeared one day by himself. He lived in a public housing area near the community center where the preschool was located. He looked so wistfully at the preschool materials and activities that the teachers allowed him to play for a few minutes. They asked about his mother or his dad, but he responded, "They're gone." After Danny had turned up several times at the preschool, it appeared that he was unsupervised in his wanderings around the area. The Traveling Preschools' policy calls for an adult to accompany children, so there was a dilemma with Danny coming by himself to preschool. The teachers went home with him one day in an effort to meet the family and urge someone to accompany him to the preschool so he could participate. The family was not especially welcoming, and the father, who was available in the mornings, refused to come to the preschool. The teachers persisted and described Danny's participation in the program. The father finally agreed to sit on the hill near the site of the preschool and watch. He did so for a short time, and even brought some of his buddies with him, but then stopped. Danny, however, continued to appear. Several parents discussed the situation and approached the teachers with an offer to "adopt Danny" so that he could come to the preschool. He continued to attend until he was ready for kindergarten.

The Story of Close Connections

Another story is about two paramedics who visited the Traveling Preschool. The children were busy exploring their vehicle and all their equipment when an emergency call came on their radio. It was a request to assist with childbirth from a mother who was ready to give birth at home. When the teachers learned who had placed the call, they realized that it was a former preschool parent and that she was alone. One of the teachers said to the paramedics, "I'm going with you." She did and stayed with the mother throughout the birth and until family members returned.

The Final Story: In Time of Need

A final story occurred during the aftermath of a recent hurricane, Iniki. For obvious reasons, the usual preschool program was discontinued during the first month after the storm. The preschool *community* did continue, however, and the teachers assisted with child care as parents sought to meet the basic needs of their families and friends: water, medication, and temporary shelter. Several preschool parents and staff members also met to help repair other preschool families' homes, especially where roofs had blown off. Food and shelter were shared. As one parent said, "You knew that you could call someone from the preschool if you needed help."

These stories and the spirit of 'ohana observed during the preschool morning reflect a community of support and affection—a healthy community for raising and educating young children. That community is enriched in its role of guiding the early learning of children by creative and natural play materials, by interesting and appropriate play activities, and by teacher facilitators. There is respect for families shown by the accessibility of the Traveling Preschools and by the inclusion of the family's culture. All of these features seem to lead to one conclusion: We need traveling preschools in many more communities!

Questions and Issues

1. Discuss the features that contributed to the "barrier-free" quality of the Traveling Preschools. Think of ways to extend the accessibility to families in Hawaii. If you were appointed to a task force to create a traveling preschool for *your* community, what unique barriers would need to be removed for families?
2. Again, if you were appointed to a task force to create a traveling preschool for *your* community, how would you create an environment and curriculum to reflect the local culture of your neighborhood and create comfort for families of your community?
3. Discuss the examples of promoting language and literacy you observed during the morning. Put yourself in Lorna and Cathy's roles and suggest ways to extend the opportunities for language and literacy during the sample activities you watched.
4. An important priority in the ongoing development of the Traveling Preschool is the collection of assessment data on individual children. The primary purpose for gathering such information is for communication with parents, and especially when there is a need

for services or resources for a child. There are obvious difficulties in assessment with the "drop in" policy and with the brief two-hour schedule. What do you see as other difficulties to the assessment process?

5. Consider the need for assessment and make recommendations for approaches that would be appropriate for the children, for the families, and for the program.

References

Berman, P., Izu, R., McClelland, J., & Stone, P. (1988). *The Hawaii Plan—For educational excellence for the Pacific area: Summary recommendation to the Hawaii Business Roundtable.* Honolulu, HA.

Chase, R. A., & Durden, W. G. (1992) Linking a city's culture to students' learning. *Educational Leadership, 49* (4), 66–68.

Coleman, M. (1991). Planning for the changing nature of family life in schools for young children. *Young Children, 46* (4), 15–20.

Fink, G. (1990a). The child as a member of a culture. *The Kamehameha Journal of Education, 1,* 64–69.

Fink, G. (1990b). The Kamehameha Traveling Preschool. *The Kamehameha Journal of Education, 1,* 17–22.

King, M. (1989). Working with working families. (ERIC Document Reproduction Service No. EDO-PS-90-8).

Levin, P. (1992). The impact of preschool on teaching and learning in Hawaiian families. *Anthropology and Education Quarterly, 23* (1), 59–72.

McClellan, J. M., & Levin, P. F. (1992). Learning through culture in the Prekindergarten Education Program. *The Kamehameha Journal of Education, 3,* 85–92.

McCracken, J. B. (1993). *Valuing diversity: The primary years.* Washington, DC: National Association for the Education of Young Children.

Powell, D. R. (1989). *Families and early childhood programs, Research monographs of the National Association for the Education of Young Children* (vol. 3). Washington, DC: NAEYC.

Speidel, G., Farran, D., & Jordan, C. (1989). On the learning and thinking styles of Hawaiian children. In D. Topping, D. Crowell, & V. Kobayashi (Eds.), *Thinking across cultures: Third International Conference on Thinking.* Hillsdale, NJ: Erlbaum.

Springer, R. (1990). The Pre-kindergarten Educational Program: An overview. *The Kamehameha Journal of Education, 1,* 1–6.

11

A Comprehensive Program for Early Intervention and Family Services

A Case of Collaboration and "Coloring Outside the Lines"

This is a story of collaboration in Alachua County, Florida, that began in 1965, long before educators used the word *collaboration* or institutionalized the concept. It is a story of people who planned creatively and took risks by providing services to young children and families in alternative ways. It is a look at what can happen when people abandon traditional separation of services and "pool" resources for one common goal. Bebe Fearnside, the person whose vision and energy provides the leadership for this collaboration, refers to what has happened in Alachua County as "coloring outside the lines."

Before hearing about this collaboration, I will introduce some of the families who are served by this comprehensive program for early intervention and family services. As you meet them and become sensitive to their needs, you will see why Bebe and her colleagues could not remain content with traditional service approaches and why they continue to expand the collaboration and resulting services for families.

Meet the Families in Alachua County

Anita Rogers is a petite 31-year-old African American parent with four children. She was recently forced into assuming full responsibility for her children when her husband abandoned her. Anita's history is full of sadness and difficult times. Her first husband died and her second mate proved to be unstable. She lives in federally subsidized housing, keeps the home immaculate, and takes great pride in her children. Her oldest child is in middle school, doing good academic work and involved in basketball. He is a great help to his mom. Her two middle children are in first and second grades, and her fourth child is only a few months old. Anita has been battling bouts of depression and extreme fatigue. She has a few bills to handle and a car that frequently needs repair.

Mary Baldwin is a heavy-set Caucasian woman in her mid-twenties, with a husband and three children. Her oldest children are in school and her youngest child is 4 years old. Mary was severely abused physically, sexually, and emotionally until the age of 6 and then spent most of her growing years in foster care. Her husband is a maintenance worker at a local motel, a hard-working man who would like Mary to be at home full time, taking care of the house and children.

Mary's home is completely in disrepair with holes in the floor, broken windows, and leaks in the roof. The conditions are worsened by dirty clothes on the floor, food scraps left out, and a general lack of care. The few pieces of furniture are torn or broken. A number of dogs and cats roam in and out of the house. Living with Mary and her family is a young couple awaiting the birth of their first child.

Rhonda Steward is a 29-year-old African American single parent. She is tall, attractive, and self-assured. Her only child, Tanieshia, is 3 years old. Six months ago, Rhonda took her daughter and escaped from a troubled and threatening relationship with only their clothing and a car. She currently lives with her mother, who works full time, in a well-kept federally subsidized apartment complex. Rhonda lived in fear for a few months. There had been threats of harm to her and Tanieshia. She now has some peace of mind about herself but is unwilling to be very far away from her daughter.

Like Mary and Anita, Rhonda did not complete high school. Unlike the other two women, she was successfully employed for a long period of time, beginning with work in fast-food service at 15 years of age and ending with management of a retail clothing store until the birth of Tanieshia.

Meeting the Diverse Needs of These Families

Anita, Mary, Rhonda, and their families represent the population served by the Alachua County comprehensive program for early intervention and family services. As I observed them and their families participating in the program's many facets, I had an unending list of questions about the coordination of this comprehensive program. One of my first questions and one that would recur frequently was related to funding: How much money does it take to offer this kind of comprehensive approach? My next most persistent question was about collaboration: How extensive is it and how did it begin? What about issues of territorialism for the varied programs involved? How do you convince others to collaborate?

Underneath these and other queries was a nagging desire to know how the program organizers and current staff found the courage and the finesse to "color outside the lines." Many of us, as educators, have questioned how to go beyond the usual outcomes, how to "bend" the guidelines, how to live within the "system" without giving up the real goals we have for children and families. There is every indication that Bebe Fearnside and her staff have some very helpful answers. Visiting the Alachua County program will provide the insights and the inspiration for others to "color outside the lines."

The Community

Travel with me to Alachua County, Florida, and meet the many dauntless individuals whose vision and long hours support families of people like Anita, Mary, and Rhonda. We begin in Gainesville, a picturesque university community. It is a community that suffers from underemployment due to the lack of industry. Numerous and varied federally subsidized housing projects exist, and there are many dirt and gravel roads where people live in shacks without windows and utilities. Then there are the contrasting lush neighborhoods of beautiful old southern homes with the largest porches in the country. We also see the extensive 2,000-acre campus of the University of Florida, the state's oldest university, with its 800 buildings, parks, ponds, and wildlife sanctuary. Gainesville takes pride in its history and has restored many of its old homes and buildings.

Alachua County's Full-Service School Model

The main office of the Alachua County program is located in one of those historic buildings—the Kerby Smith Center, a massive white stucco complex of offices. But this story begins at another location, about two miles away—the Family Services Center. The center is situated on city land at the edge of a busy highway. Its location between an elementary school and a middle school is also central to many of the federally subsidized housing projects and easily accessible by bus. The gravel lot in front of the center is full and cars have spread to the adjoining fields for parking.

The Family Services Center is conceptualized as a "one-stop-shop" of family services. Through its on-site services and connections with other nearby facilities, over 750 preschool children and their families are served. Structurally, the Family Service Center is understated, a set of seven portable buildings connected by wooden walkways and stairs. It is difficult to imagine how the large number of families and comprehensive services are managed in this small space. I am aware that the Family Service Center is the hub of the county's holistic approach to meet the national goal: "All children come to school ready to learn." The Florida interpretation of that goal is: "Communities and schools collaborate to prepare children and families for children's success in school." Bebe Fearnside worked with the state legislature to develop the Florida goal, so I look forward to seeing it in action. Specifically, I hope to see how Alachua County works toward the goal of preparing children and families as I enter one of the portable buildings labeled Parent Resources.

Parent Resources

This morning, I find Anita, Mary, and Rhonda sitting in a circle with about 16 other women and 2 men in this portable building in the Family Service Center. I watch as Dr. Shelton Davis, a tall, slim African American, conducts a parenting class called The Developing Child. The group of parents to which Anita, Mary, and Rhonda belong is sitting on comfortable blue couches or folding chairs, and Dr. Davis is standing next to a flip chart as the class begins.

During the week between the last class and today's session, these parents were asked to reminisce about the birth of one of their children. They took home a sheet of questions about the physical appearance of their children at birth, early frustrations of their children, and sources of joy for their children. The last question asked them to think about the "unspoken messages" given by their children. Today, Dr. Davis asks for volunteers to share with the group. "Tell us what you remembered about the birth and early days of one of your children."

Rhonda is the first to respond to Dr. Davis's request to share some early memories. She begins by telling the group that her daughter's name is Tanieshia. She helps Dr. Davis spell it as he writes the name on the flip chart. He laughs and kids Rhonda and the other moms, "I think you women make up these names when you're in labor." There's an easy laughter among the group and Rhonda looks more relaxed. She holds her sheet on which she has written about the birth of Tanieshia and her early memories. She looks at it occasionally but talks confidently to the group:

"I missed the birthing process because I had a Caesarian section. My labor was hard and the last hour was painful, but I don't remember much after that. I first saw my daughter seven hours after she was born, and when I did, she had her hand in her mouth. She nursed all the time; she just loved my breasts. She was thick—she weighed 9 pounds and 3 ounces, and her face was precious. The only time she would get frustrated was when I walked out of the room. She had to see me all the time. She would smile at me whenever I smiled at her. She just looked so sweet. I can't really describe it, but I just knew she loved me."

Rhonda finishes with a large grin, and Dr. Davis thanks her. He addresses the group: "Notice that many of the things that were true at birth are true today. Remembering the birth time is a way of seeing your child clearly—another way of understanding their development."

Anita raises her hand and indicates that she wants to share. Before she reads from her sheet, she heaves a big sigh and says, "Oh Lord, my boy," and laughs with nervousness. The group laughs with her and she's ready to begin:

"Eddie is 6 years old now and he's very complicated. He was two weeks overdue and when he was born; he looked old. He was so wrinkled, he just looked old. He was a baby that was always moving, like he does now. Sometimes it was like he was shakey, and he got frustrated easily. If I woke him up to feed him, he acted frustrated. If I stopped what he was doing to change him, he acted frustrated. Mostly I just remember him as active."

At this point, Anita asks Dr. Davis about the label *hyperactive* and about the possibility of having Eddie tested. She pleads, "I don't know what to do." Dr. Davis encourages her to look at Eddie's nutrition for sources of sugar—candy, cereal, colored punch, and so on. "Look at the quality of his food and get him to eat fresh fruits and vegetables." He addresses the group with, "You remember when we role-played hyperactivity and had our bodies moving and wiggling." The group responds with heads nodding and a comment from one of the mothers, "I remember that it was impossible to notice or hear anything else but my own movement." "Yes, that's what it's like for a hyperactive child," responds Dr. Davis. He concludes this conversation with advice to Anita to work with the staff at Eddie's school and a promise to find her some books on the topic.

Two more parents share their writing with the group, and each one sparks a discussion of the uniqueness of each child. Dr. Davis concludes the session with a reminder to the parents, "Keep in mind the individual nature of your child." He uses the words on the flip chart from the parents' descriptions and assures them, "It's OK if she's bright, it's OK if she's confusing, it's OK if he's independent, and it's OK if he's active and unpredictable." He also reminds the group of his suggestions about nutrition:

"Be patient and don't give up. I've been trying to get rid of 'hog knees and greens' from my diet and I do fine for about two weeks and then I can't stand it. I have to eat them and then I have to start over."

The group chuckles over Dr. Davis's story and several women ask, "What are hog knees?" He laughs with them and says, "Oh, that's what I call ham hocks so they won't sound so good." With that, the group laughs even harder. It is obvious to me that there is mutual trust and caring among this group of parents and Dr. Davis. I am also keenly aware that the course is designed to be as personal and relevant to the parents as possible. Their ideas and needs give the course direction.

As the group members bid each other good-bye and leave, I look around the small portable building. A partial kitchen is on one end, and next to it are four racks of plastic bags of books and toys. It's a "toy lending library" stocked with a variety of materials for children from ages 0 to about 6 years. There are also books for parents, as well as video equipment for loan. I am told that everything available is organized into a computerized check-out system. "We are trying to make this like a real media center so that parents get accustomed to the media center/library concept. Then they will be comfortable using the resources of the public library or the elementary school facilities."

My guide, Phyllis McKnight, also points out the parent bulletin board and a section titled "Published Parents." She explains that parents are encouraged to write about their children, about themselves, or about parenting. Several of the essays are published in a brochure each month and displayed on the bulletin board. I am touched by one of them:

> On Monday, August 23, I came back to school for the first time in a long time. I came back to study hard and get my GED. I was nervous at first, but after my first week I was comfortable with all the ladies and my teacher. I am very happy that I chose to come back to school. I'm not coming for myself. I am coming for my children, because that makes me a positive role model for them. They see me going and enjoying school, they will do the same.
>
> by Tracy Woods

The poignant writings of the "Published Parents" begin to communicate to me the importance of the Family Service Center in the lives of individuals like Anita, Mary, and Rhonda. I am also aware of some of the effort toward building parent confidence and self-image. The essays spark my curiosity about the adult education programs available to the families, so I move on to another portable building to observe the kind of classes described in the essays.

Adult Education

The adult education class is in progress and I immediately notice the fast pace and interactive quality of the session. The teacher, Enid Corbin, is reviewing math processes needed for solving typical questions on the GED exam. She reads a problem and asks, "What do you use whenever you need to find out the difference?" This is soon followed with, "When it asks for the price of one, what do you have to do?"

It becomes obvious that Enid is not working toward "right answers" but emphasizing how to solve the problems. She frequently reminds the adults in class, "Take it out of English and think it in math." When she gets to a problem that involves geometry, one of the women gives an enthusiastic, "Yeah." Enid Corbin responds, "Lisa's ready for geometry—I didn't think I'd ever hear those words." She grins and Lisa grins back.

When another parent gives a quick answer, Enid's response is, "Hey, Shirley—new hair, new thinking."

This lively review session continues for about 25 minutes, and at the end, the group talks about their feelings and their fears about the GED exam. Enid listens and agrees that it is scary and hard to think when you feel like that. She reminds them, "In case you freeze up on the test, remember to pull out the grid, plug the numbers in, and you will feel more in control." The grid is a strategy she has demonstrated several times during the review session, when the group was uncertain about how to begin solving a problem.

For the last part of the class, the group splits into small groups to work together on problems. Several individuals go to work at the row of computers across the back wall of the building. There is a serious work climate in the room, and an inspirational example of the power of cooperative learning. I listen in to a group in which Rhonda is working, and hear her explain how to begin working a math problem. "Remember, we need to use the grid." She continues, "Now what do we know already in this problem?" Rhonda has learned well from her teacher and is now instructing her peers.

On the shelves around the room are abundant resources and a collection of photographs taken at celebrations for those students who passed their GED exams. I learn that 21 families have been successful. There are also photos of former students graduating from the local community colleges.

As this morning's session ends, I follow Rhonda to a preschool classroom in another portable building. She has this time in her morning schedule to play with Tanieshia and have lunch with her. She encourages me to come along and see her daughter.

Early Childhood Education Programs

The preschool rooms are in the adjoining portable building, and for Rhonda, that feature was critical in her first months at the center. She was worried that Tanieshia's father might try to take her away. "It was important to know that she was right next door," Rhonda confides. "I like the fact that we come here together and that I can see her and play with her, and we even have lunch together."

When we enter the preschool room, Tanieshia and five other preschoolers have just finished a snack and are helping to clean the table. The room is a traditionally furnished preschool environment and there are two teachers with the children. Before their snack, the children had painted and played with blocks and manipulatives. Rhonda and two other moms from the adult education class begin to read stories to their own children and are immediately joined by other children in the group. After the stories, parents and children gather in a circle on the floor with the teachers. One of the preschool teachers brings out a bag of puppets, and the children take turns using them for a related song or fingerplay. When the black, furry spider puppet is held up by Tanieshia, I hear the familiar "Itsy Bitsy Spider." I leave the singing and decide to explore the other preschool room.

In the other half of this portable building is a room for infants and toddlers. It is a cozy setting with cribs, tiny tables, high chairs, soft mats, and appropriate toys. At this time, a father is stretched out on the mats reading to his young toddler. An infant is being rocked while another is being changed. There are two adults and a parent here for the four children.

Just before lunch, children and parents and caregivers from both rooms go outside to an area behind the portable buildings. The youngest children seem to enjoy the playground equipment and the large grassy area. There is a colorful blanket on the grass for some parents and an infant. Much of the parents' conversation is about their children or is part of interaction with their children. Rhonda and Tanieshia roll a large rubber ball back and forth, laughing and enjoying the play. When Tanieshia gets tired and wants to sit in her mom's lap, I have a chance to talk with Rhonda about the Alachua County program and what it means to her.

An Intimate Look at One Family's Dreams

Rhonda lets me know that she is new at the center, having arrived only a few months ago. When I ask how she found out about the program, she answers, "I drove by, saw the sign, and stopped and asked." Rhonda's quite open with me and confesses, "I'm comfortable now, but at first, I was afraid it would be something against me—threatening, you know—but now it's really great." With little prompting, she shares her goals and intentions:

"My mother had 10 kids and I'm the baby. I looked at my life and what I grew up wanting and couldn't have, and that's what I want for Tanieshia. For example, you know those Queen Victoria beds? I always wanted one, so I got one for Tanieshia. Or a swing set! I never had one, but I got one for her.

"I don't remember much about school—it wasn't positive or negative. When I started making money at 14, it got comfortable to work full time and have that paycheck, so I quit school. But a lot of things I thought I knew either didn't work or took the long way, so after 11 years, I'm back in school. Now my goal is to get my GED and go on to Sante Fe Community College. I want to be a funeral director, so I'll take all my science courses and other basics there. I'll have to transfer to a program in Miami and do an apprenticeship. There's a good preschool on both of the campuses, so Tanieshia can be with me. I figure that by 1996, she'll be in elementary school and my business will be getting started.

"You know, she studies when I study, so I think seeing me will help her. It's been good here at the preschool for her to be around other children and other adults. When I get my car paid off, I'll sign her up for some art classes. I'm on track at this place, so I know I can make my goal. And the staff here are real—they're on your side."

At this moment, Tanieshia needs all of Rhonda's attention, so I leave the two of them to play again. As I look around, I notice that other adults from the classes this morning have come outside to enjoy the pleasant weather.

Integrated Social Services

Some of the parents from the adult education classes are sitting and visiting at a picnic table outside one of the other portable buildings. While they are sitting there, my guide, Phyllis McKnight, who is a family liaison specialist and part of the staff of the Family Service Center, comes to chat with Mary Baldwin. Mary's 4-year-old daughter, Lucy, is in a nearby Head Start program that I will be visiting later today. Phyllis asks about Lucy and hears that she is happy in the preschool.

Phyllis asks Mary if she has had a chance to think about her requests for the "Hope for the Holidays" program. Families who are interested and in need may develop a list of items that would help make their home more comfortable. They may also request one gift item for each member of their family. "Hope for the Holidays" volunteers work throughout the community seeking donations in response to the family requests. When Phyllis asks about her family, Mary is hesitant to list anything for her home, saying, "It needs so much work but my husband wants to do it." Phyllis suggests that maybe they would like some building materials or tools, and Mary's face brightens. She responds with, "I'll have to check with my husband about this," and seems pleased about the possibility. When Phyllis asks about furniture, Mary says, "No, it will just get ruined with the kids around."

Mary has made a list of gift requests for the family, however, and Phyllis copies her list on the appropriate form. Mary asks for a watch for herself, a doll and tea set for Lucy, Walkmans for her two sons, and tools for her husband. She asks Phyllis for help with one additional item—a folder or file to keep her family's important papers together. She pulls out a stack of identification cards, social security papers, and other forms held together in a rubber band. She points to Phyllis's manila file folder, saying, "Something like that would help me keep these together." Mary is assured that she can have several folders and Phyllis tells her, "I'll bring them to you in your class this afternoon."

Mary has brought all her papers with her today because she has an appointment at the clinic and needs identification. I learn that the clinic is in the portable building just across from the parent resource building, so I decide to continue my exploration of the Family Service Center.

Health Clinic

The clinic is small, limited to the size of the portable building that houses it. Within its confines is a waiting room and a receptionist area, two examining rooms (one for adults and one for children), and a small office for consultation and resources. Today, a nurse practitioner and a doctor are attending the needs of the families who wait for their appointments.

My observations here are sensitive to the families' need for privacy, but the receptionist is happy to describe the services available to families. These include physicals, immunizations, well child care, family planning, and general medical care. The services are available to Medicaid-eligible families five days a week from 8:00 A.M. to 4:30 P.M.

At this time, Mary Baldwin is called for her appointment and shown to the examining room. As I sit in the waiting room, I begin to realize how well the Family Service Center is achieving the goal of "putting the services where the people are." Bebe Fearnside explained to me earlier that one aspect of their approach is to get the agencies together for the "one-stop-shop" concept. Here, in the Family Service Center, families certainly have access to a wide variety of services, all of which are made possible by the teaming of early childhood educators, health and human service professionals, adult educators, and medical personnel. In addition to all that is offered at this site, significant other services offered at nearby locations, such as the Head Start programs connected to the Family Service Center.

While Mary is at the clinic, I decide to visit the Head Start class where her daughter, Lucy, spends her day. It is close by, as are many of the related early childhood programs used by the families served by the Family Service Center.

Extending to Neighborhood Preschools and Child-Care Centers

Lucy goes to a program in a subsidized child-care facility, Palmer King Center, in the middle of Pine Meadows, which is a local neighborhood housing project. Alachua County's Preschool Liaison Program, begun in 1980, promoted the contracting and sharing of resources with subsidized child-care centers. By placing children who are eligible for Head Start in this existing neighborhood program, the total program is enriched for all the children. Establishing a separate Head Start center or program would not be as cost effective as this approach, so the funding buys more for children. This combination of Head Start with child-care services also accommodates those parents who work a full day and need extended hours of child care.

My guide at this location is Sandy Kolb, who is a preschool curriculum specialist and an experienced early childhood educator. Her role is one of a consultant to those neighborhood centers where Head Start children are placed. She provides in-service programs for staff members, works in the classrooms modeling developmentally appropriate practice, and is a liaison between the children's families and other programs and services. Sandy also helps enrich the program by procuring needed equipment, materials, and other resources, again supported by funding from combined sources.

As I enter the classroom for 4- and 5-year-olds, I am immediately aware of a high level of activity. The classroom is a model of developmentally appropriate practice in terms of an inviting center arrangement, rich with appropriate materials, decorated with abundant displays of children's work, and clear communication of the value of play. The extra resources available and the consultation expertise from Sandy are evident in this exemplary environment. Children and adults are involved and interacting in a wide variety of activities.

At the writing center, a senior citizen volunteer is drawing side by side with children, labeling drawings, and recording stories. I smile when I hear him say, "When I was a boy. . . ."

In the block area, two boys have built a bus and invite others to come and ride in it. Sandy accepts their invitation and the boys ask her where she wants to go. Together, the three "ride through town" in the block bus.

In a large and well-equipped dress-up area, two boys and three girls are trying on different outfits, complete with belts, ties, jewelry, shoes, and purses. They check on how they look in the large nearby mirror. They also move about the room to show the adults, or to ride the bus, or to make a phone call in the dramatic play area.

At one of the tables, children are making "pumpkin people" with colored paper, glue, scissors, and other materials. One of the teachers, Sylvia, is sitting with them and commenting on their use of glue and scissors. Cutting is a difficult task for some of the children, so each shape is a big accomplishment.

In a quiet corner furnished with a rocker, big pillows, a little table with a lamp, and a rich supply of books, another volunteer is reading to two children. The lamp gives a soft light to the corner area. Lucy, Mary Baldwin's daughter, is stretched out on one of the big pillows and she looks content and relaxed as she listens to the story.

At another table, children are making paper-towel "ghosts" with the towels, black markers, and string. Another teacher, Margie, is sitting with them, and lively conversation is taking place about whether ghosts are real. Margie tells me that the "ghost making" was a suggestion from one of the children: "He made one at home with his big brother and wanted to show us how to do it. He gathered the materials and he's in charge of this center. He's thrilled to be helping other children make them."

Just outside the door that is propped open, children are fingerpainting with orange paint. Another teacher, Jackie, is with them, commenting on their painting and assisting with hanging the paintings when finished. Jackie's enthusiasm for fingerpainting is so contagious that I'm tempted to roll up my sleeves and get into the orange paint. Instead, I decide to watch the children enjoy the painting experience. Next to the table is a pail of water that the children use to wash their hands, which seems to be just as appealing as the painting.

Near the fingerpainting activity is a sand table and four children happily filling cups and molding sand in different shapes. There is lively chatter about Halloween and costumes planned for the holiday. "I'm going to be a Ninja Turtle," says one of the boys. "Well, I'm going to be a policeman," says another.

Just before cleanup, I see one of the teachers go to the block area and coach the children who are playing there about how to put away the blocks. When the signal for cleanup is called, the classroom is taken care of with ease and in a short time. The children appear to be content, and their interactions with adults are positive and loving. I can't help but think about the benefits of this organized environment—its appropriate routines and the supportive adults for children like Lucy. I witness an abundance of hugs and receive some myself as I prepare to return to the Family Service Center.

Social/Vocational Training

Within minutes, I am back at the complex of portable buildings, and this time I want to observe an adult class focused on social/vocational goals. The rationale for this class is to provide families with experiences that will prepare them to enter and succeed in the job market after passing their GED exams or other competency requirements. The activities of the class provide opportunity to develop communication skills, decision making, leisure pursuits, planning and organizing techniques, conflict management, and leadership abilities.

Today, the parents are completing plans for a "Family Night" that will be held the following week. The parent who is in charge is running the meeting. She has listed the committees on a poster that she displays to the group. "Check and see what committee you are working on, so that you take care of your responsibilities," she reminds the parents. There is a discussion about transportation for families to the center for the event, and decisions made about the schedule for buses.

Although two Social Services staff are present at this meeting, they remain primarily in the observer/resource role. It is obvious that the parents are in charge of the coming event, which may be a unique opportunity for many of the adults. The goal of "empowering families" is certainly addressed as these adults conduct the planning, decision making, and organizing of their own social event.

After the business meeting, the group disperses to the tables to work on craft items that will be prizes or for sale at the "Family Night." Many of the women are decorating large straw hats and having a wonderful time doing so. The hats were donated, and families have gathered a colorful variety of trims, so that the hats become unique creations. I hear, "Hey, girl, that hat is fine!" "Help me with this glue gun, will you?" gets several offers of help. There is a family atmosphere here, as well as an opportunity to express individuality in the creations. It is also a time for relaxed socializing and fun—something many of these adults seldom experience in their stressful lives.

More Than a Day's Visit

It has become clear to me that this is a program that I cannot possibly observe in one day, so we will be spending a second day together, seeing more aspects of the Alachua County Comprehensive program. We will begin by accompanying Phyllis McKnight on a home visit to where Anita and her family live. The rest of the day will be spent at an elementary school with both Head Start classes and state-funded prekindergarten programs, where we will learn about the important connections being made between families and the public school system. After the programs end and children go home for the day, we will attend a parent program on nutrition. And finally, we will return to Bebe Fearnside's office to find out how all of these connections have been made and how they are funded and maintained.

Home Visits to Support Families

Anita Rogers, who was introduced early in the chapter, is a single mom with four children. She lives in a spacious apartment in a federally subsidized housing project. I am accompanying Phyllis McKnight on one of her regular home visits this morning, and when we arrive at 8:30 A.M., Anita's front door is standing open. When she hears us pull up, she comes to greet us and immediately apologizes for the strong odor in her house. She explains that her son mopped the floors before leaving for school and was too generous with the cleaning solution.

We sit in the pleasant, comfortable, living room and I notice that everything is spotless! The furniture seats are covered with towels, and hanging on the walls are numerous framed photos of Anita's children. On the coffee table she has laid out an outfit for the baby, complete with shoes and socks to match the little dress. Anita explains that the baby is napping at this time.

Phyllis and Anita begin to talk about the goals for the family. Anita states that her goal is to be ready to take her GED exam in January. Phyllis asks how she feels about that deadline, and Anita responds quickly, "I'm determined—I just have to find the time and energy to study enough."

Phyllis asks, "What kind of support do you need to help you meet that goal?" Anita doesn't hesitate. "I need a tutor for Eddie, my first-grader." She continues, "He's having a hard time with reading and writing. I'm not very good at helping him. I don't know enough about how to teach him. If someone could help him, then I could get my studying done. I can't stay up very late because I'm so tired with the baby and all."

Phyllis promises to explore some of the tutoring programs offered by volunteer groups from the university, but suggests, "In the meantime, I know that there are tutors at the public library every afternoon or evening." She asks Anita about the closest library and if she's familiar with it. Anita knows where it is, but admits that she hasn't taken the children there. Phyllis enthusiastically tells about library offerings such as story hours, and describes how she takes her own children there regularly. "It gives me a break to have them listen to a story while I browse for books for myself." Anita becomes equally enthusiastic and says, "Now that my car is running, I can go there easily and it would be good for the kids." The conversation finishes with Phyllis describing the location of the appropriate library brochures with the tutoring program information that Anita can pick up while she's at the Family Service Center later this morning.

Phyllis asks if there is any other support that would help the family, and Anita describes a need for a "Big Brother" for her two middle children. "My oldest is busy with school and basketball, but the younger two need someone," she says. Phyllis records the request and again promises to check with the appropriate organizations. She asks Anita about her depression and hears that Anita is feeling better and that she "just needs a break now and then." The home visit ends with a review of Anita's goal and the support she has requested. Phyllis and I leave just as the baby awakes from her nap. Anita waves to us, saying, "I'll see you at the center this afternoon."

Phyllis's work with Anita this morning is a good example of the work of the family liaison specialist—that is, "to assist families with appropriate contacts for needed services and agencies." She visits families like Anita's at least every three months, or more often if a need arises. The primary goal of her efforts is to "ensure that families are provided the opportunity to enhance their self-sufficiency." The conversation with Anita revealed that those opportunities are available.

Other family liaison specialists visit families with children in the public school, again assisting with needed resources, but also with transition to the public school system. For many parents, it is difficult and threatening to go for conferences or even "open house" visits, so other liaison specialists like Phyllis accompany families, or connect them with the school counselor, or support them when there are behavior problems. The result is that "families aren't so afraid—they're even volunteering because schools are more comfortable places for them." The work of these liaison specialists is just one facet of the deliberate connections with the public schools.

Important Connections with the Public School System

We drive on to a nearby elementary school in the small town of Alachua. Its socioeconomic contrasts in neighborhoods is similar to those in Gainesville. The early childhood education programs at Irby Elementary School are another example of the collaboration promoted by the Preschool Liaison Program. My guide, Marie Rizzi, a "teacher on special assignment," describes the collaboration achieved in this school. In this building are Head Start classes, state-funded prekindergarten early intervention classes, and daily visits from children and staff of Lee's Preschool, a private child-care provider in the community, together with classes from kindergarten through grade 3. A look at the floor plan (Figure 11–1) of the early childhood wing of the school begins to communicate the flexibility and fluidity of programming possible in the building.

I learn that Irby School is one of seven schools with this model of a quad for Head Start and prekindergarten children with disabilities within the elementary school. The goal is for all 22 schools in Alachua County to make this "brick and mortar" commitment to young children. I already see the potential for an easier transition from prekindergarten to kindergarten in this physical arrangement, so I

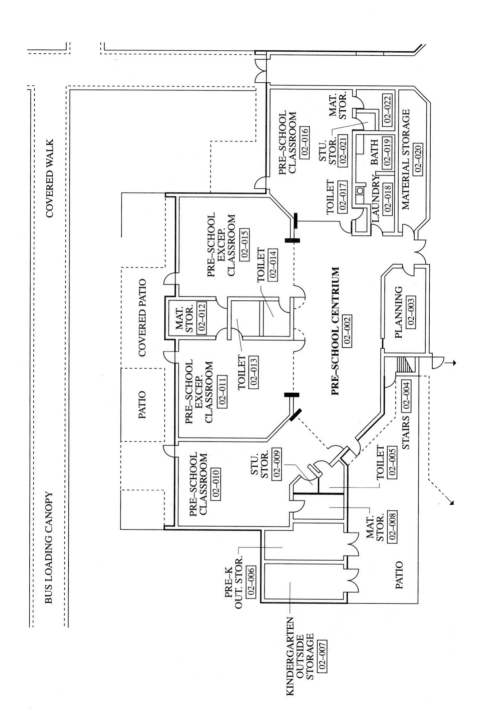

BUS LOADING CANOPY

COVERED WALK

PATIO

COVERED PATIO

PRE-SCHOOL
CLASSROOM
02-010

PRE-SCHOOL
EXCEP.
CLASSROOM
02-011

MAT.
STOR.
02-012

PRE-SCHOOL
EXCEP.
CLASSROOM
02-015

PRE-SCHOOL
CLASSROOM
02-016

TOILET
02-013

TOILET
02-014

STU.
STOR.
02-021

MAT.
STOR.
02-022

02-019

MATERIAL STORAGE
02-020

BATH

LAUNDRY
02-018

TOILET
02-017

STU.
STOR.
02-009

PRE-SCHOOL CENTRIUM
02-002

PLANNING
02-003

MAT.
STOR.
02-008

TOILET
02-005

STAIRS
02-004

PRE-K
OUT. STOR.
02-006

KINDERGARTEN
OUTSIDE
STORAGE
02-007

PATIO

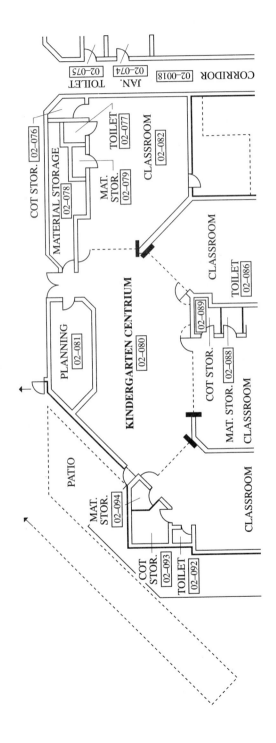

FIGURE 11-1

Source: Brame Poole Architects/School Board of Alachua County, Gainesville, Florida. Used by permission.

anticipate the much needed collaboration between early childhood education and elementary education programming. I begin my visit in the quad where young children spend their days.

Classes for Young Children at Irby Elementary School

As I arrive at the Head Start classrooms, the children are putting away manipulative materials and puzzles, washing their hands, and lining up to go to breakfast. One of the teachers asks, "What are you supposed to do with your hands when we walk together?" She hears:

"Keep your hands next to you."
"Put your hands behind your back."
"Keep your hands in your pocket."

"That's right," their teacher repeats after each answer. The children leave their bright, spacious, and interesting room for the cafeteria and a breakfast of sausage pizza and juice. They are hearty eaters, and they are joined at their tables by the children from the prekindergarten program. I hear various conversations at the tables—discussions about who's absent, about the breakfast foods, and about the weather. I also hear lots of encouragement for social skills and language use, such as one teacher commenting, "I heard you say, 'Help me, please,' very clearly and I knew what you needed." Another example I overheard was, "Thanks for telling me you like the juice. I love to hear your voice."

When Trask yells, "Hey" to his teacher, she responds with, "What do you call me?" Trask answers, "Miss Sue," and hears, "That's right, Miss Sue."

As the children are walking back to their classrooms, a van from Lee's Preschool pulls up. Children from this private child-care center and their teachers join the Head Start and prekindergarten children and their teachers returning to the classrooms. The entire group gathers in the common area to sing and to pantomime a story about a barnyard. This is a brief gathering due to the group size. The children go to their respective rooms, and those from Lee's Preschool stay in the common room (the Pre-School Centrium).

Irby's Connections with Private Child-Care Providers

I learn that many of these children from the private child-care center are also funded by Head Start; however, all of the preschoolers from Lee's come several times a week to Irby to use some of the specialized motor equipment in the common room. In addition, the staff from the private center attend the in-service sessions with all the other early childhood education staff, meet once a month with kindergarten and preschool teachers to swap ideas, share some of the materials and equipment available at Irby (such as the laminating machine, the library, and so on), and join the early childhood classes on field trips. I am impressed by this collaboration and I learn that the goal is for every elementary school to "adopt a preschool" or two in this manner. Once again, more children are being served and the quality of services is enhanced. As I consider this connection between public schools and private child care, the children's activity catches my eye and I turn to the play in the common room.

Two children are "swimming" in a plastic pool full of styrofoam. The pool sits on a large blue sheet of paper with painted waves. The paper "ocean" is surrounded by balance beams, and another child cautiously walks the beams, careful not to fall in the water.

Three children and an adult are in the block area building towers and comparing their heights.

Two children are in a fabric tunnel, giggling as each one works his or her way through to the end.

Two children are "hopping" on large rubber balls with handles. They talk about their animal potential with, "Let's be bunnies" and "No, let's be frogs."

Four children and one adult are sitting around a large Lego table. It has a Lego surface, and there are pockets around the edge of the table full of Legos. There is lively conversation about shapes, colors, designs, and size.

Today, there are 14 children from the private preschool and one staff member, who is assisted by Marie Rizzi. Marie's role is to coordinate this connection with Lee's Preschool and to model interactions with the children for the staff. Some days the children from the Head Start classes and the prekindergarten classes move in and out of the common room during this "free-choice" time so that children become part of one group, but on other days, the children from Lee's have exclusive use of the common room.

Irby's Prekindergarten Early Intervention Programs

In one of the nearby prekindergartens, children are extremely busy in the dramatic play area. Three boys push shopping carts and gather groceries. They take their purchases to the kitchen and two begin fixing dinner while a third boy begins ironing.

In a nearby center, two children and an adult are playing with dinosaur and Ninja turtle figures. The figures are "talking" to each other, and the adult watches and listens.

One child is walking around the classroom with a clipboard and a brief case, and stops to watch the other activities.

In another corner of the room, a teacher and two children are "building a town" on a large plastic map. Quiet conversation focuses on what the town needs and where to place the buildings. The teacher is using questions to elicit language from the children about their choices for the town.

The prekindergarten rooms are limited to a maximum of 12 children, but generally have 9 or 10 children and 2 teachers. The major emphasis in these programs is language development. These children share facilities, activities, and staff with the other early childhood programs for experiences within the "least restrictive environment."

Irby's Head Start Classes

In the Head Start classroom next door, four children are sitting in front of computers and playing a variety of games. One of their teachers is with them and she takes turns sitting with each child, commmenting on the game or playing with him or her.

In a carrel next to the computers, two children are using the listening center. One of the children helps the other one turn the pages of the book as they listen to the tape.

At the other end of the room, the other teacher sits at the small table in the dramatic play center. Her long hair is being combed by one child while another child brings her plates of plastic food. Both of the children are wearing dress-up clothes, complete with high heels.

The remaining four children are at a round table with colored paper scraps, markers, scissors, and patterns. One child is tracing patterns and cutting them out. Another is tracing patterns and coloring them. The other two are using the materials in their own varied ways. There is animated conversation about the upcoming holiday, Halloween:

"I'm going to a party with my brothers and sisters."

"I'm going to trick or treat and get lots of candy."

"My mom says I can't have lots of candy. I have to give it to her and I can have just two pieces."

"I'm going to make my costume tonight. It's going to be a dinosaur costume, but I don't know how we're going to do it."

In the book area, a foster grandmother is reading to two more children. The children are snuggled up to the adult in a large overstuffed chair.

There is a maximum of 20 children in these Head Start classrooms and a ratio of 1 adult to every 10 children plus frequent foster grandparents, parents, and other volunteers. The educational program is individualized with activities and experiences that promote development of language, perceptual-motor skills, and social competence.

When it gets close to lunch time, the Lee's Preschool van appears again to take the children back to the center for the remainder of the day. Here at Irby Elementary, young children eat lunch in the cafeteria, then read books and take naps, and then enjoy an afternoon of play in centers and outdoors. I am curious about the transition of these children to kindergarten, so I use this time to talk with

Marie Rizzi and one of the kindergarten teachers. I have already seen the potential for easy transition that the physical arrangement of the building provides, but I predict that these people have gone beyond the physical space in their planning for children's needs.

Irby's Transition Program

As I suspected, the School Board of Alachua County developed a transition program several years ago. The intent is to "ease the childrens' and families' move to kindergarten." At Irby, it is a six-week program for both incoming kindergarten children and those who are leaving kindergarten. Anyone who will begin kindergarten is eligible.

Marie Rizzi and Marilyn, one of the kindergarten teachers, describe the program as one with a "summer camp theme." There is lots of singing, drama, literacy, science, games, and math achieved through learning centers, as well as calendar and "daily news" routines and attention to some of the kindergarten curriculum goals. Marilyn explains that they are careful to use different materials and activities "so that there is no repetition during the academic year." They do establish similar routines so that everything won't be so new at the beginning of school. The children even use the cafeteria so that it becomes a comfortable experience.

Interestingly, the transition program is staffed by the kindergarten teachers and the Head Start teachers. This arrangement promotes a positive sharing of information about children and again a collaboration of personnel that really enhances the transition effort. The major intent of the program is to help children socialize with each other and with staff. Marilyn reports, "Many children come in and are not talking, and by the end, blossom and flourish." Marie mentions that parents are informed of the daily activities and of their child's progress in the summer program.

It is time for the parent meeting, so our conversation must end, but once again, I am impressed by the extent to which Alachua County is meeting the needs of children and families. I anticipate that the parent meeting scheduled next will provide another example of the sensitivity to families' needs and the high priority given to building relationships with families.

Positive Interactions with Parents

It is 3:00 P.M. Children are boarding buses for home as parents are arriving for the meeting. The commons room has been set up with a circle of chairs and a table of refreshments. The meeting begins on time with a presentation by Mark, who manages the food services of the school. He describes the cafeteria program, emphasizing nutrition and healthy food preparation, and makes suggestions for extending the practices at home. He speaks sincerely to parents when he acknowledges, "Cooking this way may be a real change in what you're used to, and it has been for us, too."

When Mark finishes, the program is turned over to Officer Nannette, a police officer who is a full-time staff person in the school. Her position is funded through a grant and she works to build positive relationships between children and families and the police force. Just listening to and watching her tells me that the children will definitely think of her as a friend.

The parent meeting is now opened for discussion of parent ideas for other workshops, ways to help with the program, and program suggestions from parents. Parents request help with discipline, communication with children, and inexpensive family activities. When the discussion ends, parents help themselves to "Butterfly Pancakes" and are encouraged to take the recipe and make the pancakes at home with their children. I notice that the group is quite content to sit together and chat. No one hurries to leave, which tells me that this is a comfortable situation for those adults who have come this afternoon.

I am the first to leave the parent meeting because I want to get back to Gainesville for my last stop in this visit—the office of Bebe Fearnside. Although we have talked only briefly, I feel like I have known her for some time. Everywhere I have been during these two days, her name has been mentionned and her leadership acknowledged. So, I look forward to hearing her ideas about why the Alachua County collaboration works so well.

Bebe Fearnside Shares Her Wisdom

When I express my admiration for what Alachua County has accomplished, Bebe lets me know that the collaboration has been recognized by others, too. In 1992, the program was noted as one of eight outstanding collaboration models in the country by the Bush Center in Child Development and Social Policy at Yale University. The program has also been designated as an exemplary model for collaborative services for children and families by the Southeastern Regional Vision for Education (SERVE) and included as part of a dissemination project. In her straightforward way of addressing issues, Bebe describes their work as essential in the face of the ongoing dilemma of not enough resources for children and families. She states, "We don't have a choice—we can't continue our traditional approaches to the problem."

When asked about advice for those of us who are ready to address the scarcity of resources, Bebe begins with the need to reduce and eliminate duplication of efforts. "So many of us are working toward the same goals—maybe in different ways or sometimes with the same approaches—but often we aren't even aware of what the other group is doing." She lists the projects involved in the Alachua County collaboration as examples of what she is describing: Head Start, subsidized child care, Florida's Prekindergarten Early Intervention Programs, Chapter 1 Basic PreK programs, Florida First Start, Even Start, Florida's Healthy Start, the Child Care Resource and Referral Network, and full-service schools. The major players in Alachua County's approach further illustrate the breadth of collaboration: the state Health and Human Services Boards and the Department of Education. When I consider the extent of shared resources as well as shared power and authority, I begin to understand how the program is able to meet the diverse needs of children and families.

I am feeling overwhelmed and empathize with those waiting for advice on how to begin, so I push for some simple steps. Bebe repcats, "You've got to go where the children are, or where the families are." She emphasizes, "Put the services where the people are." I listen as she advises, "First, you've got to have credibility, so you must do an excellent job of providing those first services to children. Then you can begin to draw other agencies or organizations together with your success. From there, consider alternative ways to use the resources to serve the children and families. Find people who aren't afraid to 'color outside the lines.' "

As the day ends and I prepare to say a reluctant good-bye to Bebe Fearnside, she adds one final bit of wisdom: "I like to think of children as information carriers. You know—you can send them third class or you can send them first class. And as the saying goes, you get what you pay for."

Questions and Issues

1. Consider the definition of *collaboration:* "structures where resources, power, and authority are shared and where people are brought together to achieve common goals that could not be accomplished by a single individual or organization independently" (Kagan, 1991, p. 3). Analyze your individual resources, power, and authority, and that of your immediate organization (school, center, family).

2. If you were to embark on a collaborative effort to improve services to children and families, where would you begin? Consider this question from the standpoint of your individual role analyzed in response to the first question. Ask yourself, Who is the first and most immediate person or group with whom you would share resources, power, and authority?

3. If you were to follow Bebe Fearnside's advice to "put the services where the people are," what are some places "where the people are" in your community? Go beyond the traditional places where services are provided.

4. As part of this process of preparing for collaboration, analyze the broad goal of providing services to children and families into very specific outcomes that are relevant to your community and your educational setting.

5. When you think about your own professional practices, do you find any examples of your own "coloring outside the lines"? Can you see potential for more opportunities to do so?

References

Caldwell, B. M. (1986). Day care and the public schools—Natural allies, natural enemies. *Educational Leadership, 43* (5), 34–39.

Caldwell, B. M. (1989). A comprehensive model for integrating child care and early childhood education. *Teachers College Record, 90* (3), 404–414.

Chavkin, D., & Pizzo, P. (1992). Public policy report, Medicaid and child care: Good partnership potention. *Young Children, 47* (3), 39–42.

Greenberg, P. (1990). Before the beginning: A participant's view. *Young Children, 45* (6), 41–52.

Kagan, S. L. (1991). *United we stand: Collaboration for child care and early education services.* New York: Teachers College Press.

Lombardi, J. (1990). Head Start: The nation's pride, a nation's challenge. *Young Children, 45* (6), 22–29.

Mallory, N. J., & Goldsmith, N. A. (1990). Head Start works! Two Head Start veterans share their views. *Young Children, 45* (6), 36–39.

Ramey, C. T., & Ramey, S. L. (1990). Intensive educational intervention for children of poverty. *Intelligence, 14* (1), 1–9.

Schorr, L. B. (1989). Early interventions aimed at reducing intergenerational disadvantage: The new social policy. *Teachers College Record, 90* (3), 362–374.

12

The Journey's End: Reflections on the Cases

New Hope for Children and Families— Promise for Our Profession

Now that our journey has come to an end, I would like to reflect on the places where we have visited. I could say that I have been inspired by the schools and programs described in this book, but it is so much more than that. Nel Noddings (1991) put it this way: "Stories have the power to direct and change our lives." How true. These stories have brought me to a major realization—one with enormous impact on my personal and professional life. I want to share this awareness with you as we unpack and settle back into our day-to-day routines.

This new understanding has been developing with each visit, but it remained elusive until now. My colleagues and friends have all asked the same question, and as I responded to them, I discovered what it was that I learned from this journey. They asked, "What did all the programs have in common?"

It didn't take me long to respond. It was the people—individuals with commitment to children and families. I witnessed a common spirit among the teachers, administrators, and involved parents. Asa Hilliard (1993) described it well when he talked about "productive educators"—those who go beyond wondering how to do it, and just do it. Glenna Plaisted at Riley School stopped wondering what it would be like to teach the way she truly believed best for children and built her own school so she could "just do it." Caroline Pratt did the same in 1914 in New York City. Lisa

Harjo and Irma Russell went beyond wondering in their work at the Denver Indian Center and developed the "Circle Never Ends" curriculum.

Carl Rogers (1983) gave me some additional words to describe the commonality. He ascribed three qualities to effective educators: genuineness, empathic understanding, and the ability to "prize the learner." I witnessed these qualities in Kathleen Hobbs and in all the tireless educators at Papillon Day Care in Montreal; in Bob Tourtillott, the reflective teacher of the mixed-age class in Portland; and in the parents who participate so fully in the Poe Cooperative Nursery School in Houston, Texas.

Another commonality was the importance the teachers placed on working in an environment that matched their beliefs about children and learning. Once Angela Pino discovered City & Country, she knew she could teach in a way that would encourage children's creativity. Mary Nall and Wendy Payne successfully persuaded Trevor Calkins to hire them because Rogers School sounded like the "right" environment for their team teaching. Sandy Davini chose to teach at Longwood School in Hayward because she believed in the Child Development Project. Janeen Hamel Chin reflected in her journal that she was aware of how much more she was able to offer children at Riley School.

As you probably noticed, the individuals you and I encountered in this book were very much directed by their visions and dreams of what education and care *could* be for young children. Bebe Fearnside definitely had vision as she and her collaborative team dared to "color outside the lines" in Alachua County, Florida. Those individuals who created Hawaii's Traveling Preschools had a vision that went beyond setting up a portable preschool; teachers like Kathy Javor and Lorna Hines cherish that vision in their work with children and families. Jon Hassell, the principal of Longwood School, could see beyond the curriculum and approaches of the Child Development Project to the benefits for families and community.

The individuals we have encountered in these case descriptions are only a microcosm of the many teachers, parents, and administrators who are similarly committed to children and families. I know that I could have found thousands of "out of the ordinary" programs and schools, and that these chapters could have gone on indefinitely. That realization and my increased awareness of the power of individuals gives me a new lens with which to see early childhood education. Today, our profession is overwhelmed with concerns about the adversity faced by children and families. Given the incredible stresses that young children and their families are exposed to, schools of all kinds have become a refuge, a protection for a growing number of children. Research on resiliency in children repeatedly concludes that teachers are most often the "protective buffers" or the adults who provide warmth and caring in the lives of children. Emmy Werner's classic study (1990) of the

children of Kauai revealed that for the resilient youngsters, a special teacher was not just an instructor of academic skills but a confidant and a positive model for personal identification.

Our visits to Hayward, and Montreal, and Alachua County, and all of the sites described in these pages assure me that there are those "special" educators out there. They offer far more than confident and positive models or warm caring adults. Their commitment, their spirit, and their vision enable them to have a powerful influence on many lives. With that realization, I anticipate new hope for children, new hope for families, and new promise for our profession.

References

Hilliard, A. (1993). *Responding to all children: Responsibility of teacher education.* Paper presented at Portland State University, Portland, OR.

Noddings, N. (1991). Stories in dialogue: Caring and interpersonal reasoning. In C. Witherell & N. Noddings (Eds.), *Stories lives tell: Narrative and dialogue in education.* New York: Teachers College Press.

Rogers, C. (1983). *Freedom to learn for the 80's.* Columbus, OH: Merrill/Macmillan.

Werner, E. (1990). Protective factors and individual resilience. In S. Meisels & J. Shonkoff (Eds.), *Handbook of early childhood intervention.* New York: Cambridge University.

Appendix A

Matrix of Cases

Chapter	Program/ Location	Focus	Age/Grade	Sample Issues
2	City & Country New York City	Creativity Blocks	3	Teacher Decisions Routines
3	Ruus & Longwood Hayward, California	Prosocial Curriculum	K. 1st 2nd	Discipline Cooperative Learning Family Involvement
4	Indian Preschool Denver, Colorado	Cultural Curriculum	4 5	Transition to Kdg. "Centered Learning"
5	Riley School Glen Cove, Maine	Children as Source of Curriculum	4–7	Teacher Reflections First Day of School
6	Rogers Elementary Victoria, British Columbia	Personalized Assessment	K. 1st	Teacher Team Literacy
7	Poe Cooperative Houston, Texas	Parent Involvement	4 5	Holiday Curriculum Transition to Kdg.
8	Sabin Elementary Portland, Oregon	Mixed-Age Grouping	K. 1st 2nd	Classroom Management Math Assessment Learner Independence
9	Papillon Day Care Montreal, Quebec	Inclusion	3–5	Resources Self-Concept
10	Traveling Preschools	Parent Education	2 3	Language Development Cultural Components
11	Alachua County Early Intervention Florida	Integration/ Collaboration	0–adult	Diversity of Needs Public/Private

Appendix B

Suggestions for Using This Book

- For university courses
- For in-service programs
- For individual professional development

Introduction

As I proposed in Chapter 1, these case descriptions may be used for varying levels of professional development, depending on the experiential background of university students or classroom teachers. Walter Doyle (1986) described three levels of responses teachers make when they visit other classrooms. The cases in this book *are* visits to classrooms. As visits, they can be used for the three levels suggested by Doyle:

1. To develop knowledge, specifically "how to's" (first level)
2. To develop beginning analysis approaches to use in decision making and problem solving (second level)
3. To develop further analysis approaches for reflection (third level)

Because they are detailed stories of a day in a classroom, these cases may serve as "proxies" for practicum experiences, and, as such, may provide a common experience for a group.

In the next few pages, I will describe examples of case approaches to teaching and learning using Doyle's three levels as a framework. For each kind of approach, reference will be made to incidents, strategies, individuals, and issues from specific chapters in this book. I will demonstrate how to use a few specific chapters with the intent that you will be able to generalize the approach to the other chapters of this book. I will use the term *participants* to indicate students of teaching, teachers, parents, and other professionals. The words *instructor* and *leader* will designate the person who facilitates these approaches. Many of the activities will be appropriate and effective with groups of varied experience and expertise.

Case Approaches to Teaching and Learning

Level 1: Specific Knowledge or Strategies

A. List of Strategies
First, have participants develop a list of interesting or innovative strategies from a chapter. For example, a list from Chapter 8 might include:

1. Children record attendance and lunch request on the computer, then print it when everyone has arrived.
2. The class splits into two groups for journal sharing with an established routine for taking turns and asking questions of the writer.
3. Individual math contracts are developed collaboratively by the teacher and individual student, and are used and completed by students at their own pace.

After participants have developed lists individually or in groups, use the individual/group lists or develop a large group composite. Discuss the message behind each strategy that has been listed (i.e., What does this communicate to children?). For example, when children are responsible for recording their own attendance and lunch count on the computer, it communicates to them that they are trusted to handle classroom routines, that they are capable of doing so, and that they are in charge of themselves. Another possible message in this strategy is that technology and computers are here to help us do our work.

B. Looking for Alternatives
Using individual or partner lists, or a group composite, ask for appropriate alternatives to the strategies. The directions may be: Think of three other ways to record attendance and lunch requests (or to have children share what they have written in their journals) (or to provide individualized practice in varied math skills). Ask for inappropriate alternatives to the strategies. Discuss the rationale for why the strategy is not appropriate. The directions may be: Think of one inappropriate or ineffective way to record attendance and lunch requests. "Why?"

C. Rationales for Strategies
With respect to the strategies identified by the group, the following kind of role-plays may be set up:

1. Your colleague has observed you using the strategy of _____ (insert example from lists) and asks why you use it. Respond to her question and address concerns she may raise.
2. A parent has heard from his child that you use the strategy of _____ (insert example from lists) and his child has complained about it. Explain your strategy, provide a rationale for it, and respond to the parent concerns.
3. Your university supervisor observed your teaching today and comments on the strategy of _____ (insert example from lists). He suggests another strategy with which you do not feel comfortable. Respond to him.

In each of these role-plays, participants will need to take the perspective of the teacher or student teacher as well as that of the colleague, parent, or university supervisor. Role-plays are most effective if played, then discussed, then replayed.

Level 2: Problem Solving and Decision Making

A. Locating Problems and Potential Problems
This approach may be initiated with a sample problem or potential problem identified by the instructor/leader. From there, participants can identify additional problems or potential problems in a particular chapter. For Chapter 2, some examples may be:

1. Elizabeth always role-plays the baby with her peers. This behavior carries over to cleanup time, stories, and other activities. Her peers consistently respond to her as the baby.
2. Devon appears to dominate the group times and discussions. However, he does not seem to interact much with others when there is unstructured time. He wanders more during the "free-choice" time than the other children.
3. Because children are not asked to pick up materials while they are working, there is a large amount of materials out when it is time for cleaning up. There may be days when several children don't carry out their responsibilities for the pick-up tasks.

The first step, of course, is to ask participants to decide if there is a problem or the potential for one. This may take some discussion to achieve agreement within the group. If the decision is made that there is a problem or the potential for one, then ask the group to identify what other information is needed before working on solutions or preventions. From there, have the group brainstorm possible solutions or preventions and prioritize them in terms of effectiveness and appropriateness. This activity will be ideal for small group work.

B. Reading for Reanalysis
For each of the chapters, at least one focus topic has been developed and listed in the matrix in Appendix A. There are also suggested references for each focus at the end of the chapters. Participants may work individually or in groups to read more about the focus topic, then reanalyze the classroom case using the information obtained.

C. Creating Problems for Role-Plays
Have participants create problems to be solved by the teachers in individual chapters. The problems will be connected to the context of the classroom situation in the chapter. Some examples include:

1. A parent who is taking his turn to volunteer at Poe Cooperative Nursery (Chapter 7) begins to scold his own child angrily in front of all the other children.
2. At Riley School (Chapter 5), Reggie has made a choice to go outside when he is having trouble in the classroom. On his way out, he convinces two other children to go with him.
3. At Longwood School (Chapter 3), one of the kindergarten children expresses a dislike for her third-grade buddy and eventually refuses to participate in activities with her.
4. At Papillon Day Care (Chapter 9), one of the children with disabilities refuses to do anything for himself. Although he is capable of participating in many of the class activities, he will not attempt to do so.
5. At one of Hawaii's Traveling Preschool sites (Chapter 10), a toddler wanders from mat to mat, disturbing other children's activities. Her mother is usually busy visiting or doing an activity herself and ignores her child's behavior, even when asked to supervise the child.

Before beginning the role-play, both individuals involved in the situation may request more information. For example, the person playing the child or the child's parent at Longwood School may request information about the age and background of the child and the child's buddy. The person playing the teacher at Longwood may request information about the kind of activities that have preceded this situation. It will also be important to determine if the teacher role is to be played in the context of the classroom case or according to the individual who is playing the role. As previously suggested, role-plays are most effective if played out, discussed, and played again.

Level 3: Reflection

A. Self-Evaluation Role-Plays
Ask participants to put themselves in the role of the teacher or other professionals and visualize themselves at the end of the day. Ask participants to conduct a self-evaluation either in writing or verbally. They may use a checklist or set of criteria with which participants can frame the evaluation process. On a more general basis, suggest that participants consider the individual teacher's concerns, strengths, limitations, and awareness.

B. Teacher Comparisons
Have participants compare a pair of teachers from two specific chapters. The comparison should include an analysis of teaching philosophy, values, priorities, strengths and limits, goals for children, and unique characteristics. Teachers who would provide interesting comparisons include Bob Tourtillott (Chapter 8), Janeen Hamel Chin (Chapter 5), Angela Pino (Chapter 2), and Mary Nall and Wendy Payne (Chapter 6), Sandy Davini (Chapter 3), and Irma Russell (Chapter 4).

C. Perspective Taking
Describe the classrooms in specific chapters from the perspective of children in those classes, from the perspective of parents of those children, or from the perspective of an administrator. After participants have written or presented those perspectives, highlight the emphasis of the descriptions as a way of analyzing the cases.

D. Debating the Issues
Have participants debate the following issues using the appropriate chapters as context for the arguments. Debaters should have well-developed arguments for supporting one side or the other of the issues suggested here.

1. The use of paraprofessionals in many of the preschool programs (Head Start, subsidized child care, neighborhood private preschools) in the Alachua County program (Chapter 11).
2. The lack of diverse art materials, dress-up clothes, and science materials in the classroom for 3-year-olds at City Country School (Chapter 2).
3. The focus on only Native American culture at the Denver Indian Preschool (Chapter 4).
4. The intense focus on caring behaviors, attitudes, and values in the curriculum and teaching and learning approaches of Longwood and Ruus Schools in Hayward (Chapter 3).
5. The lack of letter grades and other comparative data provided by the Rogers School assessment and reporting process.

It is important that debates are concluded with a summary of both sides of the issues, either by the debater, the group of participants, or the instructor/leader.

E. Action Research Projects

For those participants with the background and experience to do so, ask them to develop an action research project for a particular teacher in one of the chapters. This process will include the following:

1. Focus the research: Framing questions that the teacher may want to pose; identifying approaches that the teacher may want to study; or recommending change that the teacher may want to make.
2. Consider the knowledge base related to the focus: Asking, What do we already know about that focus?
3. Design a research method to include data sources, time line, data collection, data analysis, and so on.

An example of an action research project is one that Gaby and Lois at Papillon Day Care (Chapter 9) may conduct to find out if the children with disabilities are accepted by their peers. Their questions may be:

Do the other children choose to play or work with the children with disabilities?
How do the children describe the children with disabilities?
How do the children with disabilities feel about their acceptance in the class-room?

There is a substantial body of research literature about peer acceptance of children with disabilities. A number of relevant studies are cited in the chapter references. The conclusions are mixed so that there is no clear answer to the questions posed by the two teachers.

Gaby and Lois design their study for February, so that the children have had ample time to get to know each other. The procedures they will use to answer their questions include: developing a sociogram of children's peer choices by asking each child to name three friends; having children draw pictures of their peers with and without disabilities; and interviewing the child with disabilities about their accep-tance. Needless to say, the interview and the sociogram questions will need to be worded with sensitivity and in appropriate language. The drawing activity will be conducted over several days.

The sociogram will determine if children with disabilities are chosen as play-mates. The drawings will determine whether the children emphasize the disability when they visualize the child with disabilities. And the interviews will reveal the feelings of the child with disabilities about interactions with peers, and ultimately his or her perception of acceptance.

From there, Gaby and Lois will have information that can be used to plan curriculum and activities, to select children's literature, and to examine their own practices for influence on the children's acceptance of peers with disabilities.

Using the case descriptions in this book for developing action research projects will be especially useful for those who do not have their own classroom to study or for those who are just developing research understandings.

Additional Features for Teaching and Learning

In addition to the specific approaches just described, there are sections called "Questions and Issues" at the end of each chapter. For each set of questions and issues, there are multiple levels of difficulty. That is, varying levels of experience are needed to respond to the questions or issues. In addition, in the matrix in Appendix A, general issues for discussion are listed for each chapter.

At the end of each chapter, you will find a reading list of related research and development literature, again at varying levels of sophistication. The literature extends the knowledge and understanding related to the focus of each chapter.

These suggestions are intended to extend the potential uses beyond the traditional case approach and to initiate those who have not used cases previously. The stories of programs and practices in these case descriptions can focus the approaches in many directions. The intent is for the participants' background, philosophy, and interest, and that of the instructor/leader, to guide the approach. This book invites the creativity of those who read and use the case descriptions in this text.

Reference

Doyle, W. (1986). *The world is everything that is the case: Developing case methods for teacher education.* Paper presented at the annual meeting of the American Educational Research Association, San Francisco.